# The Future of University Credentials

# The Future of University Credentials

*New Developments at the Intersection of Higher Education and Hiring*

SEAN R. GALLAGHER

Harvard Education Press
Cambridge, Massachusetts

*Library of Congress Cataloging-in-Publication Data*
Names: Gallagher, Sean R., author.
Title: The future of university credentials : new developments at the
   intersection of higher education and hiring / Sean R. Gallagher.
Description: Cambridge, Massachusetts : Harvard Education Press, [2016] |
   Includes bibliographical references and index.
Identifiers: LCCN 2016016048| ISBN 9781612509679 (pbk.) | ISBN 9781612509686
   (library edition)
Subjects: LCSH: Labor supply—Effect of education on. | Education,
   Higher—Evaluation. | Universities and colleges—Evaluation. | Degrees,
   Academic—Evaluation.
Classification: LCC LB2331.62 .G36 2016 | DDC 378.2—dc23
LC record available at https://lccn.loc.gov/2016016048

Published by Harvard Education Press,
an imprint of the Harvard Education Publishing Group

Harvard Education Press
8 Story Street
Cambridge, MA 02138


Cover Design: Ciano Design
Cover Images: iStock.com/4x6
The typefaces used in this book are Frutiger and ITC Legacy Serif

# CONTENTS

# FOREWORD

Education can be an end in itself. Knowledge, culture, civic engagement, and personal growth are all valuable outcomes. But for most learners and their families, education is also a means to an end—greater professional, personal, and economic opportunity. Typically, a person's first job will build on knowledge and skills gained in college while also requiring new knowledge and skill development. Those capabilities, in turn, will lead to the next opportunity.

Higher education plays a crucial role in this process, contributing to an ever-evolving continuum of people, skills, problems to be solved, interactions, and ongoing learning. Sean Gallagher's important new book focuses on a crucial part of this continuum: the rapidly evolving intersection of higher education and hiring. As Gallagher notes, while the degree and a transcript have long been the gold standard in college and university credentialing—and the best insurance for a good job and growing wages—new options are emerging. Gallagher provides a fascinating and indispensable guide to that evolving sector.

One of the critical catalysts for change in the economy, the labor market, and higher education has been information technology (IT). Recall *The World Is Flat*? IT enabled globalization. Boundaries have become more porous; financial transactions and communication instantaneous; and traditional notions of speed and scale were upended. And although e-mail, online learning, and social media have not replaced campuses, courses, or faculty, these IT innovations have challenged our assumptions about information, hierarchies, and empowerment. Without a doubt, IT has changed work and the labor market. Routine jobs have been automated; robots and algorithms have displaced workers. While even highly skilled jobs can be displaced by advanced computational power, growth of the hybrid job market (which includes positions that blend two or more skills such as analytics and marketing) is explosive.

As the world has changed around us, our notions of what it means to be educated have evolved as well. Intellectual skills are a must in today's world, but so too are interpersonal skills. A complex world requires complex skills. Historically a college degree was the best proxy for those complex skills. But today's jobs require the meshing of multiple disciplines and skills, with frequent upskilling. Organizations are less hierarchical, with the need for rapid forming, and dissolving, of distributed teams. Fluidity rather than stability characterizes the environment. Employers find little time to grow talent—they need to hire the right match of skills, competencies, and attitudes to remain competitive. Because an organization's success depends on its people, the stakes are high for employers to find the right match in job prospects. Increasingly they are adopting sophisticated tools such as predictive analytics to improve their selections based on competency matching and quality of hire analysis. And as we achieve greater clarity between business needs and workforce capabilities, our notions of competencies and credentialing shift.

In this environment, it is not surprising that educational options have also grown. Competencies, certificates, boot camps, and badges augment traditional options. Do-it-yourself learning opportunities are readily available (for instance, Google, Khan Academy, Lynda.com), making it more convenient to keep up with rapid skill changes. Both within and outside of higher education, guidance is available for those seeking additional skills. Stackable credentials, degree pathways, course selection tools, and new services such as Training Finder seek to offer learners more certain pathways to credentials and opportunities.

Verifiable credentials have value in the marketplace. Competencies, certificates, diplomas, and informal learning are being integrated into digital identities. Online talent platforms, such as LinkedIn, can scan these credentials and match candidates with employers, as well as provide feedback to institutions on their alumni and educational programs. Online talent platforms are becoming the "operating system" of this interconnected ecology.

Common competencies (such as problem solving) may be critical in multiple industries (for example, health care, IT, advanced manufacturing, and so on). These competencies form the basis of the many "stackable" and flexible job pathways. As common terminology and taxonomies emerge, a new language is being developed that will speed the adoption and use of competencies. Employers, students, and educators are interested in a transparent system that allows each to understand the competencies needed, how they are assessed, and a marketplace that enables multiple paths to career success.

In some ways, much of this is not new. Communication skills, problem solving, and critical thinking have long been goals of education. Employers have not been oblivious to their desirability, either. For example, competency-based education has been available for decades, and many colleges and universities offer hundreds of credentials. Two shifts are significant, however. One is the economic implication of a strong link between hiring and higher education. The other is a market dynamic.

The wage premium of a college education has been persistent and significant, even as the number of college graduates has grown. However, there is increasing skepticism about the cost and value of a college education in light of reports of unemployment, underemployment, and high student loan debt. At the same time, employers are finding it difficult to pinpoint the employees they need, hampering their growth and profitability, which in turn impacts individual wages, tax receipts, and community vitality.

Markets need information to work. One significant impact of IT is the sharing of information. Access to information, whether about the price of steel or the likely salary in marketing versus medicine, affects behavior. Clearly business, industry, and the workplace are markets.

But increasingly, higher education is perceived as a market; the currency might be applicants, graduates, or those deemed most likely to succeed. Job seekers, including those with college credentials, are in a marketplace that seeks to match talent with opportunities.

In a world needing complex skills that are rapidly changing and an economy closely linked to innovation and services, education is an imperative. Credentials signal education and skills. And the emerging digital credentialing ecosystem provides an increasingly better opportunity to align pathways, needs, and skills. This ecosystem is just forming. Colleges and universities, employers, and job seekers are part of this complex system, along with governments, venture capital investors, and foundations. By focusing on the intersection of higher education and hiring—an area of great importance and rapidly accelerating change—Sean Gallagher's book is timely, insightful, and an important addition to the literature.

We cannot afford a one-sided dialogue about education or the workplace. This book brings into clear and compelling focus the limits of how our system works today, how it has evolved in recent years, and how we might do better tomorrow. It should be used as both a guide to our current situation and as a catalyst for a broader and richer conversation about education and employment, individuals and communities, and both the public and private good of education. Our future depends on it.

—Diana G. Oblinger
*President Emerita, EDUCAUSE*

# At the Intersection of Higher Education and Hiring

*As formal teaching and training grow in extent, there is the danger of creating an undesirable split between the experience gained in more direct associations and what is acquired in school. This danger was never greater than at the present time, on account of the rapid growth in the last few centuries of knowledge and technical modes of skill.*

—JOHN DEWEY, one hundred years ago in 1916[1]

As much as this book is focused on education, it is also about hiring—an activity that is at the core of how our economy works. It explores the intersection of two distinct but related spheres: colleges and universities, including the students they serve and the credentials they issue; and the world of employers and how they make hiring decisions based on university credentials—as well as the broader ecosystem in which these parties operate.

Historically, how the two sides of the equation work together at this intersection has been understudied. Educators and educational researchers typically concern themselves with topics such as curriculum and policy, whereas the world of employment is evaluated by economists and sociologists and often focuses on wages and hiring practices. However, the bottom falling out of the job market in the global financial crisis of 2008 heralded a new era in the search for understanding how the job market relates to higher education. Suddenly, terms like *workforce development* were at the top of the headlines. The unprecedented spike in unemployment during what would become referred to as "The Great Recession" contributed to a significant surge in higher education enrollment.[2] Economists and higher education researchers had long known that college enrollment has countercyclical tendencies: in bad times when job opportunities are scarce, higher education becomes most appealing; in good times when jobs are plentiful, the ease of finding a job discourages stepping out of the workforce to study.[3]

Yet, even while the state of the economy was driving more students to pursue college and university study, it was also challenging the system's foundation. With incomes and tax receipts down, states faced massive budget deficits, forcing public colleges and universities—which educate more than 70 percent of students in the United States—to substantially increase tuition.[4] Similarly, private colleges and universities that were heavily reliant on endowments or were overleveraged struggled, and they too boosted tuition. Meanwhile, as costs were increasing, reports abounded about recent graduates struggling to find jobs.[5] Talk of a "college bubble" began, as the media, policy makers, and others began to question the return on investment of higher education.

Questioning the value of higher education and the power of educational qualifications in the job market is nothing new. In 1903, William James, the giant of American psychology and philosophy, wrote, "America is thus as a nation rapidly drifting towards a state of things in which no man of science or letters will be accounted respectable unless some kind of badge or diploma is stamped upon him, and in which bare personality will be a mark of outcast estate."[6] After World War II, the work of sociologist Harold Wilensky questioned the pattern of occupations seeking professional status through the escalation of their educational requirements.[7] By 1976, when the US economy was beginning to recover from the severe recession that marked the end of the long postwar boom era, a famous cover story in *Newsweek* provocatively asked "Who Needs College?" and pictured two college graduates in caps and gowns ironically operating a jackhammer and performing construction work, reporting on the "dismal" job prospects for college graduates.[8]

In more recent years, it has become sport to question the value and utility of college credentials in the job market—and further, to challenge the very sustainability of higher education and the college business model as we know it. In 2010, Silicon Valley venture capitalist and PayPal cofounder Peter Thiel captured headlines with his Thiel Fellowship program, which encouraged and funded twenty talented students to drop out of college to pursue entrepreneurial activities.[9] In 2011, Clayton Christensen and Henry Eyring's *The Innovative University* burst onto the scene and became required reading for college leaders, with its application of Christensen's theory of disruptive innovation to the higher education "industry."[10] The *New York Times* declared 2012 to be "The Year of the MOOC,"[11] as massively open online courses threatened to revolutionize higher education. Assaulted by technology, it seemed the sky was falling—and as the Board of Visitors at the venerable University of Virginia became obsessed with disruptive innovation and "strategic dynamism," it briefly cost president Teresa Sullivan her job.[12] Stoked by a growing, multibillion dollar torrent of venture capital investments in educational technology, innovation in higher education—the topic that I had dedicated my career to—was *en vogue*.

A number of authors and thought leaders have recently taken to exploring the fundamentals and future of the higher education business model in depth. The idea that we are at the leading edge of a potentially significant reshaping of the university landscape is reflected in the sometimes apocalyptic titles of books such as Kevin Carey's *The End of College*, Jeff Selingo's *College (Un)bound*, and Ryan Craig's *College Disrupted*.[13] Each of these books (alongside similar works) argues in its own way that the higher education system in the United States is broken and points the way toward innovative and often technology-driven solutions.

Indeed, much of the dialogue about reforming or remaking higher education revolves around technology, online models, and the general idea of innovation within a centuries-old business model. But what is not as often addressed is one of the core and highest value (if sometimes inefficient) functions of higher education: the role of degrees and other higher education credentials as qualifications in the job market. Universities serve many purposes, but degree production is paramount. US colleges and universities confer more than four million degrees per year, and the majority of college and university revenues and government support is focused on students earning credentials.[14]

It is this major aspect of higher education—credentialing—that this book explores. As we will see, perhaps the relative resilience of higher education institutions in this era of technological disruption is explained by the ensconced nature of how college credentials work in the job market. Yet, the primacy of university credentials is increasingly fragile in an era of unprecedented technological change. Understanding the future of higher education and the possibilities of new models requires a deeper understanding of the credentialing ecosystem and colleges' and universities' place within it.

## MARKET PERSPECTIVES AND "HIRE" EDUCATION

After completing my undergraduate degree in business, I was trained as a consultant. I was lucky enough to find my way into the education sector at a fascinating moment when technology and market thinking were just beginning to transform higher education during the dot-com era of the year 2000—from the first major forays into online degree delivery to the idea of eBay-like higher education marketplaces and the rise of degree-granting for-profit colleges. This consulting journey would take me through corporate boardrooms, the offices of college deans and presidents, and Wall Street conferences. Along the way I earned an MBA and then later a doctorate in education—a fairly unique combination. For the most part, MBAs hold sacred the notion of markets and economic theory. On the other hand, many educators often view businesses and the profit motive as an anathema.

A number of higher education scholars have effectively straddled these business and academic mindsets: for example, George Keller with his application of business strategy to the academy in the 1980s; the work of Robert Zemsky and his idea that universities can be "market smart" while also remaining "mission centered"; and the writings of Lloyd Armstrong examining change in higher education through a business model lens.[15] Historically, however, the prevailing view about markets in higher education has been more aligned with Sheila Slaughter and Gary Rhoades's critique of an ascendant "academic capitalism" that threatens to erode classic academic values by focusing on students as customers.[16] Yet, as colleges and universities have become more complex enterprises operating in much more turbulent competitive environments and serving an array of stakeholders, the ethos of market orientation and business-like thinking has emerged as especially relevant and increasingly accepted.[17]

Personally, I believe that the market is an appropriate, relevant, and timely lens through which to view higher education, and I can appreciate the still present debate about this, having worked in both for-profit companies and academia, and having specialized in the intersection of these two worlds over many years. Colleges and universities are certainly unique institutions in our society and have a special status given their focus on the public good and the advancement of knowledge. But indeed, one of colleges' and universities' principal purposes is not only the transmission of knowledge, but also the delivery of certified, reliable credentials that have a special role and standing in our society. Further, the language and concepts of business—particularly economic theory, competitive strategy, and marketing—are increasingly relevant for colleges and universities. For example, higher education institutions face competitive dynamics and resource constraints, and they must generate revenue from a variety of sources to sustain themselves. Colleges and universities are also impacted by emerging alternatives and substitutes in the classic economic sense, an issue that is especially pertinent to this book. Likewise, brand is an extremely important concept, and this has also been recognized in recent years. And, as a final example, the notion of return on investment (ROI) is prominent—if not dominant—in today's public discourse about higher education, from policy stances, to rankings schemes, and academic discussions about mission and new program development.

My first decade of work approaching higher education through a business lens eventually led to a role creating an institutional strategy and innovation function at Northeastern University. This took me from researching and advising on degree programs and credentials to the work of actually creating and managing them—and at an institution with a unique market orientation and focus on employer needs, given Northeastern's experiential character and history founded on more than one hundred years of cooperative education.

In 2009, we at Northeastern headed down the path of growing our online degree programs and entering new geographic markets across the United States with professional degree offerings. This strategy would require a very deep and nuanced understanding of the relationship between the job market and university credentials. Even though there is a recognized trend toward the master's degree becoming "the new bachelor's degree," graduate/professional degree attainment rates vary greatly and generally correspond to the knowledge and service intensity of a regional economy: from 7 percent of the adult population in Las Vegas, to 14 percent in Denver, and 23 percent in Washington, DC.[18] Advanced credentials are attained and valued differently in different regions, and coming from the Boston area—a statistical outlier that is home to eighty colleges and universities, and where one in five adults holds a graduate degree— it was critical for our expansion process to assess how employers value certain qualifications and credentials in their hiring process. Over three years, I explored this question in different regions of the United States, by personally meeting with and interviewing more than three hundred employers and industry associations and their senior human resources leaders, chief executive officers, divisional managers, and the like. Did they value degrees, and did they need more of them?

The answer, largely, was yes. And the major employers we were speaking with—from Fortune 100 firms to small start-ups and government agencies—were hungry for universities to leave their ivory towers; to have this dialogue about skills gaps, leadership development, and human capital; and to collaborate more closely with them. As we explored this intersection of higher education and employment, the conversations and the possibilities were thrilling. This work understanding the skills and credentials demanded in the job market is what inspired my later doctoral work on this same general topic, which in many ways formed the foundation for this book.

Each year, US employers spend more than $120 billion annually on hiring, and US higher education is a more than $400 billion segment of the economy.[19] Given the scale of these figures—and the time, effort, and number of lives impacted that they represent—it is critical that we better understand how the higher education system's production of credentials and the job market intersect. Many argue that higher education is on the precipice of significant change, and technology and market forces are bringing change to hiring as well, especially in an increasingly global market for talent. It is a pivotal moment, and that is why I am writing this book now. More than ever before, there is a pressing need to understand and create a dialogue between the world of employment and higher education. In the chapters ahead, we will ground ourselves in history to understand the present, and ultimately, assess the future.

# A Pivotal Moment in the University Credentialing Ecosystem

On any given day, a company such as Cree, Inc., a publicly traded multinational with more than 6,000 employees and $1.6 billion in annual revenue, may have more than 100 open jobs that it is looking to fill in the United States alone.[1] Cree is a developer and manufacturer of light-emitting diode (LED) lighting and semiconductor products. Headquartered in North Carolina's Research Triangle region, the company has operations ranging from research and development in its headquarters to manufacturing facilities in North Carolina, Wisconsin, and China. As a result, its talent needs span a wide educational spectrum, from roles that require no or a few years of postsecondary education, to leadership and R&D positions that rely on master's and PhD degrees. Over the course of 2015, approximately 18 percent of Cree's job openings preferred high school or vocational training, and the majority—another 82 percent—preferred a college degree at some level.

As firms such as Cree expand in the knowledge economy—seeking talent in areas such as manufacturing, software development, and engineering—they draw on the market of both experienced talent and the more than three million new college graduates annually in the United States.[2] For US firms, this talent market is increasingly global, with hiring activity and applicants spanning multiple continents. Potential hires come to the table with a wide range of experience levels and with a variety of credentials from an extremely diverse pool of higher education institutions. Some of these individuals come from elite schools; others may have completed only part of a degree at a state university; others may have completed an online program in leadership or a vocational certificate in a leading-edge area of manufacturing.

It is within this complicated context that professionals such as Tom Mathews, senior vice president of human resources at Cree, operate. With his more than thirty years of experience in human resources at firms such as Shearson Lehman Brothers (an American Express company) and Time Warner Cable, Mathews, like other executives who are charged with finding and developing their companies' talent base, increasingly rely on colleges and universities and the credentials they issue—as indicators of skill, capability, trainability, or leadership potential. At Cree, like many companies, a job with educational qualifications at the college level may likely seek strong skills in data analysis, communication, writing, problem solving, or project management. As Mathews notes, "Degrees still matter, from a credentialing perspective, from an intellectual capacity perspective"—and as a signal showing "the ability to stick with something and get it done."[3] While the hiring processes of the future may be more driven by deep analysis and optimization based on sophisticated technological algorithms operating across a network of data on jobs and credentials, in the hiring activities of most firms today, university-issued credentials—particularly degrees—are central job qualifications, whether as a proxy for ability or as a direct measure of skill.

How did we arrive at a moment in which university credentials are the key currency and gateway to professional jobs? How meaningful is a degree, and are real alternatives to the degree emerging? Answering these and other related questions is the focus of this book.

## THE PRIMACY OF UNIVERSITY CREDENTIALS

Producing degrees is one of the principal products of colleges and universities, and the foundation of the business model for most higher education institutions. University-issued credentials such as degrees possess a strong and unique market power, backed by the quality assurance of accreditation.[4] Whether one believes that degrees are pure certifications of skill and knowledge, or more pessimistically that they are simply an elaborate signaling mechanism, in either case, the degree and other types of university credentials are critical and nearly universal occupational qualifications in the modern job market.[5]

As educational researcher and sociologist David Baker argues, educational credentials are at the center of the transformation of work in modern society. According to Baker, "With its vast culture of education, a distinctive feature of postindustrial society is the primary requirement of formal educational training for access to increasingly more occupations. Over time and across many occupations, educational credentials have gone from mostly irrelevant, or at best supplemental, to now dominant."[6] University credentials are deeply ensconced in the workings of the job market and our economy, and despite prognostications to the contrary, the legitimacy of degrees is only growing.[7] Similarly, the research of MIT economist David Autor makes a convincing case that transformations in the modern economy have escalated the demand for college-educated workers—especially those with advanced degrees. According to Autor, waves of innovation are indeed automating jobs that require lower levels of manual and routine cognitive labor; however, at the same time, these dynamics are simultaneously increasing demand for higher-level jobs that require college-level skills in problem solving, critical thinking, communication, and so on.[8]

Although the movement to a knowledge economy and the transformation of professional work has been playing out over many decades, we are today at a pivotal and unique moment in the evolution of the role of degrees and other educational credentials in the workforce. Technological innovation has been a defining characteristic of the economy in the 2000s, and technology is simultaneously enhancing the value of degrees and college credentials in the workforce, while also challenging how the entire credentialing landscape works.

Beyond just degrees, colleges and universities award a wide range of credentials that educational experts place in the broader category of postsecondary awards, which includes various certificates and diplomas. A great deal of attention is currently being focused on certificates and other types of higher education credentials, as colleges and universities increasingly experiment with—and as employers demand—shorter forms of learning. However, a significant majority of university-issued credentials are degrees. Despite their shorter nature, all forms of certificates from the undergraduate to postmaster's level account for only 21 percent of postsecondary credential conferrals each year, with most of them at the sub-baccalaureate level. Of all higher education credentials issued by colleges and universities each year, bachelor's degrees account for nearly 38 percent; associate degrees, 22 percent; master's degrees, 16 percent; and doctoral degrees, less than 4 percent.[9] Historically, the US higher education system has been a degree production machine, with certificates, diplomas, and other credentials representing an important but relatively small segment.

Thus, in using the term *university credential* throughout this book, it is typically in reference to degrees. Yet, the use of the broader term *credential* purposefully captures the other categories of postsecondary award, and also acknowledges that the dynamics of credentialing are changing and that the future does appear to include many new types of programs and credentials well beyond the traditional degree or certificate. Further, the term *university credential* bounds our discussion to the programs and credentials offered by or in affiliation with *universities*. This focuses our analysis on the issues for—and offerings of—the higher education sector, rather than the broader, highly diversified and fragmented landscape of professional credentials, certifications, and vocational licenses awarded by industry organizations, companies, and government bodies. These types of credentials are important substitutes or alternatives to college study and are held by about a quarter of the US population, but they are beyond the scope of this higher education–focused analysis, although we touch on them many times in this book.[10] Finally, in a semantic sense, the term *credential* importantly invokes the job market function of degrees, certificates, and other university program offerings. For students, university credentials certify their completion of a course of study and provide them with a portable currency of value in the job market. Employers rely on these credentials to interpret the ability, skill, potential, or other attributes of the credential holder in hiring decisions. Understanding how university credentials work in the job market is the core focus of this book. Figure I.1 is a conceptual illustration of the credentialing landscape and the area of growing convergence in short-form university-issued credentials and those from noninstitutional providers.

This book also takes the perspective that the environment in which university credentials exist and operate is a multisided market, or *ecosystem*. The ecosystem principally consists of the colleges and universities that issue university credentials; the employers that use them in making hiring decisions; the students that need them; and the government and quality assurance bodies that provide a policy and quality assurance framework for them, among other parties—which include, for example, various technology firms and investors. Understanding the value and future of university credentials requires understanding the overall environment and the components of the ecosystem, including its relationships, intersections, and momentum flows.

Before we dig into analyzing the workings of the university credentialing ecosystem, it is first important to establish context. The role played by university credentials in the job market is a central issue within a much larger higher education policy and economic

**Figure I.1** The credential landscape: Market size and orientation and credential duration

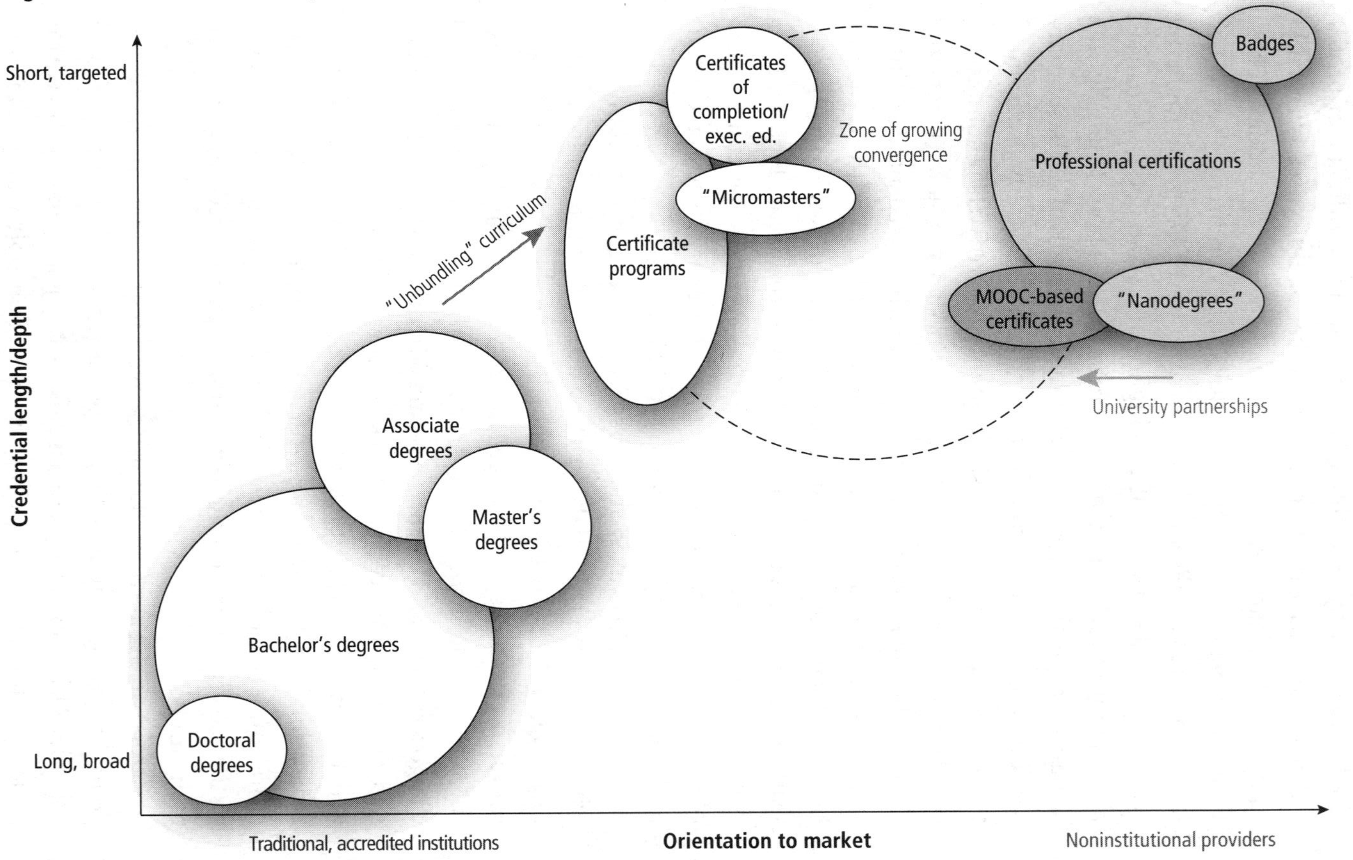

Credential length/depth

Short, targeted

Long, broad

Badges

Professional certifications

"Nanodegrees"

MOOC-based certificates

University partnerships

Zone of growing convergence

Certificates of completion/exec. ed.

"Micromasters"

Certificate programs

"Unbundling" curriculum

Associate degrees

Master's degrees

Bachelor's degrees

Doctoral degrees

Traditional, accredited institutions

Noninstitutional providers

**Orientation to market**

dialogue concerning how university study aligns with economic outcomes and the themes of greater transparency, value, and innovation.

## THE RISE OF THE CREDENTIAL AND THE JOB MARKET OUTCOMES OF HIGHER EDUCATION

Interest in how higher education relates to job market outcomes has been building over the past decade and a half, as a result of various trends that have now reached an inflection point.

After bottoming due to a demographic low in the early 1990s, US higher education saw a rising tide of demand that extended from the second half of that decade through the first decade of this century. College and university enrollment experienced fifteen consecutive years of growth, from 14.3 million students in 1995 to 21 million in 2010.[11] Although the vast majority of this growth was in domestic students, the inflow of international students to the United States has been a fairly significant contributor as well, especially in recent years. The number of international students studying in the United States grew 72 percent over fifteen years, from just over 500,000 in 1999–2000 to nearly 900,000 in 2013–2014.[12] It was around and shortly after the year 2000 that a number of long-running and newly emerging demand-related dynamics converged to both drive enrollment growth but also begin to disrupt the foundations of the traditional higher education business model.

The dot-com era that lasted from the late 1990s into the year 2000 brought the first major wave of technology-driven transformations and innovations to higher education, a period that we will explore in chapter 3. Hundreds of educational start-up companies raised a total of $5.5 billion in venture capital and private equity between 1999 and 2000 alone, with many of them targeting higher education; however, very few of these firms were able to find a sustainable business model.[13] Many of today's entrepreneurs and pundits who are champions of "disruptive innovation," massively open online courses (MOOCs), and next-generation online credentials are unfamiliar with many of the experiments and lessons of this era. For example, in 1999, Jones International University became the first purely online university to gain regional accreditation—and indeed one of the only such institutions to ever exist, despite the preponderance of the term *online university*.[14] Stanford University, Columbia University, the University of Chicago, and a few other elite universities and their business schools came together to fund and build UNext/Cardean University, which raised more than $100 million in private capital but ultimately did not succeed in scaling its innovative online executive MBA program.[15] Meanwhile, a decade before the first MOOC, the notion of high-end online personal enrichment classes was advanced with AllLearn, a collaboration between Oxford, Stanford, and Yale (AllLearn quietly closed down in 2006; Rick Levin, president of Yale at the time, would later become the chief executive officer of Coursera).[16] Across the pond, the government in the United Kingdom established and funded UK eUniversities as a state-sponsored online learning vehicle in 2000 with £50 million of public money, but it attracted only 900 students before folding in 2004.[17] The consensus view was that the market was not yet ready for these new forms of online learning and nontraditional approaches to credentials.

This period saw a number of bold prognostications about the future of colleges and universities—often relegating higher education institutions to endangered species status. In the late 1990s, management guru Peter Drucker had suggested that traditional universities wouldn't survive the Internet era, while Cisco Systems CEO John Chambers was christening e-learning the Internet's next "killer app."[18] At this same time, a parallel postsecondary universe of information technology (IT) certifications was emerging, providing a viable alternative to traditional degree study as students pursued Cisco, Microsoft, A++, and other technology vendor–sponsored certification programs to forgo traditional college study and secure high-paying jobs.[19] Between 1997 and 2000, an estimated 2.4 million IT certifications were issued worldwide, and this was an early and notable example of professional credentials successfully substituting for university credentials, as millions of workers found their way into high-paying IT jobs without degrees.[20]

These technology-enabled market developments were just one sliver of the much broader activity across the higher education landscape at the time, but they were a signal of what was to come in the years ahead. One of the catalytic impacts of this era was inspiring the idea that legitimate university credentials could be delivered and earned online, when in the mid-2000s traditional institutions with traditional brands moved into online delivery with full degree offerings.[21] Much like how the recent boom in Silicon Valley technology start-ups was built on the foundation of cheap bandwidth and computing power created by the overbuilding of first-generation telecom/fiber/Internet infrastructure companies, the online education experimentation of the early 2000s laid the groundwork for the leaps forward in the years ahead.[22] Indeed, because so much of the future of university credentials is associated with online education, the history and present evolution of online education and its credentials are significant characters in the chapters ahead.

The recession, stock market decline, and changing employment landscape that brought an end to the dot-com era in 2000–2001 also set the stage for the direction that the higher education market would evolve. Classically, higher education enrollment had been countercyclical—with student enrollment increasing during challenging job markets.[23] As the economy contracted, college enrollment grew at a significant rate.[24] Further, demographics—in addition to economics—were now strongly on the side of higher education enrollment growth. Enrollment in colleges and universities had bottomed out in 1995 due to the relatively low number of births in the mid-1970s. However, the baby boom echo was coming—with record numbers of high school graduates throughout the 2000s creating the strongest pipeline for college study ever.[25] The attention of policy makers was turning to preparing for this coming demographic wave, as well as meeting the needs of a knowledge economy that was, in the postrecession recovery, demanding more college-educated workers.

The economic expansion of the 1990s had been characterized by growing tax receipts and higher government funding levels for higher education, but in the early 2000s that funding, including state appropriations, peaked and began to significantly decline—a particularly significant fact as the vast majority of students in the US postsecondary education system attend public institutions.[26] As a result, tuition began to escalate at rates above the historical norm, as costs shifted to students and families. Increasingly, higher education was being seen as a private good—generating a return for the individual who invested in it—as much as a public good.[27]

Just as higher education demand was increasing and costs were escalating in the early 2000s, the "college wage premium" (the economic value of college education versus just a high school diploma) was flattening. According to education and workforce expert Anthony Carnevale at Georgetown University, the value of college education over a high school diploma reached a premium of 73 percent by 1999 (and the value of an advanced degree reached 124 percent).[28] The college wage premium had grown relatively steadily throughout much of the 1980s and 1990s, but as Jonathan James, an economist at the Federal Reserve Bank of Cleveland, pointed out, the rate of growth for the college wage premium has been much slower since the late 1990s.[29] In fact, while the wage advantage of a college degree "persists at historically high levels," rather than growing, the premium of a four-year degree alone has remained flat over the last decade.[30] Bachelor's degrees have maintained a very strong economic premium over the alternatives, but advanced degrees have accounted for virtually all of the recent growth in the wage premium. Since the most common credential produced by universities is bachelor's degrees, this trend could be considered a significant driver of the recent attention given to the return on investment of college education and the importance of credentials.[31]

Amid all of these aforementioned market dynamics—recession and recovery, the emergent online delivery of credentials, pressures on financing, and shifts in the economic value of degrees—Congress was due to reauthorize the Higher Education Act in 2003, a process that would ultimately take until 2008. The Higher Education Act is the federal regulatory foundation for colleges and universities, including the framework for billions of dollars in student and institutional aid. At the time, key issues associated with the reauthorization process included expanding access, managing tuition price increases, encouraging accountability and standards, and responding to growth in distance education.[32]

In 2005, these prominent policy themes tied closely to the creation of "The Secretary of Education's Commission on the Future of Higher Education," colloquially referred to as the Spellings Commission, after US Secretary of Education Margaret Spellings. The commission's work consisted of studying the state of higher education and its intersection with the economy as well as making recommendations for reform. It was envisioned as having a watershed impact similar to the publication of *A Nation at Risk* in 1983. The founding charter was particularly focused on meeting the needs of developing a more educated American workforce, as well as the themes of access, affordability, accountability, and quality.[33] This focus was driven by the fear that higher education was failing to adequately prepare students for the workforce and that reforms were needed. Appointed by the Secretary of Education, the commissioners consisted of a mix of college presidents, policy and thought leaders, CEOs, and others. The commission issued its final report in September 2006, using the term *credential* on the first page, within the first point of the report's findings:

> The transformation of the world economy increasingly demands a more highly educated workforce with postsecondary skills and credentials. Ninety percent of the fastest-growing jobs in the new information and service economy will require some postsecondary

education. Job categories that require only on-the-job training are expected to see the greatest decline. In high-demand fields, the value of postsecondary credentials and skills is likely to rise. The Department of Labor projects, for instance, that by 2014 there will be close to four million new job openings combined in health care, education, and computer and mathematical sciences.[34]

In addition to setting the tone regarding the value of postsecondary credentials in the workforce, the Spellings Commission's making the case for broader educational access and scaling up the US system of higher education would shape much of the dialogue in the years ahead, even as the commission's process and the report's reform-oriented tone were criticized within some higher education circles. The commission did appear to achieve its goal of generating a national dialogue about the future of higher education, and its conclusions suggested a future in which credentials were the ticket to workforce success and American economic competitiveness.

By 2008, citing the same job market and competitive imperatives as the Spellings Commission, the Bill & Melinda Gates and Lumina Foundations were defining their higher education missions as focused on higher education attainment, and specifically, using the language of credentials. As the Gates Foundation began to move beyond innovation in K–12 education and was ramping up its Postsecondary Success program in 2008, it defined its goal as "to help double the number of low-income adults who earn postsecondary degrees or credentials—meaningful credentials with value in the workplace and labor market."[35] In the Lumina Foundation's first four-year strategic plan in 2009, the foundation defined its mission around what it now refers to as "Goal 2025"—which aims to "increase the proportion of Americans with high-quality degrees, certificates and other credentials to 60 percent by 2025."[36] Again, the term *credential* and the focus on the job market were central because thought leaders and policy makers were defining success as not exclusively being based on college *degrees*—which were increasingly seen as an expensive multiyear proposition—but rather, being built on other forms of educational credentials.

If the Spellings Commission was the spark that began to kindle the vision for scaling up educational attainment levels and encouraging stronger job market alignment, it was the Great Recession of 2007–2009 that poured fuel on the fire. By the start of 2009, bold educational attainment goals related to credentialing were ensconced in national policy when in the State of the Union address—amid a growing recession and the national unemployment rate at 8.1 percent—President Obama called for every American to have at least one year of postsecondary education, with the goal of America becoming the most educated country in the world again by 2020.[37] By 2010, the National Governor's Association had announced its Complete to Compete initiative, heavily framed around the language of credentialing.[38] In the years since these developments, this college completion agenda has been the primary focus of most national-level education policy, driving substantial new investments and funding; calls for innovation; and support for new models such as competency-based education, all in service of the educational attainment goals.[39]

Independent of the policy undercurrents that had been brewing for years, the financial crisis and recession were certainly the tipping point that brought the employability of college graduates to the fore as an especially urgent issue. Suddenly, college graduates were having difficulty finding jobs in a time that was regarded as the worst in many decades to begin a career, with the unemployment rate for recent graduates in their twenties reaching nearly 20 percent.[40] Colleges and universities—even the most prestigious ones— found that they were underprepared to place their students in jobs in such a turbulent environment, and many—from the University of Southern California to Brown University—began to invest heavily in career services.[41]

Today it is well accepted that one of the primary purposes of higher education is to prepare students for and connect them to jobs, in service of both the student and the broader economy. Among incoming college freshmen, 88 percent cite "to get a better job" as a very important reason for attending college—up from 68 percent in 1976, according to long-running national surveys by the Higher Education Research Institute at UCLA.[42] At the same time, however, nearly 90 percent of business executives believe that college graduates lack the skills to succeed.[43] A widely cited McKinsey report in 2012 characterized the global "education to employment" system as in great distress, with graduates who can't find jobs and employers who can't find skills—and suggested that this disconnect escalated the risk of global unrest.[44] As Peter Stokes documents in his recent book *Higher Education and Employability: New Models for Integrating Study and Work*, the perception of a skills gap and needing to align higher education with job outcomes has become a central theme in today's higher education dialogue.[45] In particular, the prompt for higher education to play a stronger and better role in workforce development has inspired a particular focus on innovation and new business models, including new approaches to credentialing.

As the economic forces of the last decade brought an elevated focus and intensity to the intersection of higher education and the job market, the government, media, and consumers have been focused more than ever on jobs—and key to jobs are university credentials.

## UNIVERSITY CREDENTIALS IN FOCUS

Market forces, the college completion movement, and the drive for innovation in higher education are resulting in new approaches to the development and delivery of university credentials. The credential is emerging as a key character in the evolving story of American higher education.

The opportunity associated with new forms of university credentials is increasingly front and center among senior institutional leaders. The American Council on Education's Presidential Innovation Lab recently acknowledged the emergence of new types of credentials as a significant trend, and the Association of Governing Boards has similarly pointed out that the emphasis on new forms of online learning such as MOOCs is catalyzing new approaches to credentials and bears monitoring by those who govern institutions.[46] Many universities—even the most elite institutions—have begun to aggressively experiment with developing and issuing new forms of credentials. Harvard Business School has launched HBX CORe, which stands for Credential of Readiness, and is a short, intensive, MOOC-inspired online program that now translates into credit at Harvard Extension School.[47] Universities such as Johns Hopkins are offering specialization certificates through online platform company Coursera.[48] And, as another example, leaders at the Georgia Institute of Technology, Northwestern University, the University of Wisconsin, the University of Washington, and two University of California campuses have partnered to develop a joint project focused on new forms of online credentials and digital badges.[49]

In the higher education trade press and general media, it seems not a week goes by without some discussion of the future of university credentials. The *Chronicle of Higher Education*'s September 2015 special report kicking off the new academic year was titled "The Credentials Craze," and featured a package of thoughtful articles on trends and issues associated with new forms of credentials.[50] In that same month, an article in the *New Yorker* discussing the return on investment of college covered some of the finer points of human capital theory in discussing how degrees work as signals or measures of skill.[51] One month later, an October 2015 symposium convened by the *Economist* in New York City featured panel sessions of policy, academic, and business leaders discussing topics such as the value of traditional degrees and nanodegrees, while the influential magazine's pages were exploring the credentials offered by technology start-up Udacity in partnership with major employers.[52]

In addition, substantial funding streams are both following the alternative credentialing trend and driving it. Arguably one of the more significant developments in this area in years occurred in mid-2015 when the US Department of Education announced the development of a pilot program to create experimental sites that would through new quality assurance mechanisms and partnerships open up access to noninstitutional educational providers such as technology boot camps and MOOC providers.[53] If this effort progresses beyond an experimental pilot stage, it could be a game changer not only because federal financial aid for higher education in the United States is a $150 billion funding stream, but because it would begin to break the monopoly that universities have on producing accredited credentials and access to federal financial aid.[54] As President Obama noted in his remarks launching an initiative called TechHire, the desire of policy makers is to leverage faster, cheaper alternative methods to teach skills and link individuals with jobs, rather than rely only on traditional qualifications such as a degrees.[55]

Significant private capital is also flowing to innovations in university credentialing and the adjacent professional credentialing space. The education sector set records in 2014 with $1.4 billion in venture capital and private equity raised by US educational technology firms, a pace that continued through 2015.[56] Some of the largest funding rounds of 2015 went to higher education and professional skills-focused firms, such Pluralsight (an online training provider) and Udacity, which coined the term *nanodegree*.[57] Parchment, a company that describes itself as offering a credentials management system in service of students, institutions, and employers, raised $40 million over the course of 2014 and 2015; while Degreed, another learning tracking and credentialing system, raised $28 million over the course of 2015 and 2016.[58] Meanwhile, publicly traded behemoth LinkedIn, which has been busy disrupting the hiring and recruiting space for years, is increasingly defining its business strategy as developing and owning the economic graph that connects job seekers, employers, and institutions.[59] LinkedIn has been creating an interesting set of tools and databases for potential college students and professionals. In 2015, the firm turned heads when it spent $1.5 billion to acquire Lynda.com, an online professional skills provider, as part of a strategy to link training and skills development with credentials and jobs.[60]

Employers are last but certainly not least in the cresting wave of momentum. Human resources/hiring expert Peter Cappelli, a professor at the University of Pennsylvania's Wharton School, has studied the intersection of higher education and hiring for many years and suggests in his recent book *Will College Pay Off* that the "burgeoning world of skill-based credentials" is important to monitor.[61] There is a great deal of opportunity for improvement in how employers assess their workforce and make hiring choices, and HR/talent analytics is emerging as a top area of focus in corporate strategy given the strengthening economy and the more than $125 billion annually that US companies spend on hiring and recruiting, according to Deloitte.[62] Further, in a growing number of cases—while they remain the exception—major employers are transforming how they consider university credentials in their hiring process. For example, professional services firm Ernst & Young's United Kingdom operation announced in August 2015 that it was scrapping traditional academic credentials as a qualification and moving toward online testing, following an eighteen-month-long analysis of its hiring process.[63] In the academic world that studies how corporations hire and manage their workforce, there has been for many years a call for deeper and more descriptive analysis of how managers and human resources professionals actually make hiring decisions: much of the hiring process, as critical as it is, is a "black box."[64] Particularly in today's global market for talent, employers need an appropriately prepared workforce and also need to better understand how to assess and use new forms of university credentials in an increasingly fragmented landscape. Moreover, to ensure that programs and student outcomes are aligned with market needs, universities—many of which have historically viewed a focus on workforce issues as vocational and below them—must do more to align with the changing employment landscape.

## THE IMPERATIVE FOR A DEEPER UNDERSTANDING IN AN INEFFICIENT AND RAPIDLY EVOLVING ECOSYSTEM

This book is built on the recognition that the higher education market and critical aspects of the economy revolve around university credentials. However, given how important this topic is, it is quite surprising that our understanding of how employers use university credentials in hiring is not well understood. Analyzing the role of university credentials in hiring sits at the intersection of multiple academic domains—including sociology, education, economics, and business. Expert researchers who have focused on hiring and credentialing, such as Lauren Rivera, David Brown, and David Bills, note that the empirical research on how employers use credentials is very limited and that much more research is needed.[65] Moreover, most of the limited academic research on this topic dates to the 1980s and 1990s and often focuses on hiring processes in sectors and at levels below the professional roles that prefer or require university credentials. The economists who study the issue tend to focus on quantitative analyses and formulas related to years of schooling and human capital, whereas sociologists are often more interested in how credentials relate to occupational status or class.

Further, although there appears to be consensus among key parties that the future higher education landscape will include a proliferation of new options and university credentials beyond the monolithic degree, frequent prognostications about the "death of the degree" and the brave new world of digital credentialing are very often not built on empirical evidence or data, but rather on anecdotes and speculation.[66]

It is this problem that this book aims to solve, by analyzing the future of university credentials in an evidence-based fashion. As this introduction has established, understanding the future of university credentials is crucial for a wide range of parties who must plan and adapt to the changing environment. Academic leaders within universities are tasked with designing, delivering, managing, and assessing credential programs. As a result, they must think strategically about the design and delivery of academic programs based on a strong understanding of how credentials and their curriculum intersect with the job market. In addition, university administrators, boards, and government leaders have a major role and interest in the oversight and production of university credentials, and they can benefit from a systematic view for better-informed administration, oversight, and strategic planning. Policy makers and regulators also have a special need to understand the future of university credentials, as they seek to optimize the structure and financing of higher education and workforce development, and also provide appropriate frameworks for quality assurance and innovation.

Additionally, business leaders and major employers rely on university credentials as the backbone of millions of critical hiring decisions and billions of dollars in learning and development investments made each year. They also need an understanding of future directions in the market for talent, and how their actions and voices as key stakeholders can have an impact on universities and higher education policy. Finally, other parties—such as the growing number of start-ups, established education companies and publishers, and investors—view the credentialing ecosystem as a major and growing market opportunity. As they shape their business strategies, they too can also benefit from a timely and comprehensive review of trends in the environment to influence their business ideas and strategy.

## THIS BOOK AS A SOLUTION

As a range of leaders in higher education, government, and industry encourage innovation in higher education, many are claiming that higher education—in the United States, if not worldwide as well—is broken or in crisis. It follows then that insofar as credentialing is a central feature of higher education, perhaps it is the credentialing mechanism that is in need of innovation and key to understanding and generating new models and greater value. This is precisely why MOOCs, digital badges, $10,000 bachelor's degrees, and the like are often positioned as harbingers of healthy disruption and potential saviors of higher education and workforce development in the twenty-first century: evolving the credential ecosystem is key to optimizing higher education.

To have the modern credentialing ecosystem that so many seem to desire—one that is high quality, is more efficient and transparent, enables greater access, and is relevant globally—the US system as it works today needs to adapt to change. This will require the various parties ranging from educational institutions and government agencies to employers themselves to work more closely together.

In the pages ahead, we will explore how the university credentialing ecosystem is evolving—with an eye to the future that is grounded in an analysis of current market trends and an understanding of history. We will do so based on evidence and hard data: the academic and industry research literature, various surveys and other data sources, the voice of employers themselves based on extensive qualitative interviews, and a behind-the-scenes examination of how the academic and quality assurance worlds have approached and are approaching innovation in the development and delivery of university credentials.

Chapter 1 sets the analytical foundation with a brief history of university credentials and the demand for and value of them in the job market, tracing the growth of mass higher education and the rise of college degrees as a key occupational qualifications. Chapter 2 deeply explores what we know about how employers actually make hiring decisions and how and why they use university credentials as key occupational qualifications. With those critical dynamics established, chapter 3 establishes the lessons learned from the rise of IT certifications and early efforts in online education. Next, chapter 4 evaluates the maturation of the online credential market. Chapter 5 profiles the technology solutions and innovations that are shaping both university-side credentialing and employers' hiring strategies. Chapter 6 focuses on examples of how the higher education system—universities, quality assurance entities, and so on—are responding to changes in credentialing via various new forms of university credentials. Finally, chapter 7 synthesizes the findings and analytical themes and focuses on implications and recommendations for the future.

ONE

# The Rise of the University Credential in the Knowledge Economy

The higher education system in the United States as we know it today arguably traces its beginnings to the late 1800s. The Morrill Act of 1862, passed during the American Civil War, was significant in creating land grant colleges and universities that would focus on agricultural, mechanical, and professional education.[1] Rather than focusing on educating the elite, the higher education sector was starting to become more vocational in its focus, expanding to educate the masses. Into the 1870s, many colleges and universities were still operating with a classical curriculum that required, for example, Latin and Greek language proficiency.[2] As Julie Reuben documents in *The Making of the Modern University*, the scientific thinking emerging at that time and a crisis of relevance brought about significant evolutions in curriculum and governance.[3] Building on the German model, the American research university was born, characterized by the addition of graduate education and research, with transformations at Harvard and Johns Hopkins among the best examples.[4] This new university model aligned higher education more tightly with economic and industrial interests. Beyond the birth of the modern research university, this era also saw a proliferation of new private colleges, normal schools, and state universities.[5]

According to credentialing expert David Brown in his monograph *Degrees of Control*, it was only in the 1890s that bachelor's degrees began to gain wide acceptance as hiring qualifications and professional credentials in business and government.[6] This would become a major factor in future college enrollment growth as employers started to prefer hiring college graduates. The master's degree—which was initially a terminal qualification for college instructors—was also relatively new on the scene in this time frame, experiencing significant growth in the second half of the 1800s alongside the first US-based PhD programs.[7]

Growth in higher education was enabled by the dramatic expansion of secondary education in the United States during the twentieth century, given the dependence of college- and university-level enrollment on a pool of qualified high school graduates.[8] High school completion had not even been widespread until the early-to-mid 1900s, when it became more universal through "the high school movement."[9] By World War II, half of the American population was completing high school (and by 1970, this number rose to nearly 80 percent of the population).[10] In addition, the postwar economic expansion, the GI bill, and substantial Cold War investments in graduate programs later drove continued dramatic expansion in college programming and enrollment. It took about one hundred years, but higher education in the United States had "massified," a relatively unique achievement in the scheme of the economic development of nations. Higher education—and the earning of college degrees—was now deeply ensconced within the fabric of the economy.

College enrollment flattened for a period immediately following the Vietnam era, since military draft deferments had artificially inflated college participation, and the large baby boom demographic cohort had moved through its peak college years.[11] However, enrollment surged through the 1990s and 2000s, with approximately 70 percent of high school graduates continuing to college.[12] Later, driven by economic conditions, college enrollment grew at a nearly unprecedented pace between 2006 and 2011, representing growth of more than three million students—a rate of increase that exceeded the previous ten years combined.[13] Total enrollment declined in 2012 and 2013: in the most recent year, the decline was driven by lower enrollment in two-year colleges, whereas four-year enrollment grew 1 percent.[14] This surge and then leveling off still places total college and university enrollment in the United States near all-time highs. With the exception of brief pauses and periods of contraction, the history of American higher education is generally one of growth and expansion—as measured by enrollments, institutions, and credentials produced.

As higher education in the United States scaled, various types of college- and university-issued credentials developed for different purposes and at different paces. If we rewind three hundred-plus years, the early American colleges were essentially secondary schools that granted the traditional bachelor of arts degree borrowed from the European model.[15] The bachelor's degree, normally requiring four years of college-level work, remains by far the most popular and the most commonly understood credential in higher education. With some variation, the bachelor's degree typically consists of 120 credit hours of study, and it comes in forms ranging from bachelor of arts (BA) degrees, typically in the humanities, to bachelor of science (BS), bachelor of fine arts (BFA), and many other diverse varieties.[16] Once a relatively rare credential, the bachelor's degree has become the norm for entry into the middle class workforce, while it is still attained by only about 30 percent of the US adult population.[17]

Interestingly, the two-year associate degree was born out of an interest among elitist research university reformers seeking to align the first two years of undergraduate college study with secondary schooling, allowing universities to focus on upper division coursework. The first associate degree was therefore awarded at the University of Chicago in 1900, after president William Rainey Harper designed this credential as a terminal offering to be received at the end of sophomore year—and later seeded the idea in the broader market with the creation of Joliet Junior College in Chicago, which was effectively the first community college in the United States.[18] The associate degree blossomed as the core credential of community colleges, which grew from numbering seventy-four nationwide in 1915 to nearly one thousand by 1968.[19]

Master's degrees, meanwhile, were originally research-focused terminal credentials—and later consolation prizes awarded en route to research PhDs. The first master's degree offered in the United States was awarded at the University of Michigan in 1859.[20] As bachelor's degree attainment became more common across the twentieth century, master's degree attainment increased correspondingly, with the master's becoming a key professional credential for leadership roles in business and government.[21] By the 1980s and 1990s, most master's degrees awarded were no longer principally research-oriented masters of arts (MAs), but rather, enrollment was more concentrated in professionally and practically focused master of science (MS) degrees and other credentials such as the increasingly popular master of business administration (MBA).[22] The variety of master's degrees also exploded, and in just a ten-year period between 2000 and 2010, master's degree enrollment in the United States surged 46 percent.[23]

Although doctoral and professional degrees such as the PhD (scholarship), MD (medicine), and JD (law) make up a critical and well-known segment of higher education, they account for only 7 percent of all degrees awarded each year.[24] Enrollment at this level of higher education has generally grown as well over the years, but these types of credentials serve a very particular audience and of course require a significant number of years of schooling beyond the bachelor's. The educational model of doctoral and professional degrees has largely been tradition-bound, smaller-scale, and relatively slow to evolve, with these terminal credentials and training methods solidified within their professions for many decades. Of course, change may be ahead.

In the thirty-year period between 1980 and 2010, the number of associate degrees awarded in the United States more than doubled; the number of bachelor's degrees nearly doubled; the number of master's degrees awarded surged 140 percent; and the number of doctoral degrees increased by two-thirds.[25] In the 2010–2011 academic year, nearly 1 million associate degrees, 1.7 million bachelor's degrees, and almost 1 million advanced degrees were awarded. This total of nearly 3.6 million degrees issued is exactly double the figure (1.8 million) from thirty years prior.

In addition to degrees, much of the diversification in higher education credentials has come through various types of certificates, which span from the vocational/prebaccalaureate levels all the way to the postgraduate. Higher education institutions can be especially nimble in developing and offering new types of certificates because the canvas is so wide, and given that certificates are typically short form in nature. The US Department of Education defines a certificate simply as "a formal award certifying the satisfactory completion of a postsecondary education program," and this is in a descriptive rather than prescriptive sense.[26] This definition suggests the wide variety of forms and levels in which certificates can be found. Certificates exist in both a for-credit and a noncredit basis, with standards and governance oversight often loose for noncredit offerings. For example, at one institution, a for-credit graduate-level certificate might be linked directly to a degree program, with similar admissions standards as the degree program, and requiring the completion of three semester-length courses. At another institution, the same type of certificate may require the completion of four or five courses, with no connection to a degree program and loose admissions standards. A noncredit certificate might be issued for either the completion of an intensive multiweek executive education program; a short one-day seminar; or, increasingly, a single self-paced online course. Whereas degrees have much greater standardization and consistency, the depth and scope of certificate programs can vary substantially within a given state—or even across departments and colleges within the same educational institution.

It is important to note that many in industry—as well as in higher education, government, and media circles—often mistakenly conflate the term *certificate* (program) with *certification*. A certification, by contrast, is a credential issued by a professional, occupational, or government body, and many times certifications can be obtained through the completion of an exam and very little in the way of connectivity to postsecondary institutions. And, to complicate matters, college-delivered *certificate* programs may often be usefully aligned with industry certification standards. For example, a university-delivered certificate program in project management or financial planning might help a student prepare, qualify for, or earn credit toward Project Management Professional (PMP) or Certified Financial Planner (CFP) industry certification. The breadth, market alignment, and flexibility of certificates are key to their status as a category full of experimentation and variety, but this also creates potential confusion in the marketplace.

The expansion of the higher education system and the variety of credentials it produces have, of course, been shaped and influenced by various quality assurance and governmental bodies. Like many other developments briefly reviewed in this chapter, much of this originated a century ago, around 1900.

The Association of American Universities (AAU) was itself founded in 1900, in part out of a desire to set needed standards due to the proliferation of degrees and higher education institutions.[27] The academic establishment in Europe looked down on the lack of consistency in PhD and master's degrees at fledgling American research universities, and this led to what came to be known as the "standardization movement" in the United States. The standardization movement evolved into what we today know as "accreditation," as groups such as the North Central Association (one of the six major regional accrediting agencies, and still in existence as the Higher Learning Commission) came into being. In 1916, the North Central Association set admissions and curricular standards for member institutions that included, for example, that college admission be based on the completion of fourteen units of high school credit and that a bachelor's degree would be constituted of 120 credits.[28] As Judith Eaton, an accreditation expert and president of the Council for Higher

Education Accreditation (CHEA) articulates, one of the core roles of accreditation is giving students confidence that a given degree or credential has value and meets a set of standards.[29] According to Eaton, the "gatekeeping" role of voluntary private sector accreditors emerged in the 1950s when the federal government sought an authority to certify the quality of higher education institutions, positioning accrediting agencies as arbiters of all-important federal funding.[30]

Although there have been loud calls for reforms to accreditation in recent years—US Senate hearings in 2015 and prior years focused on the need for and potential of reform—standards set by the triad of accreditation agencies, the federal government, and state regulators keep the definitions and terms related to most university credentials, particularly degrees, fairly uniform.[31] It is for this reason that assuring the quality of new approaches to university credentials (such as competency-based education) must involve collaboration across a host of organizations and agencies, from institutional governing boards to state agencies, accreditors, and the federal government—not to mention the role played by industry groups, employers, and other parties. It is for this reason that the most innovative and leading-edge new university credentials are often of the noncredit variety—requiring little in terms of institutional governance or outside regulatory approval.

The growth and multiplication of American higher education institutions, enrollments, and credentials over the past century is not simply a story of universities engaging in an unbridled, land-grabbing expansion. Rather, this growth is a direct result of the rise of a knowledge- and service-driven economy and the institutionalization of education and occupational credentialing in the twentieth century.

## THE KNOWLEDGE ECONOMY AND THE INSTITUTIONALIZATION OF CREDENTIALS

The evolution of the American higher education system and its credentialing function is intimately related to the growth of the knowledge economy and the expansion of professional work over the past century. In *The Race Between Education and Technology*, economists Claudia Goldin and Lawrence Katz credit educational expansion and the ensuing growth in degree attainment with driving the United States' economic success over the last hundred years, terming the period "the human capital century."[32] Goldin and Katz establish and dissect the strong link between educational attainment, productivity, and earnings—attributing benefits that have accrued to more highly educated workers to "skills-biased technological change."[33] In essence, the technological and economic transformations that have occurred in recent decades have favored more highly skilled, highly educated workers. This has in turn escalated the demand for educated workers and advanced the level of education required for economic productivity, as the economy builds on the newly available stock of human capital.

Between 1910 and 2000, the share of the workforce made up by professional and service workers grew from one-quarter to three-quarters, as the US economy transformed from a reliance on agriculture and manufacturing to being driven by services and knowledge. Growth was especially significant in professional and technical occupations—exactly the types of occupations that tend to require or prefer college degrees.[34] Anthony Carnevale, director of Georgetown University's Center on Education and the Workforce, is one of the foremost experts analyzing how higher education relates to the job market. Over a variety of studies, Carnevale and his colleagues have documented the value of college education in the modern workforce. An analysis by Carnevale and Stephen Rose illustrates that postsecondary education is now typical for middle class and white collar workers: between 1967 and 2012, the share of workers with some college or a degree grew from to 25 to 61 percent, owing to the number of high-skill managerial and professional jobs in the workforce nearly doubling.[35]

It is not just that the changing demands of work shape the need for credentials: in a self-reinforcing cycle, the availability of credentialed workers in turn reshapes work. Sociologist and credentialing expert David Baker argues that not only has the growth of knowledge work transformed the economy, but also that the growth and institutionalization of education has in turn transformed the nature of work itself, resulting in a "schooled society."[36] Drawing on a range of empirical findings, Baker argues that mass education, especially higher education, has created the human capital capacity to shape the evolution of the economy and changes in the nature of work. Similarly, Carnevale and Rose characterize economic and societal trends—such as the rise of information technology, the power of societal and business networks, and the growth of high skill office work—as mutually reinforcing in escalating the importance of postsecondary education.[37]

While these economic trends have been playing out over many decades, the value of education and training and university credentials has been particularly pronounced lately. MIT economist David Autor has demonstrated that especially in recent years, job market growth in the United States has polarized between high-skill, high-wage jobs, which require college education, and low-skill, low-wage jobs, a trend that has been exacerbated by the Great Recession.[38] According to Autor's analysis of decades of economic data, as well as more recent trends, the financial benefits of educational attainment are now highly concentrated among four-year and advanced degree holders; that is, the more educated groups in the job market are economically pulling away, and the returns to education below the bachelor's degree level are not what they once were and are in fact declining.

The arrival of a knowledge economy and the power of postsecondary education to drive earnings and job placement have established university credentials as central to occupational mobility and career success. In addition, the power of credentialing is also evident in nonuniversity credentials, for example, occupational and professional credentials. Many occupations and fields have sought to be seen as professions—by creating specialized techniques and bodies of knowledge, regulation, continuing education requirements, and sets of standards.[39] As a result, countless professional credentials and designations have emerged, especially in the 1980s and 1990s. They include, for example, the Certified Financial Planner (CFP) designation, the Project Management Professional (PMP) credential, and the Senior Professional in Human Resources (SPHR). These credentials and others like them serve both as complements to and substitutes for traditional college degrees. They have proliferated to include, for example, Geographic Information Systems Professionals (GISPs) in the geospatial field, the Certified Nurse Midwife (CNM) in health care, and the Certified Property Manager (CPM) in real estate. A 2012 US Census Bureau analysis found that 22 percent of the US adult population held a professional certification or license—often in addition to a degree.[40] David Baker's analysis suggests that this trend toward occupational and professional licensing is a key hallmark of the schooled society and the educational transformation of work: whereas many decades ago access to occupations tended to be controlled by unions, occupational access and station are today driven by educational and professional credentialing.[41] In the current market, knowledge work is entrusted principally to educationally credentialed individuals in educationally created areas of expertise.[42] While the focus of this book's analysis is on university credentials, professional credentialing and licensing are an adjacent domain that has many points of intersection with the future of university credentials.

## GROWING DEMAND FOR UNIVERSITY CREDENTIALS AND THEIR VALUE IN THE JOB MARKET

A strong argument can be made that in our knowledge- and technology-driven economy, the demand for college-educated workers is growing—and that the value of university credentials is as high as ever. However, there is great debate about the "value," or return on investment, for university credentials, given escalating tuition rates, frequent critiques by politicians, and rampant anecdotes about underemployed baristas with master's degrees and six-figure college debt. Headlines in major media outlets are illustrative of the attention the anticollege argument is receiving. Pieces titled "Is College Worth It?" or variations on that language have been featured everywhere from the *New York Times* and *Time Magazine* to the titles of numerous high-profile books over the past few years—not to mention this topic's prominence in Silicon Valley or Washington, DC, conference panels and political speeches.

Are all types of degrees economically valuable or necessary in all circumstances? Of course not. Is it appropriate to question the return on investment of college study when the investment portion of the equation (tuition costs) continues to escalate while the college wage premium has stopped moving ever upward? Yes. But on the whole, the economic evidence that degrees are highly valued in the economy is compelling. And much of this value derives from degrees' status as professional credentials that are useful to employers in hiring and developing their workforce—a value that shows up in occupational qualifications and salary levels.

## Job Market Demand for University Credentials

University credentials are essential qualifications in today's professional job market. Yet, of the approximately 150 million individuals employed in the overall US labor market, two-thirds (66 percent) of jobs are concentrated in occupations that typically do *not* require a college-level education for entry—occupations such as home health aides, electricians, retail salespeople, construction laborers, and so on.[43] However, for many years, job market growth—not to mention wage advantages—has been highly concentrated in jobs that prefer or require postsecondary education.

In one of the US Department of Labor's most recent occupational summaries, bachelor's degrees were the typical *entry-level* educational qualification for 18 percent of jobs, followed by associate degrees at 4 percent, doctoral and professional degrees at 3 percent, and master's degrees at 2 percent. Postsecondary nondegree awards and "some college" account for another 7 percent.[44] Looking forward, over the ten-year 2014–2024 forecast period, jobs that typically require graduate degrees for entry are projected to grow at the fastest rate: 12.8 percent, versus just over 8 percent for the categories of bachelor's and associate degree and "some college" level jobs.[45] The growth prospects for non-college-level occupations are expected to be relatively dim, with a growth forecast of only 3.9 percent for roles that typically require a high school diploma or equivalent, and 6.9 percent for less-than-high-school jobs (such as restaurant cooks, bartenders, and landscaping workers).[46]

Importantly, a majority of the occupations with the highest forecast growth rates for the 2014–2024 period—nine of the top fifteen—typically require a postsecondary degree.[47] They include, for example, statisticians (master's degree), financial advisors (bachelor's degree), physical therapy assistants (associate degree), physical therapists (doctoral degree), and nurse practitioners (master's degree); and the pattern holds true further down the list in terms of occupations with the strongest expected growth prospects.[48] Although forecasting the job market on a long time scale can be notoriously fickle, the growth in knowledge and service occupations will demand the production of millions of new university credentials, many of them in new and emerging fields.

Evidence indicates that employers are demanding greater numbers of newly minted college graduates, based on tracking surveys that have annually benchmarked employers' hiring activity or intention to hire. The National Association of Colleges and Employers (NACE)—a significant industry association of university career services offices and employer university relations professionals—reported a positive job outlook for the class of 2016, with 72 percent of employers reporting they planned to hire more (36 percent) or the same (37 percent) numbers of college graduates compared to the prior year.[49] NACE also reported that the MBA job market had been continuing to grow in 2015, with schools reporting an increase in on-campus recruiting activity.[50] Similarly, the 2015 Michigan State

University Recruiting Trends survey found an expected 15 percent increase in hiring across all degree levels due to economic growth and turnover and retirements.[51]

In this discussion about educational qualifications for jobs, a critical distinction is to be made between required and preferred levels of education. The illustrative Bureau of Labor Statistics data cited earlier is based on the typical *entry-level pathway* for a given occupation. Outside of regulated occupations, most jobs rarely *require* a particular level of educational credential per se, but they may very well *prefer* a certain level of education. You need only think of the commonly found phrase in job postings, "bachelor's degree required, advanced degree preferred." Most occupations have individuals who enter the field with a wide range of credentials, and large shares of professionals within the occupation typically advance to a higher level of credential during the course of their career. For example, the bachelor's degree is clearly the typical *entry-level* credential for advertising managers, held by 61 percent of these professionals in the workforce. However, fully 20 percent of professionals in this occupation have no degree at all, whereas another 14 percent hold a graduate degree, representing quite a wide variety.[52] Similarly, if we examine construction managers as an occupation, a relatively equal proportion of these individuals have either only a high school diploma (27 percent), some college education (25 percent), or a bachelor's degree (28 percent).[53] A further 6 percent of construction managers hold an advanced degree, and graduate-level offerings in construction management have represented an in-demand growth area for a number of colleges and universities.

Compared to more static datasets and forecasts, real-time labor market analytics are especially useful in describing the current demand for university credentials, especially at the professional level. Burning Glass Technologies is a leading firm that has developed an innovative technology and reliable database based on "scraping" millions of online job advertisements, deduplicating, and classifying them. Based on Burning Glass's data, more than twenty-six million discrete job openings were posted in the United States over the course of calendar year 2015.[54] Based on both the preferred or minimum/required level of education referenced in these job openings, it is clear that job openings largely favor credentials at the four-year level and above (note that totals add to more than 100 percent since required and preferred qualifications overlap). Across many millions of job postings, among those that specified an educational level, fully 56 percent referenced a bachelor's degree; 21 percent, a graduate degree; 15 percent, an associate degree; and another 33 percent advertised high school or vocational training. This snapshot illustrates the extent to which economic growth depends on university credentials. These preferred levels of educational attainment in recent job openings represent a significant gap above the educational attainment rates of the US population, given that only 20 percent of the population over age twenty-five holds a bachelor's degree as their highest credential; and only 12 percent have an advanced degree.[55]

Burning Glass researchers have conducted studies dissecting the growing demand for bachelor's and advanced degrees at the more detailed level of specific occupations, including a 2014 analysis that quantified the upcredentialing trend. This analysis identified gaps as high as 20 to 25 percent in many fields between the percentage of job postings *requiring* a bachelor's degree and the percentage of job holders in that occupation with a bachelor's degree.[56] For example, while only 42 percent of individuals in management occupations hold a bachelor's degree, 68 percent of job postings require them—a gap of 26 percent.[57]

One of the most talked about findings from this study was the example that 65 percent of job postings for executive secretaries and executive assistants required a bachelor's degree, compared to just 19 percent of individuals in that occupation who hold one.[58] Arguing that this is a prime example of unnecessary credential inflation—since secretarial roles clearly used to require no more than a high school diploma or vocational degree—one media outlet ran a story titled "The Reason Why Peggy Olson Would Never Get Hired Today," referring to the character in award-winning television drama *Mad Men* who began as a secretary and worked her way up through the ranks at the advertising firm to become a copywriter and partner.[59] Although it is a fair point to question whether employers should require or prefer a bachelor's degree for administrative assistant labor, this example (even at the relative lower rungs of the knowledge work ladder) actually offers a useful case study of the skills-biased economic and technological change referenced earlier, as it relates to demand for educational credentials.

In the *Mad Men* era of 1965, an administrative assistant likely would have been responsible for basic tasks such as typing correspondence, transcribing dictated notes, performing basic accounting tasks, and scheduling appointments.[60] She or he likely may have had only a high school diploma or a credential from a specialized one-year program at a secretarial school. By contrast, administrative assistants today—especially those of the executive variety—are often expected to author correspondence, assist in preparing presentations and written deliverables, conduct research, perform basic data analysis, interact with outside clients and vendors, manage purchasing, and potentially supervise other administrative staff.[61] These are certainly higher-order tasks that require significantly more advanced communication and writing skills, judgment, technical knowledge, and professional acumen than in the past, and these are the types of characteristics that could be readily found in most bachelor's degree graduates. This notion is confirmed, for example, by a quick review of a handful of randomly selected executive assistant job openings in New York City as of October 2015. This exercise finds employers seeking executive assistant candidates who will (yes, in addition to scheduling appointments and processing expense reports) manage projects, oversee consultants, interact with donors, oversee monthly revenue tracking, execute special projects, manage day-to-day operations of the office, build presentations, and assist with regulatory compliance.[62]

Of course, the demand for university credentials hinges far less on the evolution of executive assistant roles and more on the growing need for professionals such as software developers, business intelligence analysts, marketing managers, nurses, accountants, engineers, and the like. Is the nature of executive assistant work and its educational requirements or preferences the best illustration of occupational demand for university credentials? Most certainly it is not. But the stretch and perhaps extreme example of the executive assistant goes to show how much nuance is under the surface when we consider the mapping between job requirements and educational credentials. Using stories about the overqualified executive assistant or the cab-driving PhD, the anticollege narrative suggests that employers are irrational and that markets are inefficient. Employers see university credentials not only as reflections or certifications of skill, but also as useful indicators of other productivity characteristics and proxies for ability and potential. Employers have every reason to be rational and profit-minded, rather than overpaying for educational qualifications that are not actually necessary; and the economic value of university credentials manifests itself in the still-strong earnings premium for college degrees.

## The Economic Value of University Credentials

Postsecondary educational attainment, it is commonly understood, results in greater earnings and increased economic opportunity. This fact is generally true across a wide range of nations, from highly developed to emerging economies. Comparative education studies from the Organization for Economic Cooperation and Development (OECD) indicate that similar to trends in the United States, high school attainment has become the norm in OECD countries, making postsecondary education required to reap the economic rewards of advanced schooling. OECD analysis has also found that among all countries, the wage premium for college-level education over lower levels of educational attainment is highest in the United States.[63] Harry Patrinos, economist and education practice manager at the World Bank, attributes this to the fact that the US economy is the world's most innovative and competitive: "In the US there is definitely a demand for labor that is skill-biased, the changes in the economy are putting a premium on skills that are not easy to automate or contract out or off-shore. The spread is much higher in the US."[64]

College degree holders are rewarded by higher salaries indicative of demand for their skills; they are also much less likely to be unemployed, and likewise benefit from the economic opportunity of job growth that is increasingly centered on occupations and industries that require advanced levels of education. Scholarship shows that this positive relationship between degree attainment and economic success has been made more prominent by recent economic trends.

According to the US Department of Labor's Bureau of Labor Statistics, for the year 2014, the unemployment rate stood at just 3.5 percent for adults who held a bachelor's degree, 2.8 percent for those with a master's degree, around 2.0 percent for those with doctoral or professional degrees, and 4.5 percent for individuals with an associate degree.[65] This compares to a headline unemployment rate of 5.0 percent for all workers, and unemployment rates as high as 6.0 percent for those with only a high school diploma, and 9.0 percent for individuals who have not graduated from high school.[66] Analyzing how the recession of 2007–2009 and the ensuing recovery had impacted employment prospects, Anthony Carnevale, Tamara Jayasundera, and Ban Cheah found that through 2012, holders of a bachelor's degree or above had gained more than two million jobs in the recovery, whereas those with associate degrees or only some college had recovered only 1.6 million jobs, while those with a high school diploma or less had lost nearly two hundred fifty thousand jobs.[67]

Many economists consider the college wage premium—the earnings differential between those holding college-level credentials compared to high school graduates—to be the best indicator that the economy values credentials and higher levels of educational attainment. Anthony Carnevale notes that in the 1960s and 1970s, an oversupply of college graduates led to a decline in the wage premium for postsecondary education: in 1979, a postsecondary degree provided a 43 percent earnings premium over a high school diploma.[68] Carnevale asserts that contrary to basic economic theory—which contends that when supply increases, price declines—it is remarkable that the college wage advantage doubled even as more than ten million individuals with a bachelor's degree or higher entered the workforce between the 1990s and 2008, and this illustrates the increasing advantage to earning university credentials.[69]

While remaining near an all-time high, the college wage premium has flattened in recent years. David Autor's analysis suggests that this may be due to the much faster pace of college attainment between 2004 and 2012, when both a demographic boom and the economic situation contributed to a nearly unprecedented surge in college enrollment and graduation, a situation similar to the 1960s and 1970s.[70] Despite this, the premium remains substantial. According to recent data from the US Department of Labor's Bureau of Labor Statistics for 2014, the average weekly earnings premium over just a high school diploma stood at 19 percent for individuals with an associate degree; 65 percent for bachelor's degrees; 99 percent for master's degrees; and more than 138 percent for doctoral and professional degrees.[71] Even factoring in both the growing costs of college and the fact that wages have been stagnant for recent college graduates, Jaison Abel and Richard Dietz of the Federal Reserve Bank of New York found that the benefits of college do substantially still outweigh the costs.[72]

The differential in economic value between various credentials is important to note, and this is illustrative of the relative demand for and supply of these credentials in the workforce. Interestingly, despite growth and so much policy emphasis on sub-baccalaureate credentials (for example, community college certificates and associate degrees), many researchers have found lackluster value for these types of postsecondary awards in the job market. In a recent academic paper published in 2014, Mina Dadgar and Madeline Joy Trimble explored the job market returns to sub-baccalaureate credentials. They found that the economic value of associate degrees was modest for women and nearly nonexistent for men, and that short-term certificates have minimal value and generally do not lead to improved job market outcomes beyond just completing some college courses with no credential.[73]

The bachelor's degree is, of course, the most common credential in higher education and the bread-and-butter of the college wage premium—so much so that in most surveys and economic studies, all higher levels of education are clustered together in the category "bachelor's degree and above." However, when we unbundle higher levels of credential from the bachelor's, it is apparent that advanced degrees—particularly master's degrees—have increased in value, especially since the Great Recession.[74] It is also worth noting that the earnings premiums associated with associate degrees and bachelor's degrees as terminal credentials do not capture their value as critical prerequisites and stepping stones to higher-level credentials (bachelor's degrees and master's degrees, respectively).

## Not All Credentials Are Created Equal

To this point, we have largely discussed university credentials and their value with respect to the level of study (such as bachelor's, master's) alone, as if all postsecondary credentials at the same level are commodities. Yet, there are nearly 5,000 degree-granting colleges and universities in the United States—with varying quality levels, approaches, and reputations—and they award credentials across nearly 2,000 discrete areas of academic study.[75] The literature on the value of university credentials illustrates that both the area of academic study associated with a credential and the awarding institution have significant impacts on their value in the job market.

Using detailed new data from the US Census Bureau's American Community Survey, Jaison Abel and Richard Dietz (Federal Reserve Bank of New York economists) found considerable variation in wages among bachelor's degree holders, and that not surprisingly, technical majors such as engineering and computer science had the greatest job market value. Health and business majors also ranked highly, while earnings for liberal arts majors were among the weakest.[76] Analyzing the same dataset in 2015, Anthony Carnevale and Georgetown University's Center on Education and the Workforce came to similar conclusions—reporting that the highest-paying majors lead to substantial wage premiums at both the entry level and over the course of one's career.[77] They also point out that the two highest-paying categories of undergraduate major—STEM fields (science, technology, engineering, and math) and business—happen to account for 46 percent of all undergraduate degree completions.[78]

Differentials in value by field of study hold true and are even more pronounced at the graduate level. A salary survey by the National Association of Colleges and Employers shows salary premiums for new master's degree graduates that are more than 20 percent higher than bachelor's graduates, with the premium in some fields (such as computer science) rising to 30 percent or more.[79] Similarly, researchers such as Katie Zaback, Andy Carlson, and Matt Crellin have analyzed state-level data and found great differences in the premium between educational disciplines with income premiums for graduate degrees as high as 69 percent in health; 62 percent in social and behavioral sciences; and 48 percent in business and communications.[80] These higher percentages represent the salary premiums of experienced talent with master's degrees.

In addition to significant variation in the value of credentials by major, the brand and reputation of a university awarding a credential are other major factors. Keeping this dynamic in mind is key when considering the proliferation of credentials and a public dialogue that often treats university credentials as commodities. It is no secret that graduates of prestigious colleges and universities tend to earn more than their peers, all other factors being equal, and countless economic analyses and salary-oriented college rankings attest to this point.

In a 2014 study, Joni Hersch of Vanderbilt University explored how the transition from a less selective undergraduate institution to later study with a more prestigious graduate institution affected individuals' earnings and career prospects. Categorizing a large and broad cross-section of institutions into selectivity tiers, Hersch found, not surprisingly, a very strong linkage between selectivity and earnings.[81] Notably, the impact of the reputation of the undergraduate institution attended persisted even when students attended a more elite graduate school.

Another example of the power of the institutional reputation and brand attached to credentials can be found in a 2014 working paper for the National Bureau of Economic Research. David Deming, Noam Yuchtman, Amira Abulafi, Claudia Goldin, and Lawrence Katz conducted an experimental study in which they assigned institution types and selectivity levels to fictitious resumes and measured the extent to which these resumes received callbacks to job applications. This analysis included bachelor's degrees as well as certificates. Within their experimental frame, these researchers found that employers particularly valued college quality and selectivity, favoring more reputable institutions.[82]

Finally, it is worth pointing out that there is a documented value to completing a university *credential*, over and above the years of schooling or knowledge and skills that the credential designates. Most economic models treat additional courses, training, and degrees equally as "years of schooling," and suggest in either simple terms or complicated models that worker productivity and economic value increase with time in school or each additional learning outcome. However, economists such as Dale Belman and John Heywood of the University of Wisconsin–Milwaukee have confirmed a "sheepskin effect"— in essence that completing a credential has a substantial premium over the completion of an equivalent number of years of schooling.[83] Earning a *credential* indeed tends to have significant value and meaning beyond the individual who might have, for example, completed most of a degree with flying colors but fell one course or credit short; or the individual who strung together an extensive series of continuing education courses. This is in great part due to the notion that to an employer, having *completed* a credential represents perseverance, determination, and other attractive attributes in a potential employee, beyond just the schooling or learning outcomes that it captures. This is the strong signaling value of university credentials—a topic that will be explored in much greater detail in the next chapter, along with other details related to how employers perceive and use university credentials in their hiring processes.

TWO

# Behind the Curtain

*How University Credentials Operate*
*as Job Market Qualifications*

$\Tau$he value of university credentials in the job market is predicated on their ability to represent and communicate a certain set of skills, knowledge, and attributes to employers making a hiring decision. Understanding how university credentials factor into employers' hiring process is central to analyzing how the role of university credentials is evolving and what the future holds. However, as noted at the outset of this book, the role of educational credentials in the hiring process is a surprisingly understudied area. Based on the existing academic literature, original research, and tangible examples, this chapter explores how employers actually view and use degrees and other university credentials in their hiring process.

## RECRUITING AND HIRING: A CRITICAL STRATEGIC ACTIVITY

Given the escalating human capital requirements in our knowledge-based and globalizing economy, identifying potential employees with the appropriate skills and qualifications is increasingly challenging.[1] In a 2015 annual survey by consultancy PricewaterhouseCoopers, US chief executive officers reported that talent strategies are central to their organizations' growth, and more than 80 percent were looking for a broader range of skills than in the past and also actively extending their search for human capital to new geographies, industries, and demographic groups.[2] From the end of 2014 into 2016, the US economy experienced its strongest stretch in hiring activity since the late 1990s, with a record number of job openings.[3] Moreover, within certain industry sectors, such as technology, health care, and finance, the war for talent is especially heated.

Allen Blue, vice president of Product Management and cofounder of professional networking company LinkedIn, frames the evolution of talent and hiring in a changing world: "Change is driving the world of hiring these days. In the 1980s and '90s you were still living in a world dominated by a hiring model and educational model that were born in the agrarian economy, serving the large-scale corporation that was a product of the industrial revolution. . . . Employers' processes were focused on talent rising up internally, and developing from within. Globalization and technological change are transforming every job and creating the requirement for greater technical literacy—it's just the beginning of the change that we're seeing."[4]

Hiring is also an area of considerable expenditure. According to a study conducted by human resources consultancy Bersin by Deloitte, companies in the United States spend more than $124 billion on hiring and recruiting, and each single professional-level job opening received an average of eighty-nine applicants.[5] Leading human resources expert Josh Bersin, principal and founder of Bersin by Deloitte, comments on changes in recruiting and the scale of hiring: "Something radical has happened in hiring in the last few years—and that is the huge transparency of employer brand and the ease of applying for a job went down by an order of magnitude. You can click on a job and apply through LinkedIn or another tool without having to write a resume or actually having to send a letter. So employers are getting one hundred applicants for every job, and many of them are not the right fit. They need tools and information to filter through which one of those people is going to be relevant."[6]

In addition, researchers have estimated the costs of making bad hiring decisions at well over $100 billion annually, as measured by lost managerial time, the need to manage poor performance, and job vacancy.[7] The cost of employee turnover in the United States is consistently about 20 percent of a given worker's salary.[8] This scale of resourcing, complexity, and risk makes hiring, recruiting, and screening a critical area of concern and focus for employers—and a major area of significance within the modern economy.

Microsoft is one example of a company that has reached an uncommon level of scale and maturity. But it is also experiencing strong growth and reinvention as it fends off new technology rivals, in a war for talent both in its Seattle backyard and globally. Chuck Edward, head of global talent acquisition for Microsoft, describes this new hiring landscape: "This intense pressure on finding the right talent has never been stronger—the iteration is all around new capabilities and cloud computing and optics or machine learning and data science: these are topics and capabilities that companies are betting their future on. So companies are looking at their talent strategies and asking, 'Where do I find those capabilities?' You need the right executives and industry experts, but you also need an early in career strategy—finding the best and the brightest. Can I develop talent myself or do I acquire it? Strategic workforce plans are critical."[9] Across the country in Illinois, within a very different industry, Tom Hanna, staffing manager at Robert Bosch Tool Corporation, frames the challenge similarly: "Having the right people in place is the most important thing any organization can do. You can invest in processes, you can invest in equipment, etc.—but the right person, at the right time, in the right role in the organization has the greatest impact on the productivity of the business."[10]

In human resources parlance, employee *recruitment* is the practices that identify and attract employees—an activity that is often indivisible but distinct from *selection*, which is the paring down of the pool of job candidates.[11] Not surprisingly, the recruiting and selection environment has heightened in complexity in recent years as dynamics such as online recruiting and growing employer complexity are making the process more challenging.[12] Human resources expert Peter

Cappelli has argued that employers' approach to the hiring process is fundamentally broken in many ways, including the growing reliance on computerized job application systems that screen and sort candidates in an environment where hundreds of individuals apply for every job opening.[13] Cappelli also laments how picky employers can be in selecting candidates for jobs, suggesting that the challenge of matching candidates and employers is one of the most significant issues facing the economy.[14]

Many employers have well-developed college recruiting functions that focus on hiring individuals as they graduate from colleges and universities. However, the vast majority of an organization's talent base comes from recruiting experienced talent in the open job market, and this type of recruiting is often decentralized.[15] Although a central human resources function often provides guidance on job qualifications (including educational requirements), the level of desired educational qualifications is often set by individual line managers.[16] Tim Howe, a leader at GE Distributed Power, describes how this interplay often works: "You rely on the knowledge that your HR manager has in terms of the resources you're looking for. When I'm looking for someone for my own team, I typically have a really good sense of what I want—but HR people might be covering multiple functions. There's a back and forth, and there are company policies, and you have to dig in and put in some hard work."[17]

## Education Versus Experience

The research literature and my own extensive work and research with employers indicate that educational credentials are indeed among the most important qualifications for jobs. As Adrienne Alberts, director of talent acquisition for the American Red Cross, explains, "When we consider qualifications, ultimately what I and our leaders care about is, Will individuals be capable of performing the work at a high standard? Unlike some other areas—the technology sector is definitely one of them, where people can be more flexible about formal training because they can be self-taught—in traditional organizations leaders tend to think about traditional education and educational credentials, that people have a formal education related to the topics we have an interest in."[18]

As much as formal education is valued, the utility of education as a hiring criterion is closely interwoven with—and often difficult to decouple from—work experience. All other factors being equal, many employers favor experience—the most direct measure of relevance, fit, ability, and potential productivity—over education. As described by an HR executive in the health-care industry, "We like to look at experience more than just education—somebody with a bachelor's degree and 5 years experience running a multi-million dollar business is preferable over somebody with a master's and no experience."[19] Similarly, Felby Chen, a technical recruiter at Facebook, notes: "Experience is valued greatly—we look at direct and transferrable skills. Education in all forms is also important—we want to know how you've picked up the necessary skills to perform the job. Both help in giving us a better understanding of how you've created or taken advantage of opportunities to pursue a profession."[20]

In assessing the total package of education and experience that a given job candidate brings to the table, extricating educational qualifications from professional experience can be difficult. While formulaic approaches are rare, many employers consider degrees as part of an equation that substitutes for years of professional experience.[21] For example, as a manager at a pharmaceutical company explained: "If you're looking at somebody with 3–5 years of experience and a master's degree and management, vs. somebody that has 10 years of management experience—they'd be considered on the same level."[22]

For many employers, degrees appear to be most valuable in the early part of a professional's career, when candidates lack a significant amount of professional experience and quantifiable results. In the middle and later stages of an individual's career, a candidate's potential value and productivity can be better assessed based on that person's track record, regardless of educational level. This flips on its head the investment industry disclaimer that past performance is not necessarily indicative of future results: in hiring, past performance is considered the best predictor of ability and future productivity.

The fact that employers appear to place greater emphasis on educational credentials for less experienced, earlier-career candidates goes to the heart of the notion that educational credentials serve as *proxies* for performance and acumen that is otherwise difficult to observe.[23]

Researchers Dale Belman and John Haywood have outlined in their work on "sheepskin effects" in education economics that work experience trumps the signaling value of educational qualifications as workers gain experience over the course of their career.[24] Tom Mathews, the senior vice president for human resources at Cree, Inc, describes: "After five or ten years, education doesn't matter as much. It's more about 'What have you done, what have you accomplished?' School starts to fade. The importance of 'What was your GPA at Brown or Trinity?' Tell me instead about the last three jobs you've had, what you've accomplished, what you bring to us."[25] Similarly, Tom McCleary, vice president for Strategic Partner Alliances at Salesforce.com, observes, "As you get further out from your first gig to your third or fourth job, then the skills and experience start to take on more value than the educational pedigree."[26]

## To Prefer or Require a Degree?

As the pool of individuals in the workforce with college-level education has expanded, the bachelor's degree has emerged as a baseline requirement, or floor, for a great number of professional roles. This is evident in the approximately 50 percent of job openings over the course of 2015 that *required* a bachelor's degree, according to Burning Glass Technologies.[27] For many employers, bachelor's degrees are often written into what are referred to as formally defined basic requirements for hiring. For example, many human resources leaders refer to bachelor's degrees using terms such as a *prerequisite* or *minimum expectation*. As one employer with a retail presence describes, "we view a bachelor's degree as a strong foundational qualification for success as a future leader in our organization, whether for our stores, distribution centers or global headquarters."[28] Patrick Walsh, director of operations HR and talent acquisition at Pizza Hut, describes these dynamics: "As more people have gone to college over the years and the population grows, it's become a general minimum expectation for certain type of roles that you should have it. It's become a societal norm."[29]

In addition, many employers are placing a greater value on advanced degrees as the supply of individuals in the workforce educated at this level has escalated. An HR professional in the health-care industry remarks, "When I first started in this business 20 years ago, nobody had advanced degrees. And then along the way . . . people have realized that it looks great on a piece of paper and oftentimes it will get you that interview, and it's a differentiator."[30] Tom Mathews of Cree further describes this dynamic: "For many roles, these days it's almost like bachelor's degrees are table stakes. Master's degrees are what separate you. You're going to need that to break out from the pack."[31]

One of the most universal items in a given job description or posting is the preferred or required level of educational qualifications. Interestingly, the determination of what level of educational credential is necessary or preferable for a given job is fluid—and often a decision left to individual hiring managers, in consultation with central human resources groups.[32] Often, great variation and individual discretion exist in this process, even within a firm: while the marketplace and external benchmarking often set the standard for deciding on educational qualifications, internal deliberation, benchmarking, and policies also play a role.[33]

Given the relatively substantial market of individuals with a bachelor's degree, a bachelor's can commonly be listed as *required* for a job. However, most often employers operate in terms of stating a *preference* for a credential, to keep their options open. By contrast, advanced degrees such as the master's are more often preferred versus required, since only 12 percent of the US workforce holds an

advanced degree, and stating this level of credential as required for
a role would severely limited the pool of candidates that could qualify for a job.[34] Across all educational levels, the size and diversity of
the recruitment pool are real legal and policy concerns for employers. In this way, regulatory dynamics are among the forces that drive
how employers establish educational requirements, with the need for
compliance firmly ensconced in corporate hiring policies.

A hiring leader at a pharmaceutical firm offers the following example: "'Required' is a very fine line . . . because it could drastically
limit your candidate pool that doesn't have that required M.B.A.,
let's say. We can't technically hire them unless we repost the job for
10 days publicly in order to go to offer, just due to some compliance
reasons. So a B.A. is typically always required and an M.A. or M.B.A.
is typically always preferred. We'll never require an M.B.A., but we
will require a B.A., or Ph.D/M.D. for some science positions."[35] Similarly, as a recruiter at a finance firm described: "Once you put . . .
a minimum requirement of an advanced degree . . . your hands are
tied, and you can't hire even the perfect candidate if they don't have
that minimum. So it's not really allowed to be honest with you, from
a legal standpoint."[36]

The legal and policy dynamics that employers cite in these examples relate not only to corporate policy but also to the US Equal
Employment Opportunity Commission's (EEOC) prohibited employment practices, which exist to prohibit discrimination by ensuring that there is not a disproportionately negative effect on
individuals of a protected class.[37] In this way, it is important that
minimum qualifications map directly to the essential functions of
the job. Legal experts have noted that many regulatory interpreta-
tions in this area are recent and can represent a potential legal landmine for employers.[38] Over time, a variety of changes in the legal and
regulatory environment have arguably helped establish degrees and
other forms of third-party credentials as preferred signals of ability
and skill, in an environment where direct testing of ability is considered risky or prohibited, depending on how it is constructed.

As sociologist David Bills observes, when employers are reviewing candidates' qualifications in making hiring decisions, visible screening criteria—such as job history—are not only socially acceptable but also cannot be challenged legally (as in the use of race, gender, age, or other criteria).[39] This same ease of observation and legal acceptance extends to educational credentials, which signal otherwise unobservable information about candidates to employers.[40] Over time, US employers have come to rely much more on college credentials than on direct ability testing—which was common prior to the 1971 *Griggs v. Duke Power* United States Supreme Court case.[41] Prior to this court decision, employers routinely directly tested potential employees for their ability, with one survey reporting that 84 percent of employers used ability and intelligence tests in recruitment and hiring in 1963.[42] However, the Civil Rights Act of 1964 placed theoretical limits on testing due to the discriminatory nature of such tests, since minority candidates disproportionality performed worse. In 1971, the US Supreme Court ruled that any employer testing must bear a direct relationship to job performance. As a result, fearing potential litigation, employers strayed from the use of testing in hiring, and this behavior was further driven by subsequent court decisions and additional legislation such as the Equal Employment Opportunity Act of 1972.[43] According to legal experts, one clear impact that this had was to end poor and clearly discriminatory testing practices that many employers had in place.[44] In addition, college degrees took on an additional importance as one of the best available measures for employers to ascertain worker ability, aptitude, and general intelligence, in addition to the content or form of the educational study.

## A REFINED TAKE ON HUMAN CAPITAL

The growth of an educated society and the significant supply of individuals in the workforce with a college degree created the opportunity for employers to use degrees—just as they had used other levels of education or licensure—to infer certain capabilities in hiring. In making a hiring decision, employers use educational qualifications as a screening criterion—a proxy that they can use to maximize their chances of making the right hire.[45] In the emphasis on the direct relationship between the skills and knowledge gained in a college educational program and job requirements, this critical screening or signaling value of credentials is too often unexplored. Harry Patrinos, lead education economist at the World Bank, describes: "It's been clear for a long time that the degree is a signal of someone's productivity and ability to undertake complex work—and I use the word *signal* not in the sense that it's hiding something, but that it saves the employer a lot of time and effort; otherwise, they'd have to test thousands of people before they employ anyone. With degrees, you're reducing that uncertainty about someone's skills."[46]

Analysis and dialogue about the value of education and university credentials in the workforce typically revolve around the direct relationship between knowledge and skill to on-the-job productivity—which is the foundation of *human capital theory* in economics. In the 1960s, economists developed this theory as an explanation of the link between educational investments and occupational status and earnings. This included economists such as Jacob Mincer, who focused on the economic returns to on-the-job training; Theodore Schultz, who explored how human capital drove productivity; and Gary Becker, whose seminal book *Human Capital* focused on the economic value of education and training.[47] Schultz's and Becker's work on human capital theory would win them Nobel prizes in economics. Human capital theory—and its assertion that skills and knowledge acquired through education and job experience drive productivity—is the primary basis for educational and economic policy in nations around the world.[48]

Since the essence of human capital theory is that education and training make workers more productive, all other things being equal, employers will prefer and seek more educated employees. Education is typically measured and represented by years of schooling, courses taken, and credentials earned, thus giving educational credentials their value as important currency in the job market. As a result, students and workers rationally invest in greater levels of education so that they can qualify for jobs and increase their value to employers, and employers rationally select the best-educated students aligned with their job needs.[49] Literally thousands of studies support human capital theory and the linkage between education, earnings, and productivity. However, not as often explored is the fact that human capital theory does not perfectly describe all of the relationship between education, jobs, and why employers value degrees.[50]

## More Than Skills and Knowledge Alone: Screening and Signaling Through Credentials

A key extension of human capital theory is the notion of *screening* or *signaling*—concepts that various economics and sociology scholars have addressed separately but are essentially coupled and synonymous. In this framework, as economists Kenneth Arrow and Joseph Stiglitz proposed, higher education is a filter: in addition to driving labor market productivity, employers are making hiring decisions based on incomplete economic information and incorporating the notion of education as socialization.[51] In other words, aside from skills and productivity alone, higher education is a screening device that communicates other attributes about potential employees, such as writing and communication abilities, punctuality, and so on. Employers can use educational qualifications to screen more productive workers, and workers can in turn make a strategic choice to invest in education to signal, or distinguish, their ability from less productive workers.[52] Credentials document aspects of individuals' intellectual ability and attest to their perseverance.

My own research with employers has provided particularly strong support for employers' emphasis on the screening value of degree *completion*, in particular the idea that completing an educational program at a certain level signals an investment in one's self and the ability to complete a long-term effort to reach a goal—an achievement that is distinct from simply mastering the knowledge and skills in a particular educational program. As one senior recruiter at a major financial services company explained, "What the degree is in itself is not as important as you made it through a 4-year program . . . (that) you stuck to it and you finished it says something about the character . . . there is something to be said about the individual, and the characteristics of completing something; stick-to-itiveness, set up a goal and did it; got through all of the diversions that students go through . . . got to the goal line."[53] As Harry Patrinos, the World Bank economist, further describes: "An obvious indicator of the productivity of a degree is that when people don't complete a degree, they aren't rewarded. It's not that you went to college, it's that you completed the degree, attained that certification. The ability and motivation to be able to successfully undertake a course of study is what is being rewarded in the labor market, and we see that from the wages."[54]

The role of university credentials as signals and screens has been empirically supported through studies by researchers such as David Bills in the 1980s, and Lauren Rivera more recently. They both found that employers valued the utility of degrees in reflecting candidates' general abilities (such as communicating, meeting deadlines) or cultural/professional fit.[55] In fact, Rivera's deep research—which consisted of 120 interviews plus participant observation over a two-year period embedding her within corporate human resources functions—illustrated that within certain elite sectors of the economy, such as law firms, consultancies, and investment banks, degrees are often principally used as tools in a cultural matching process that is less focused on educational outcomes and more on prestige.[56] This cultural matching dynamic is underscored by Paul Edelman, Managing Director of Edelman & Associates, a boutique search and technical recruiting firm: "Prestige still matters a lot with certain employers. It's about performing well on the job, but also fitting well with the culture. There's a certain tribal affinity."[57]

As a test of employers' premise that degree completion correlates with productivity and ability, a 1999 study by Jeremy Arkes investigated if credentials reflected workers' *precollege* cognitive abilities, through linking performance on longitudinal national education surveys with data on degree attainment. Arkes found that high school diplomas, college attendance, and bachelor's and master's degrees did in fact signal precollege cognitive ability to employers and resulted in higher wages.[58] Arkes concluded that because information on workers' true productivity and skill level is essentially impossible—and costly—for employers to discern prehire, more productive workers can indeed differentiate themselves to employers by completing a credential.

That educational credentials signal and differentiate candidates as much as they document the completion of a course of study and the affiliated skills and knowledge prompts the critique that many credentials are unnecessary; that workers are overeducated; and that employer requirements are inefficient. This argument has a long history and is known as credentialism, or describing the trend toward unnecessary credential inflation. Well-known critiques include Ivar Berg's *Education and Jobs: The Great Training Robbery* and Randall Collins's *The Credential Society,* both written in the 1970s.[59] These scholars and others argue that many workers are overeducated and that education is principally a means of social reproduction. More recently, workforce experts such as Peter Cappelli have characterized the drive to earn additional credentials to secure jobs even if jobs don't require them as an "arms race."[60] Thus, the fact that credentials can operate as a powerful screen or signal in hiring is sometimes portrayed as a challenge to the skills-driven theory of human capital. In fact, the concept of signaling and screening explaining how employers use university credentials is more of an incremental adjustment, according to experts such as David Bills.[61] As Bills notes, in the screening and signaling view, employers still make rational economic decisions based on credentials that reflect worker productivity, but the process of how this takes place differs: the screening and signaling view also does not preclude the basic idea that increased levels of skill and economic value come through education.[62]

Indeed, some risk of qualification inflation occurs as job seekers earn higher-level credentials in pursuit of increased economic opportunity, and employers then demand higher levels of education for the same jobs.[63] However, a wealth of evidence supports the contentions of human capital theory.[64] In the 1990s, David Bills tackled the question of credential inflation in an analysis specifically focused on how employers responded to educationally overqualified candidates.[65] Bills found that while many hiring managers establish ceilings on qualifications, almost half of managers would accept educational qualifications one full level of schooling above that required for the position (for example, a bachelor's degree in place of an associate degree), and another 28 percent would accept credentials two levels higher.[66] This research suggested that that too much education rarely hurts candidates, with employer interviews showing that only 25 percent of candidates, at most, would have been forced out of contention for a job if they were educationally overqualified.[67] In addition, Bills cites examples of employers who believed that people with master's degrees, for example, would be more aggressive and promotable, and that more highly educated workers had higher goals and broader worldviews. One of Bills's fundamental conclusions was that employers often hire based not only on *minimum* qualifications, but also with career progression and promotability in mind.[68]

## The Hard and Soft Skills and Attributes Valued in College Degree Holders

While signaling and screening have their place, employers, of course, value university credentials because these programs tend to produce a reliable set of skills and abilities, irrespective of area of study, alongside specific technical skills—the skills gained through a credential program in a purist human capital sense. Although there is much debate about the value and purpose of higher education, a variety of data sources attest to the hard and soft job-related skills and other attributes that employers associate with university credentials.

The National Association of Colleges and Employers' annual survey of the skills and qualities that employers seek in *new* college graduate hires is useful in understanding the package of attributes connected to degrees within this audience. For the class of 2015, key priorities were leadership, teamwork, written communication and problem solving, followed closely by analytical/quantitative and technical skills.[69] Looking to the broader market for experienced talent, based on the skills referenced in millions of job openings requiring college degrees over the course of 2015, we similarly find employers associating skills such as collaboration, communication, writing, problem solving, and research with these roles, as well as the addition of skills such as planning and project management.[70]

Notably, academic research has found that employers tend to be more satisfied with employees who possess creative, critical thinking, and leadership skills *over* those who possess specific technical skills.[71] In my research efforts focused on advanced degrees, it is clear that employers particularly value soft skills such as critical thinking, problem solving, communication, and leadership, as well as a higher level of business acumen and professionalism.[72] As underscored by Stanley Litow, a vice president at IBM and president of the IBM International Foundation, "Soft skills are 'essential skills.' The people we're most interested in hiring don't have just one hard skillset, but are problem solvers, are able to present effectively, write effectively, work in teams, and adapt and continue to learn."[73]

It is interesting to consider that these sorts of high-level skills are present in traditional liberal arts education, and in nonprofessional, nontechnical programs of study, suggesting that employers value credentials and educational experiences that are not overly specialized or myopic. Major employers value interdisciplinary, cross-functional perspectives and understanding, as in the example offered by one firm: "You can't just be a scientist coming in here. You have to be able to collaborate with marketing and supply chain and sales—all the different functions, because it's so collaborative."[74] In appreciating these liberal arts types of skills and mindsets over raw technical skills, Tom McCleary of Salesforce.com provides the following example: "What it really gets down to is agility and rapid learning, comfort with the unknown. Collaboration, collaboration, and collaboration are more and more important. Our technology-intermediated world is driving the value of personal skills."[75]

### Digging Deeper: Beyond the High-Level Credential, Do Details Matter?

Now that we have established a framework for understanding why employers value university credentials in hiring, we can move beyond the gross level of the credential or education generally. We can now consider some of the other levels of detail and signals embedded within university credentials beyond their completion alone.

Given employers' desire to ascertain details about potential performance, one might assume that details associated with the credential, such as courses taken, full transcripts, and grade point average (GPA), would be highly valued. However, perhaps surprisingly, my research—and that of others—has shown that employers often do not look beyond the credential itself when making hiring decisions. Certainly, there are exceptions to this practice, especially in the college recruiting world where employers hire directly from campuses and programs they know, and in which a review of GPA (how well a credential was completed) at least is reported as influential.[76] In my research, many employers said that they *did* tend to focus on grades and transcripts at the undergraduate/bachelor's level, since academic performance, in lieu of experience, may be the only indicator an employer has to work from, but that the same scrutiny typically does not apply at the master's level or with more experienced hires.[77] The work of Peter Cappelli and Lauren Rivera has found little linkage between grades/GPA and on-the-job performance/hiring decisions.[78] Google and its influential senior vice president of People Operations, Laszlo Bock, have championed the idea of GPA and test scores being irrelevant in the hiring process, after extensively crunching the data and finding no correlation with posthire performance, thus doing away with this category of information in the firm's hiring activities.[79]

Microsoft's global talent leader Chuck Edward explains: "The degree carries a ton of weight, but less so the detail within the degree—GPA, transcripts, etc. GPAs don't matter as much. Interviews will always assume some basic level of proficiency, and it's more about 'How do you lead? What do you do outside of work?' We're more interested in leadership and intangibles. Transcripts, too, the more we know about a curriculum, we might be familiar with some certain pivotal classes and project experiences, but it's really about the depth of knowledge of a school."[80] Similarly, Stephanie Pallante, assistant vice president for global college recruiting at Aramark, describes: "Each academic institution is different, so being able to validate that GPA is extremely difficult."[81] And, as Shelly Holt, a recruiting veteran and senior director with Concur Technologies, an SAP Company, notes: "You can look at a transcript, but I wasn't in those courses and I don't know hard they were. I'd have to ask them. It becomes subjective and doesn't really add value."[82]

On this interest in transcripts and course and project-level detail, many new technology firms and universities have worked to create e-portfolios and deeper, digital forms of the resume, but these new offerings remain in the nascent stage. An early 2014 article in the *Wall Street Journal* cited the lack of awareness or interest in these solutions among hiring managers, despite the promise of these tools, a finding consistent with my own research and experience.[83] However, this landscape is evolving rapidly, and these dynamics will be explored later.

## Reputation and Prestige: A Second Layer of Signal

One of the most fascinating dynamics in higher education is the power of reputation. Institutional reputation is a driving focus of many higher education institutions—particularly in an era when global university rankings are creating worldwide competition for prestige, and rankings and reputation are impacting student choices and professional outcomes.[84] In a more competitive marketplace, colleges and universities are increasingly focused on brand positioning and reputation.[85] Previously, we reviewed some of the academic re-search connecting selectivity and college quality with earnings. It is considered common knowledge that reputation matters when it comes to degrees, but how does it factor into employers' hiring process? Yes, the reputation of the institution associated with a credential does matter—but in nuanced ways that vary by credential level and context, and operating along general tiers of prestige.

Reputation, or brand, is in many ways the ultimate signal. A brand, according to the management research literature, stands for and communicates the promise of a certain level of quality or identity, ideally reducing risk and creating trust for the product buyer—something that is particularly apparent with products that are difficult to assess and in markets with imperfect information.[86] The market for degrees meets both of these conditions. The substance and details behind a degree are certainly routinely difficult to assess—especially with hundreds or thousands of unfamiliar institutions awarding degrees—making strong reputations/known brands powerful in higher education. Further, as the literature on educational credentialing discusses, in the job market, employer "buyers" of talent have imperfect information on job seekers, making the reputation of an awarding institution a useful indicator of potential performance.

Further, in a landscape where college attendance is normative and millions of degrees are issued annually, a commodity credential on its own is at times no longer enough. Rather, the admissions process and institutional prestige signal students' abilities and potential to employers, especially as found recently in work by Lauren Rivera.[87] Yet, because of the thousands of academic institutions that exist and the many multiples of programs and credentials available from them, a given employer (even a large global one) or hiring manager is likely able to understand or measure reputation only in a very general sense—a situation that may be changing with the growth of hiring analytics.

Indeed, my research has found that many employers are, somewhat surprisingly, fairly dismissive of institutional-level academic reputation in hiring, while acknowledging that the top, elite brands—household names like Harvard—stand out on a resume or from a candidate pool.[88] As a hiring leader at a major financial institution shared, "the Harvard or Stanford or Ivy League school if you will, yes, of course that stands out . . . I think it definitely helps jump off the page a little bit, that brand name."[89] Or, in the case of a pharmaceutical company: "when you have a certain prestige to it, does that increase someone's position in that group? Yes. It does stand out. You see some of the top names, the Stanfords, the Harvards and Yales—yeah, it does stand out and maybe even rise to the top when you put those people in one bucket."[90] Many employers view reputation along a series of tiers, with reputation and brand mattering most at the extremes of the bell curve—for example, elite or poor; Yale versus the University of Phoenix. There's a vast middle ground.

This thinking, of course, should not be a surprise. But what may be a surprise is that distinct from institutional brand (such as a credential from the University of Minnesota or Pepperdine), it is clear that many employers, especially as they recruit for specialty talent needs, place greater emphasis on individual *program-level* reputation and excellence. That is, while a given university may not be nationally known or top-ranked, employers recognize and seek out when an institution or program produces high-quality students in a specialized domain, and these best-in-class programs become privileged in the attention they receive from major employers.[91]

Further, the reputation of a school rarely outweighs other attributes (for example, degree, experience) when considering two hypothetical candidates against each other. Employers often make the point that an individual would *never* be hired based only or principally on the reputation of the school that awarded the degree. Instead, reputation is often used as a sorting or filtering mechanism when prioritizing candidates and applications from a broad pool, and when targeting specific schools for direct recruiting.

How reputation and brand operate is complicated and difficult to simplify, and of course it varies considerably across industries,

employer types, and credential levels. When asked about the importance of prestige or selectivity, many employers are quick to answer
"it depends." The important takeaway here is that university credentials are not commodities: brand and prestige often have impact in
an environment driven by signaling, yet sometimes not as much as
we think. Insofar as university brands are often defined by rankings,
we may increasingly see traditional notions of prestige and quality
upended by data and new levels of transparency on quality and outcomes. As Michael Housman, a leading workforce expert and data
scientist at hiQ Labs, a people analytics firm, reports, "More and
more employers will be listening to the data. For example, *U.S. News
& World Report* has dominated for years, and reputation is a large
chunk of that ranking, but there's more data being brought to bear
showing what the best schools truly may be for a particular hire or
position, showing the value of their education."[92]

## A NUANCED AND EVOLVING SET OF DYNAMICS

In this chapter we have established a strong baseline for how university credentials factor into employers' hiring process—a hiring process that over time is becoming more complicated, data-informed,
and central to many organizations' overall strategies. Given that education and experience are often difficult to decouple; whether to
make a degree or credential a preference or a requirement can be
fluid and subjective; and that credentials operate as screening and
signaling mechanisms in addition to indicators of hard skill; not to
mention the dynamics of prestige, the environment is complicated.
Furthermore, this environment is beginning to evolve rapidly, with
many new forms of experimentation. On the employer side of the
equation—whether informed by long-standing internal policy, recent
external or internal benchmarking and job audits, or outside regulations—the setting of educational qualification is increasingly being
informed by more rigorous data and analysis, but today this remains
the exception rather than the rule.[93] And, on the university side of

the ecosystem, new forms of credentials are proliferating, creating new options for employers to consider, but also potentially introducing confusion and complexity. With this foundation in place, we can dive deeper into understanding these issues and how innovative forms of university credentials and the ecosystem have evolved historically, as well as the directions that they are moving in the future.

# THREE

# Higher Education's Information Age

*Lessons from the Dot-Com Era*

To this point, we have reviewed why an urgent need exists to study the current state and future evolution of university credentials; traced the evolution of university credentials and their scale, scope, and value in the economy; and established how educational credentials are actually used by employers in hiring decisions. The change and opportunity driven by technology are common themes across these areas. Over the past fifteen years or so, technology, particularly the evolution of the Internet, has certainly been the primary force in shaping both the demands placed on educational credentials and the new models through which to earn them. So much of the current innovation and future of university credentials relates to Internet-based business models and online delivery that it is informative to understand how the early years of the commercially available Internet shaped and evolved the market for higher education credentials. This is true particularly in terms of the influence of industry and the impact of private capital and profit motives, both themes that are recurring today.

## THE FIRST WAVE OF DISRUPTION: IT CERTIFICATIONS

In the late 1990s, the US job market became extremely tight, with hundreds of thousands of new jobs created each month.[1] For the year 2000, the unemployment rate hit a record low of 4.0 percent.[2] Amid a strong economy generally, an information technology (IT) boom was in full swing. The Internet had become commercially available to nontechnical users in 1993 with the launch of the first web browser, Mosaic; and the growth of the Internet and other new technological factors (such as evolutions in e-commerce, telecommunications, and preparations to fix the Y2K bug) contributed to the booming IT job market.[3] A special report from the National Research Council at the time documented rapid growth in the prior eight years, with a more than 60 percent expansion of jobs in the tech sector.[4] Given this explosion of technology jobs, colleges and universities could not produce IT workers quickly enough.[5] As a result, numerous IT certification and training programs began to fill the gap, and these IT certifications emerged a fast-track credential to IT jobs. Between 1997 and 2000, more than one million individuals are estimated to have earned an IT certification.[6]

The Certified Netware Engineer (CNE) certification from networking company Novell was one of the first of the major IT vendor certifications to be launched, in 1993, setting the stage for many other credentials to follow later in the 1990s.[7] Novell's CNE and the Microsoft Certified Systems Engineer (MCSE) certifications became two of the most dominant IT credentials, held by hundreds of thousands of individuals by 1999.[8] For professionals looking to break into or advance in the world of IT, these certifications and those like them—whether the Cisco Certified Network Associate (CCNA), Certified Computing Professional (CCP), or literally hundreds more that emerged—began to be valued as much as or more than degrees.

To understand how the certification market mapped against degrees, Cliff Adelman of the US Department of Education engaged in a content analysis of job postings in the technology employment section of the *Washington Post* between 1998 and 2000: an old-school form of today's big-data-driven real-time job market analytics. Adelman analyzed thousands of entry- and mid-level IT job postings and found that bachelor's and master's degrees were rarely mentioned as preferred credentials, and nearly 80 percent of job postings did not mention a degree at all.[9] In addition to IT vendors' own efforts, dozens of chains of IT training centers (such as New Horizons and Computer Learning Centers) emerged to meet the market need. Typically, earning certifications would cost only a few thousand dollars. Universities themselves even got into the game, tying certification examinations to credit; incorporating them into bachelor's degree programs in technology; and providing preparation and training for certification themselves, with examples ranging from Pima Community College in Arizona, to the University of Colorado, and Boston University.[10] The opportunity to offer practical training and certification created a revenue opportunity for many universities and aligned with their educational mission. Kevin Currie, a leader of certification programs at both Boston University and Northeastern University in the 1990s, recounts: "You could get someone who was an unemployed house painter and put them through this program in ten to fourteen weeks and get them hired as an engineer or developer somewhere at a high salary. You could also go back to your alumni who might have graduated with a technical degree that was now really outdated and get them up to speed quickly, as well as go into corporations and cement relationships by offering certification programs on-site."[11]

Networking company Cisco Systems was one of the quintessential firms defining the Internet boom. Cisco built a robust certification business that it still maintains today: the firm's Cisco Certified Internetwork Expert (CCIE) was one of the more prestigious certifications in the 1990s IT market. When the CCIE certification program was launched in 1993, current chief executive officer and then senior vice president John Chambers likened it to higher education in its selective, experiential, and signaling-oriented nature. Chambers noted, "It can be compared to completing a university course versus taking college entrance exams. Prospective CCIE candidates must be highly qualified just to enter the program, and then, after taking an intensive troubleshooting course, must pass a rigorous hands-on lab test conducted by senior support engineers. This very stringent set of requirements ensures that only the best professionals are selected."[12] Today, Cisco alone awards more than forty-five different certifications, and the company has issued more than two million credentials since 1993.[13]

The initial vision for the CCIE and many similar credentials was to certify elite specialists. However, as IT certifications from many organizations proliferated in hundreds of varieties and also became easier to obtain, the market became oversaturated. David Lucey, vice president of Talent Acquisition at Epsilon, who was at the time a recruiting lead at Nortel Networks, recalls: "Many companies overpaid just because someone had that label, hiring people out of those programs almost sight unseen without a real depth in the interview. The value of those certifications really became watered down. Companies realized what mattered more was the hands-on experience: Have you done this? Can you do it? If you've shown you're flexible, adaptable, a quick learner, etc., you can come in and do well with our technology."[14]

Indeed, the IT certification market circa 2000 offers an interesting example of the supply and demand for skills and the dynamics between experience versus education and training. When few workers with the certification were available, certifications were one of the best proxies for presumed ability. However, the certification system began to churn out individuals with short-term credentials representing theoretical knowledge and the ability to pass a test—but little in the way of hands-on experience, diluting the value of the credential as a marker of professional competency. As an IT manager reported in a March 2000 interview with *Computing Magazine*, "Interviewing one freshly-printed (Microsoft) MCSE, I soon discovered he had never used a command line. The quality of these applicants is variable, and they often have unrealistic salary expectations . . . people trying to get into IT are taking these exams in droves, but IT companies dismiss them as 'paper MCSEs.' So if you don't work in

IT and think an MCSE is a way in, you're wasting your time."[15] This terminology of a "paper" professional became common in the later years of the boom and highlights the gap in relevance between mastering theoretical knowledge versus having practical experience.

As just one example, the Microsoft MCSE was initially the marker of a fairly elite technical specialist, but it became commonplace: to maintain the credential's differentiation, over the years Microsoft introduced a number of changes to its tests and a variety of different versions or tracks for the MCSE. Well beyond Microsoft, the proliferation of an alphabet soup of certifications meant that hiring managers practically needed a reference guide to decode them, and this confusion—the lack of familiarity with various credentials and thus an inability for them to serve as shorthand reputation-driven signals—often eliminated their utility in hiring. Many hiring managers and human resources professionals were in the position captured by the title of an August 2000 *Crain's New York Business* article that declared, "When hiring techies, check the certificate: MCP? CCNA? It's hard to gauge an employee's skills without a guidebook."[16] The challenge of employers sorting through a sea of various credential types and terms is a concern that should resonate with universities and industry players that are experimenting with new varieties and semantics of credentials today.

The IT certification boom introduced an alternative fast track to professional jobs and prompted useful debates about the value of specialization versus broader knowledge, the value or portability of vendor-specific skills versus general technology skills and theoretical understanding, and the shelf life of professional expertise and credentials. In a dynamic market in which the protocols, programming languages, and fortunes of various technology vendors rose and fell quickly, it ultimately turned out that broader credentials such as degrees had more staying power.

Yet, for many hiring leaders, one of the lessons driven home from this time period was that the talent pipeline could be expanded beyond traditional college sources. Mark Johnson, director of talent

acquisition with Fresenius Medical Services, then a senior recruiting manager with Andersen Consulting/Accenture, recalls: "It was a
huge transformation from a recruiting standpoint for a number of
different reasons. The competition was tremendously fierce for those
types of skills. The lesson was, from a talent acquisition standpoint,
to not be afraid to expand your sourcing pools: you've got to be open
to other talent pools that you may not have considered in the past."[17]
This is a spirit that continues today with the rise of coding boot
camps as a new source of talent for software development jobs. Another lesson was that a system could spring up and be responsive
to an explosive need in the job market, and these alternative pathways that emerge in a strong job market can siphon enrollment away
from traditional postsecondary institutions yet also present opportunities for them. It was also clear that this type of short-term job
market training could be big business, with technology vendors, testing companies, training centers, and universities becoming involved,
and a healthy blurring of boundaries occurring in many cases.

The ultimate decline in demand for IT certifications of course
hinged on the economic cycle and the fortunes of the broader technology market more than anything else. The certification boom
went hand-in-hand with the rapid growth in telecommunications
and Internet start-up work, which came to a screeching halt with
the collapse of the NASDAQ index and the early 2000s recession. It
could also be argued that the proliferation of *technology* certifications
and credentials twenty years ago set the stage for the acceptance of
many other types of short-term professional credentials in other
nontechnology sectors that would gain momentum in the years
that followed, such as in project management, Six Sigma, or supply
chain management. IT certifications also foreshadowed the type of
shorter-form, job-oriented credential models that are today becoming more popular in higher education. Certification programs were
employer-aligned, competency-based, lower-cost compared to university degrees; and the instructor model was reliant on expert practitioner instructors and self-study rather than tenured faculty—all

characteristics that are common in many of today's professionally oriented university credential programs.

The same Internet technologies that drove the IT certification boom also spawned another innovation that would have an even bigger and more lasting impact for higher education: the online degree.

## THE ONLINE EDUCATION GOLD RUSH

Distance learning has a long and storied history in higher education, evolving over centuries to take advantage of the communication technologies of the day, from correspondence study by mail in the 1800s, to later modes such as radio, broadcast and cable television, and satellite transmission.[18] Universities were often among the first organizations to take advantage of leading-edge communication technologies. In the 1940s, television was seen as the future of higher education, and later, technologies such as videoconferencing were embraced.[19] By the second half of the century, numerous university extension and continuing education units and even new, adult-focused institutions were providing distance-based college courses and degrees.[20]

Ostensibly, the first online degree offered by a regionally accredited higher education institution was the online MBA program launched in 1986 by John F. Kennedy University, an institution in the San Francisco Bay Area. In 1983, Ron Gordon, former CEO of game manufacturer Atari, had pioneered the dial-up modem-based concept when launching a company called Telelearning Systems and its Electronic University Network, which was praised as an innovation by US Secretary of Education T. H. Bell.[21] As John Ebersole, who was dean of the John F. Kennedy University School of Management at the time (and currently president of Excelsior College), recalls, "I went before the Western Association of Schools and Colleges (WASC) accreditation commission to have the program approved and the reception was skeptical to say the least, but ultimately the people sitting on the commission were curious enough and research-oriented, and they saw this as an opportunity to get some insight and experience into something that they correctly foresaw they would be seeing more of in the future. So they gave us permission to offer the MBA with the understanding that we'd file monthly reports on what our progress was, what worked, and what didn't work."[22] In 1989, the campus-based University of Phoenix (an institution later synonymous with online education) began offering online degrees via the national CompuServe Information Service, a precursor to the Internet.[23] Like so many other areas of innovation, it was the enhanced technological capability and interactivity of the World Wide Web that changed the game beginning in the mid-1990s. Until the arrival of the web, the distance learning that most consumers were familiar with was the train-at-home correspondence schools pitched on late-night TV commercials by Sally Struthers or on the back of matchbooks.

The first fully web-based course is attributed to art professor Jerrold Maddox, offered at Pennsylvania State University in the spring of 1995.[24] Understandably, the activity of most universities and faculty in this time period focused on using web-based course materials to augment traditional classroom study, and this demand and experimentation gave birth to the first course or learning management systems such as WebCT and Blackboard. The catalyst for a number of the first fully web-based *degrees* was the Alfred P. Sloan Foundation's Asynchronous Learning Networks (ALN) initiative. Beginning in the early 1990s and continuing into the 2000s, the foundation made more than $75 million in grants to scores of institutions, seeding the development of the online education market through what would become known as the Sloan Consortium (and is today known as the Online Learning Consortium).[25] Early program participants included Pennsylvania State University, Drexel University, the University of Maryland, and the University of Illinois, among others.[26] One of the first fully web-based master's degrees—a professional master's degree in library science from the University of Illinois at Urbana–Champaign was funded by an ALN grant and launched in 1996.[27] Also in 1996, Duke University launched its Global Executive MBA, one of the first forays into the online blended/hybrid delivery of a credential by a top-ranked business school.[28] In 1998, Stanford University launched an online master's degree in engineering, under the leadership of engineering dean and later president John Hennessy.[29]

The growth of online courses and programs continued through the late 1990s, but most of the activity continued to be in supplementing the on-campus experience with online components. Institutions with long histories in other modes of distance learning and engineering schools were particularly active. Until around 1999, awarding accredited credentials via fully online study was still relatively rare. Rather, most online learning efforts were mainly the experiments of research universities with a new pedagogy. To develop, deliver, and scale up the delivery of traditional degrees and credentials online, universities would need to wrestle with fundamental business model issues and questions about mission, strategy, technology infrastructure, financial capitalization, governance, and intellectual property. The same dot-com boom that stoked the flames of the IT certification boom would force traditional universities and entirely new types of higher education institutions to confront these issues.

## University.com

As the Internet boom drove technological development and business model experimentation across a range of industry sectors, it also began to shape higher education, especially through new firms that emerged as partners for or competitors to universities. Education companies—publishers, online learning platforms, services firms serving universities, and so on—raised $5.5 billion in venture capital and private equity investment in 1999–2000 alone.[30] These record totals were only recently surpassed by the current wave of fervor for educational technology (or edtech) investment from around 2010 to the present day. A significant portion of this investment went to enabling firms that provided technology infrastructure to or worked with universities to develop online courses and programs. For example, online course management system provider WebCT raised $125 million from its founding through the end of 2000 alone, and was later acquired by Blackboard.[31] Blackboard itself raised more than $100 million before successfully going public in 2004 (and ultimately generating billions of dollars in equity value), flourishing through both organic growth and an aggressive acquisition strategy.[32] Firms such as eCollege (which went public in 1999) and EMBANet focused on enabling fully online distance learning programs. Many years later publishing giant Pearson Education acquired both eCollege and EMBANet for $477 million (2007) and $650 million (2012), respectively.[33] These were among the major platforms that enabled the delivery of many of the first fully online university credentials.

Meanwhile, some of the biggest bets were being placed on companies focused on the delivery of online higher education, executive education, and corporate training: new businesses, often affiliated with or funded by universities, that were aiming to deliver entirely new sorts of online course experiences, and ultimately, credentials. A company called Pensare was behind the plan to build on the success of Duke University's Global Executive MBA program, moving it online and taking it to the world by selling courses to corporate customers—and even licensing the curriculum to other universities.[34] This partnership included the concept of an Open MBA Toolkit, "which can be used by other business schools and degree-granting organizations to offer their own accredited MBAs and certificate programs."[35] Pensare filed for bankruptcy and shut down in 2001, so much of this vision never came to fruition, but if the dates were changed, this concept would be just as at home in 2016.[36] Caliber Learning Network, spun out of Sylvan Learning Systems (which would later become Laureate Education), partnered with Johns Hopkins University and the University of Pennsylvania's Wharton School to deliver executive education courses and certificates, but no degrees.[37] Caliber's play was a satellite- and video-based network of learning centers, inspired by the Sylvan Learning Centers tutoring center model. Caliber successfully went public but was delisted from the NASDAQ stock market and sold its assets in 2001, failing to gather momentum or generate profits as the dot-com bubble deflated.[38]

## UNext: A Unique Case Study

One of the boldest and most interesting online education enterprises was UNext.com and its subsidiary, Cardean University. UNext .com (or UNext) was notable for the scale of its ambition and funding, prestigious partners, bright minds, and technology architecture.[39] UNext's unique story presents a case that wraps together a great number of the institutional and market issues and dynamics that were prominent then and are important today and in the future.

UNext raised $180 million in funding with the vision of being a platform company that would develop and deliver business education over the Internet, leveraging the curriculum of an elite set of partners that included Stanford University, Columbia University, the University of Chicago, and the London School of Economics and Political Science.[40] UNext was one of the earliest and best capitalized plays in the online business education market, having been founded in 1997 and backed by Knowledge Universe, a significant education-focused investment firm led by Oracle's Larry Ellison and junk bond innovator Michael Milken.[41] Founded by successful entrepreneur and University of Chicago law professor/economist Andrew Rosenfield, UNext also had significant involvement from Nobel prize–winning economist and one of the originators of human capital theory, Gary Becker, along with other Nobel laureates sitting on the board.[42] In 2000, UNext recruited respected academics such as Dr. Geoffrey Cox, vice provost and dean for Learning Technology and Extended Education at Stanford University, into key academic leadership positions with the company.[43]

UNext was forged from academia, for academia, and its academic all-star team and elite business school partners (who were coinvestors due to receive a share of profits and stock, as well as no-risk payments of up to $20 million) gave the firm significant credibility and gravitas.[44] UNext invested heavily in technology and instructional design, spending a reported $1 million per course.[45] As the dean of Columbia University's Graduate School of Business, Meyer Feldberg, described in a *Fortune* magazine article at the time: "We knew distance learning was like a freight train. We knew we could get run down, get onboard, or get out of the way."[46] The initial strategy was to build a learning community. One of the preferred business models of the era was to become an Internet portal à la Yahoo.com, aggregating courses from elite business schools and taking them to the world. Courses were centered on topics such as business communications, finance, economics, and so on, and included titles such as "Understanding the Basics of Capital Markets" and "Power Plays: Shakespeare's Lessons in Leadership and Management."[47] Initially, there were no credentials.

By 2000, UNext's strategy and ambitions turned to creating a new stand-alone for-profit online university, in the spirit of Capella University, Jones International University, and the other accredited online schools founded in the 1990s. However, UNext's school, Cardean University, would uniquely have the imprimatur and curriculum of the elite business schools that were UNext's consortium partners. Echoing the vision of being an Internet portal, Cardean was so named after Roman mythological goddess Cardea, who presided over doorways (portals), in a fusion of the vernacular of e-commerce with the classical heritage of higher education.[48] In 2000, Cardean University received approval from the state of Illinois to grant its own degrees, a Cardean MBA that involved the completion of forty-five courses. It was also accredited in 2000 by the Distance Education and Training Council (DETC), a national rather than regional accreditor.[49] Interestingly, this accreditation was gained via a strategy that would years later be employed to create for-profit university titans such as Grand Canyon University. That is, Cardean achieved DETC accreditation by acquiring a small university with existing DETC accreditation, ISIM University.[50] Through these moves, accredited and state-licensed university degrees based on elite business schools' curriculum were now in play. However, there were a few caveats compared to a similar offering from a traditional institution. Students weren't earning a University of Chicago or Columbia MBA; they were earning a Cardean MBA. And, because of the national DETC accreditation, students' credits might not transfer to regionally accredited institutions if needed, and the program would not be eligible for federal Title IV student aid funds (assuming Cardean had campus-based students, a separate issue). Cardean's MBA program was accelerated, with courses offered in six- and nine-week cycles, and the total cost of the credential came in at approximately $30,000 in 2001.[51]

By 2001, enrollment in UNext programs had reached 2,000 students (most likely taking individual courses rather than a degree), and it employed 400 part-time faculty.[52] UNext and Cardean University had formed partnerships with companies such as IBM, General Motors, publishing giant Thomson Corporation (also a strategic investor), and others, giving it a direct channel to professionals for its MBA. In a 2001 news release, General Motors described this as: "GM's global salaried work force will have access to high quality executive and management development courses and an online M.B.A. program created in partnership with some of the world's leading business schools."[53] However, like other dot-com companies (the collapse of the education investment and start-up market lagged the broader economy by nearly a year), UNext had struggled throughout 2001 as losses piled up. Revenue was scant, and it was challenged as access to capital—including from its university partners—dried up, especially given that its business plan called for investments of $1 million per course. UNext laid off about half of its workforce in 2001.[54] The company continued to invest in its proprietary online technology, its expensive course library concept, and the corporate (B2B) market, uncertain if the consumer in the top end of the market was quite ready for an online MBA. As vice president of academic affairs Geoffrey Cox told the *Chronicle of Higher Education* in a 2001 article, "The greatest demand is not for the degree program in the corporate marketplace . . . and we don't know yet whether individuals will seek online M.B.A.'s."[55]

During the same time that UNext was capturing attention and trying to scale, many other significant experiments in online course delivery were happening at various leading universities, often in consortium models of a very different flavor. They included Fathom (Columbia University with involvement from the London School of Economics, Oxford, Cambridge, and others); Universitas21 Global (University of Virginia and others); and AllLearn (Oxford, Stanford, Yale).[56] All were essentially out of business by 2006, if not years earlier. Fathom focused on online enrichment courses from Columbia and other major cultural institutions and burned through more than $25 million.[57] Universitas21 ultimately developed an Online MBA and burned through $50 million.[58] When AllLearn shut down, it had burned through $12 million, concluding "the cost of offering top-quality enrichment courses at affordable prices was not sustainable over time."[59] The common thread was that these efforts were not focused on or never arrived at developing, marketing, and delivering online *credentials* that would have value in the job market. Instead, they were focused on broadcasting university content and individual courses to a consumer or corporate audience (reminiscent of many of today's MOOCs), and courses did not carry academic credit. Given all of these high-profile ventures and the others that could be analyzed—and I had the privilege of working with the institutions behind each of these efforts as a researcher and consultant in the early 2000s—what is so instructive about UNext, whose story we will resume?

As a case study, UNext is unique in the host of issues wrapped up in its business model, representing a novel bridge between two very distinct epochs: the first epoch being the initial online education gold rush and implosion, and the second being the later maturing of a sustainable online degree market. UNext spanned these epochs as it survived for a number of years, pivoting through various corporate iterations and business models. In its various incarnations, UNext also uniquely straddled both the hyper-elite university stratosphere that was so often risk-averse and focused on broadcasting courses, and the burgeoning world of online-only for-profit universities and the first online degree programs at scale—territories that were not (and are still not) often traversed.

Thus, what are some of the lessons from UNext as it pertains to our study of the history and future of innovation in university credentials? Aside from the business lessons—like most companies of its time, UNext appears to have spent too heavily too quickly, and invested far too much in R&D and too little on marketing—one of the most critical lessons relates to brand when it comes to the value and utility of credentials. Yes, UNext had the backing and could leverage the reputations and content of elite business schools, but this halo effect did not effectively translate from the prestigious consortium partners to Cardean University's MBA. A Cardean MBA was not the same as a degree or even a certificate from Stanford or the University of Chicago. The online degree/credential market is a consumer-driven one, and what has value to the consumer is a portable credential. Unless that credential is fully accredited and recognized in a traditional sense, and from an institution of some standing, it has discounted value in the market. Second, prestigious reputation is not necessarily achieved or extended through association, a lesson that could be heeded by MOOC businesses and universities, which are still often awarding their most innovative online credentials through side vehicles set up explicitly to provide a delineation between the core brand and the new (such as MITx). For example, can a packaged certificate from Coursera or MITx become as valuable in the market as a credential awarded by the traditional partner institution itself?

A minor lesson also can be learned about the price and market value of a nontraditional credential: Cardean University's initial assumption was to price its MBA at 80 percent of the cost of an MBA at top-ranked business schools. Despite its affiliations, it was clear that it could not command this in the market.[60] In 2003, Cardean offered its MBA for $24,000 total, a steep discount to most elite business schools that often cost $50,000 to $60,000 or more at that time. Yet this was also a discount to many state schools and even the University of Phoenix.[61] The UNext MBA was a strong value and high in quality, but with various identity characteristics working against it as much as for it, it appeared that it couldn't command the premium price that its business model and the expense side of its corporate ledger were predicated on.

The UNext experience also shows us that it is difficult to market and explain a new, different type of educational credential to the potential customer base—whether a business audience or a consumer audience. Cardean University was a start-up institution, and while it was state-licensed and nationally accredited, it was not the sum of its partners. In a market that values prestige and track record, it is also hard to achieve traction and momentum without an operating history or a campus. There continues to be great skepticism for start-up offerings in a domain where market value is so driven by tradition, history, and reputation.

For these reasons among others, UNext's ultimate play was to affiliate with the New York Institute of Technology (NYIT), a traditional, nonprofit, campus-based institution with regional accreditation and access to federal student aid programs, in 2003. UNext and NYIT created Ellis College of NYIT—a joint venture that powered NYIT's online strategy through UNext's capital investment, technology platform, existing curriculum, and marketing acumen.[62] However, although this arrangement experienced early growth, it ultimately failed as each organization's end goals and the governance and ownership mechanics proved too incompatible: the NYIT partnership was an interim stepping stone in UNext's plan to spin off its own accredited university.[63] The plan was that UNext would first establish Ellis College as a branch campus under NYIT's accreditation and federal financial aid eligibility and then spin Ellis College out into its own free-standing school, a strategy that was possible under the standards of the era.[64] However, the partnership wound down acrimoniously in a series of lawsuits.[65] Although the UNext/NYIT partnership was a unique situation, in the years ahead, other investors and for-profit universities would employ variations on this business strategy.

Complexity and controversy with respect to governance, ownership, structure, and profit motives were also evident early in UNext's
history.[66] In his book *Universities in the Marketplace: The Commercialization of Higher Education*, former Harvard president Derek Bok noted
that UNext's contracts were often negotiated behind closed doors
without the consultation of faculty.[67] This enhanced the pressure
from skeptics in academic leadership roles at partner institutions,
especially as it became clear to university partners that their original
expectations for returns from the venture would not be met. The role
of faculty and shared governance was becoming more central. Managing a consortium of multiple partners also proved challenging,
and this was the case at AllLearn, Universitas21, and other bold online education plays as well. Most aspects of UNext's model blurred
the boundaries between the academic world and the for-profit sector, and the type of joint venture and governance that it pioneered
is more common today in various international student pathway
program arrangements and new types of online learning vehicles.
Finally, UNext's experience with state licensing, accreditation, and
federal student aid—the triad of regulatory and quality assurance
bodies that govern higher education offerings and degree-awarding
authority in the United States—highlighted how difficult it can be to
innovate and move quickly within these frameworks.

## Lessons Learned from the Dot-Com Boom

Of course, many of the companies and partnerships during these
years were simply casualties of the irrational exuberance of the era,
which extended well beyond the higher education market. The start-
up firms raised too much money or went public prior to proving
out their business model or any path to profitability, and the "build
it and they will come" mantra was evident. For example, the *Baltimore Sun* article reporting on Caliber Learning Network's IPO in May
1998 (interestingly still nearly two years before the peak of the boom)
recounts: "shares of Baltimore-based Caliber Learning Network Inc.,
a money-losing, development-stage distributor of education and

training programs for working adults, rose as much as 21 percent yesterday in their first day of trading . . . Caliber lost $13.6 million last year on revenue of $1.2 million."[68]

The ideas and business models were also often simply ahead of their time. Why is it that Caliber's Wharton Direct partnership with the University of Pennsylvania, backed by "smart money" and one of the best business school brands in the world, didn't work in 1998, but publicly traded 2U's multimillion dollar deal to deliver an elite University of North Carolina Chapel Hill online MBA is thriving in 2016? Obviously, the market matured in the intervening time period—particularly in terms of the capabilities and costs of the technology, and significantly, the acceptance of the online mode of delivery.

When we look back on the dot-com era IT certification boom and online education gold rush as a whole, a number of takeaways are apparent that are applicable to the current state of the university credential ecosystem and innovation within it, and many of these themes have been highlighted throughout the chapter. A booming economy and the perception of huge market potential were powerful in motivating both start-up players and universities to explore new educational models, and the bold thinking of the period was exciting and truly did encourage innovation and risk taking. The easy availability of private capital was an accelerant, but the easy availability and low cost of capital often led to hastily developed business plans. The number of failures during this period shows the value of sound business models, due diligence, market research, and measured approaches. The model of venture capitalists is predicated on and expects failure—perhaps one home run out of every ten investments—but this same math may not map to the risk profile of most universities.

Despite the monopoly that universities hold on degree credentials, new entities and solutions will spring up to fill the voids when a market opportunity for professional credentials is apparent, whether this is adjacent to university credentials themselves (like IT certifications) or in the form of entirely new institutions to deliver them in different ways (as in online education). It is also clear that professional markets move quickly and that organizations must be nimble to move with the tide of changing industry needs. In addition, universities learned that the corporate training market, while compelling, can be difficult to map to and serve. Plus, it is important to distinguish between corporate and consumer buyers and their needs and budgets. Additionally, the IT certification boom showed us that a proliferation or saturation of credentials in the market can create confusion among hiring managers at employers and consumers, and volume can dilute what was once valuable (a critique that could, of course, be extended to degrees, as well, if they are not calibrated to the demands of the market). Also, third-party partner firms and their technology solutions emerged as catalytic partners for higher education, particularly in fast-paced markets or in bringing to the table new capabilities that universities did not need to develop themselves.

The strategies and actions of the elite institutions at the top of the food chain and the influence that this had on their peers were also significant drivers of activity. Brand, reputation, and prestige clearly have value in the market, but the institutional need to carefully steward and protect these can complicate attempts to scale up. Also, regulation and quality assurance systems were not a particular inhibitor of activity when accredited credentials were not the product.

Virtually all of these themes will reoccur and be further developed in our next chapter and beyond. As the economy began to recover from the dot-com bust, a number of traditional universities had relatively quietly and in more measured ways moved into online credential delivery—and degree-granting for-profit universities were also rising.

FOUR

# Modern Online Education

*Mainstream Online Degrees, MOOCS, and the Emergence of Shorter-Form Credentials*

The dot-com boom era resulted in hugely unmet expectations and saw some of the most prestigious universities in America struggle with e-learning ventures. Given this, in the early 2000s there was a feeling in higher education that online learning's moment had come and gone. In addition to the examples referenced previously, other high-profile initiatives that failed included New York University's NYUonline, Temple University's Virtual Temple, and University of Maryland University College's UMUConline.com. NYUonline, for example, was framed as more of a corporate training play similar in some ways to UNext's initial go-to-market strategy, and spent $25 million over three years of operation, yielding just seven courses and a handful of business partners.[1] One of the principal challenges with these particular initiatives was that they were conceived as for-profit ventures, distinct from the core of the university, and like most dot-com era ideas, hastily conceived and richly capitalized. Their focus, it should be noted, was also not on awarding credentials. Commenting on the profit-making distance learning aspirations of other universities upon the closing of Virtual Temple in July 2001, Temple University president David Adamany told the *Chronicle of Higher Education,* "Good luck to them . . . when they make money, tell them to call me."[2] In 2004, eminent higher education scholars Robert Zemsky and William Massy analyzed the bust in a widely cited report titled *Thwarted Innovation: What Happened to e-Learning and Why*, in which they critiqued the "if we build it they will come" mentality and questioned the market's readiness for e-learning and its ability to improve teaching.[3]

Yet, while many in traditional higher education circles were lamenting the demise of online education, for-profit universities—many of them highly focused on the online model—were experiencing explosive growth due to their willingness and ability to offer accredited degrees online. For-profit colleges had been around for centuries, but typically in trade school incarnations focused on lower-level postsecondary education and short-term training. Beginning in the 1990s, many large players from Apollo Group and DeVry to Education Management Corporation and Strayer began to reach significant scale with a vast array of degree offerings that included not only bachelor's degree completion programs and vocationally focused associate degrees, but also master's and PhD-level programs.[4] The first regionally accredited fully online schools had been for-profit, including Capella University and Jones International University. By the early 2000s, the University of Phoenix had been operating for twenty-five years and had a network of campuses and centers spanning the nation, yet it had become synonymous with online education, building on its pioneering experiments on CompuServe from the late 1980s. The scale and pace of the University of Phoenix's growth are likely unrivaled in the history of higher education. In May 2000, the University of Phoenix Online had an impressive 13,800 degree students, or more than 10 percent of the entire online education market at the time.[5] By the end of that year, this number had grown 35 percent to 18,500 students—and by May 2003, to the astonishing figure of nearly 100,000 students.[6] The University of Phoenix was adding the same number of net *new* students each year as the total headcount at some of the largest universities in the country. The Apollo

Group, the parent company of the University of Phoenix (which accounted for the vast majority of its activity and revenue), had been publicly traded since the 1990s, and on the strength of the University of Phoenix Online's growth, it became one of the best performing stocks of the early 2000s.[7]

For-profit universities had stepped in and taken risk by marketing and delivering fully online degrees where many traditional institutions had not been willing to. In the mid-2000s, for-profit universities held an incredible 40 percent share of online students in the United States.[8] They weren't dabbling in courses and certificates, but they recognized the market demand for credentials that would advance individuals' careers. In particular, their degree offerings targeted regulated fields such as teaching, nursing, and criminal justice—fields with compensation schedules that tended to award higher salaries for completing a degree, often irrespective of the institution from which the degree came. Perhaps most significantly, for-profit universities invested heavily in marketing their online education programs, especially via emerging Internet marketing channels, during a time when most universities were still debating the value of branding and were investing little in online advertising. Nearly $200 million was being spent on marketing online education programs annually, with for-profit colleges dedicating 15 to 20 percent of their total revenue—on par with the pharmaceutical industry—to sales and marketing.[9] The University of Phoenix Online's web advertisements became ubiquitous, and it became one of the single largest advertisers on the Internet, spending more than all but a few consumer-facing blue chip companies. All of this marketing had an important effect, often discussed among online education leaders at smaller and traditional universities at the time: the rising tide was lifting all boats. For-profit universities were popularizing the idea that a university credential could be earned online. Meanwhile, more reputable traditional institutions were slowly and quietly scaling their online education enterprises with increasingly sustainable business models.

## STEADILY GROWING CREDIBILITY BUT
## INCONSISTENT PERCEPTION

The entry of more nonprofit universities into the online degree market steadily made the idea of earning a degree online more credible. The most active parties were the continuing and professional education units at traditional universities that had long played a role in distance learning: the Sloan Consortium ALN grant recipients, institutions wholly focused on adult learning, and a host of others. In 2002, the online distance education market had reached nearly 500,000 students and was growing 40 percent annually, accounting for an estimated $2.4 billion in tuition revenue.[10] In addition to the aforementioned for-profit universities, this scale and growth were driven by a wide range of traditional institutions—principally public institutions, but also private. The University of Central Florida was building out a suite of online programs, and Bismarck State College in North Dakota was offering nearly one hundred online courses to almost 1,000 students.[11] Penn State's "World Campus" was growing rapidly and offering a variety of online degree programs and certificates in disciplines ranging from turf grass management to addiction studies. University of Maryland University College, a distance learning pioneer (continuing on in its original nonprofit model), was reporting nearly 40,000 unduplicated online enrollments.[12] In 2003, the University of Massachusetts system, through UMass Online, had reached a scale of 13,000 enrollments and $11 million in revenue, growing at a 40 percent rate across a variety of degree programs and courses that included, for example, bachelor's completion degrees for nurses.[13] Meanwhile, Boston University was offering online master's degrees ranging from criminal justice to insurance management.[14]

By 2005, the number of students pursuing fully online study—mainly in degree programs—continued to grow rapidly and passed the one million student mark.[15] According to the Sloan Consortium, an even larger number of students—3.2 million—was taking at least one online course.[16] The largest traditional university players in the online distance education market had grown to include institutions ranging from Arizona State University (11,000 students taking online-only courses) and the University of Florida (5,000 students) to Michigan's Baker College (3,500).[17] By 2005, fully online degrees were increasingly—although not entirely—accepted by students, employers, and university leaders alike. Understanding the patterns through which online degrees gained credibility and were perceived is key to understanding issues then, today, and tomorrow.

At Eduventures in 2005, I led the first comprehensive national survey of consumer attitudes toward online education. We found that 77 percent of prospective adult college students would *consider* enrolling in an online distance education program.[18] However, despite their willingness to consider this new delivery mode (and a preference for hybrid or blended programs, still present today), there were lingering concerns about quality. Relative to traditional classroom-based study, 38 percent were unsure about the quality of online education, and 29 percent believed online education was outright inferior—meaning only one-third of prospective students was confident about the quality of online education.[19]

Meanwhile, many employers had been engaged in online training for years, and among them, the perception of online education relative to traditional instruction was actually more encouraging, while still including doubt. In a 2005 national survey of more than 500 employers, we found that nearly two-thirds of employers felt that online instruction was either *equally* valuable (52 percent) or *more* valuable (11 percent) compared to traditional face-to-face instruction.[20] Employers' acceptance of online education was critical, as our consumer surveys from this period showed that whether or not an online degree or course would be accepted by an employer was the principal reservation or barrier to enrolling for most students: employers would be the ultimate arbiters of quality. Not surprisingly, typical employer concerns included a perceived lack of rigor or dynamism.[21] Our online survey work with employers was complemented by more than fifty telephone interviews with hiring managers. These interviews yielded comments such as, "Is it too easy to get a good grade? Is it, dare I say it, a diploma mill?" from a manager at a food company.[22] Yes, the stigma of online schools and diploma mills—this was a major dynamic in the early online credential market, and it still echoes today.

With for-profit universities such as the University of Phoenix and others dominating mindshare, there was not yet a wide awareness that online degrees were offered by more credible or prestigious institutions. At the time many of the for-profit institutions were actually producing quality programs and graduates, but the reputations of online-only schools such as Walden University, Capella University, and Jones International University simply did not, of course, carry the same weight as the University of Washington or the University of Cincinnati. A study by Jonathan Adams and Margaret DeFleur in 2006 found that employers were deeply skeptical of degrees from virtual (rather than traditional) institutions.[23] A number of years later, a *Saturday Night Live* skit comedically captured this cultural meme in parodying online schools and their advertising. In the fake commercial, one of the characters reports, "The University of Westfield Online gave me the skills I need to get the job I want—skills like not mentioning in a job interview that I went to an Internet college."[24] Of course, for for-profit purveyors of online degrees, this wasn't funny. Yet the tide was already turning: growing numbers of traditional institutions had shaken off their skepticism and were investing heavily in online degree programs. This research and development would be well timed for the unprecedented boom in enrollment in the late 2000s economic cycle.

## THE NONPROFIT EMPIRE STRIKES BACK

In the second half of the 2000s, the online higher education market entered the third stage of its evolution. The favorable perception of online learning among chief academic officers at traditional universities was slowly but steadily increasing. According to the Sloan Consortium's large-scale annual tracking surveys, the percentage of leaders who agreed with the statement "online learning is critical to the long-term strategy of my institution" rose from 49 percent in 2002 to 59 percent by 2006.[25] A majority of universities were now seeing online learning—including online credentials—as more central. Jeff Seaman, who was Chief Information Officer and Survey Director for the Sloan Consortium, recalls, "From the point of view of the chief academic officer, they were largely onboard with understanding it was critical to long-term strategy from the very beginning. And much of it was very driven by access, state or local mandates, and what their mission was. They worried about faculty, resources, how do they measure quality—but they rarely worried about student satisfaction, student demand, or acceptance. Those were not things that kept them up at night, but the other things were."[26]

Universities were responding to the clear growth in the market and the opportunity to extend their reach, meet their mission, and generate new revenue streams. Competitive concerns were also in play: in the early years of growth in online credential offerings, the assumption was that online students represented an entirely new market of students who otherwise wouldn't enroll, due to distance and a lack of access. That was somewhat true. However, now institutions without online degree programs were clearly beginning to lose enrollment to their national *and local* peers who did: online education was beginning to encroach on traditional market segments. Further, universities continued to become more comfortable with the mode of delivery as increasingly large waves of online degree graduates found career advancement and employment in the workforce.

Due to the growing momentum, the policy and regulatory environment was—quite critically—becoming more favorable to delivering credentials at a distance. For example, at the federal level, the Higher Education Act had long restricted or limited accredited institutions' ability to participate in the Title IV financial aid program if a majority of its students were in distance learning programs ("the 50 percent rule") or if its programs were delivered in nontraditional course lengths—a hallmark of many online programs.[27] In 1998, the

US Department of Education had instituted the Distance Education Demonstration Program, to experiment with waivers and alterations to statutory and regulatory requirements that would provide greater access to fully online programs.[28] This program effectively granted a set of leading institutions offering online degrees—for example, Eastern Oregon University, Capella University, University of Phoenix, and Regis University—with waivers to the restrictive limitations so that the Department of Education and Congress could study the outcomes. This effort would ultimately span seven years.

Following a positive 2005 report to Congress on the success of the Distance Education Demonstration Program, Representative John Boehner, chair of the House Education and Workforce Committee, issued a call to relax the regulations, stating, "this new report once again confirms that outdated barriers must be eliminated so that colleges and universities aren't stifled in their attempt to increase access to higher education through innovation and technology."[29] In a move accelerated by for-profit college lobbying, Congress eliminated the "50 percent rule" in a 2006 budget bill, in news that made the front page of the *New York Times*.[30] Accrediting agencies and states were also actively updating their standards to account for the growth in online higher education. As one example, in Texas, the state legislature was considering whether online law school graduates would be allowed to sit for the state bar exam.[31] Although for-profit universities were among the biggest beneficiaries of this regulatory change, Mike Offerman, former president of Capella University, observes: "The removal of the 50 percent rule may have meant more for the field—the public universities and private not-for-profits. Even though they weren't on the forefront of arguing for it, once that door did open up and you could do more than 50 percent, you suddenly had institutions realizing they could deliver full degrees online, enabling places that before wouldn't have been thinking about this. It did a lot of good."[32]

In this new era of more mainstream online education, it helped that increasingly prestigious research universities were becoming more active in the market. Higher education's institutional isomor-phism, or the idea that universities tend to mimic their peers, was a powerful force. Interestingly, movement into the online degree mar-ket roughly followed the ladder of the *U.S. News and World Report* rankings from the bottom upward, first within the top one hundred and ultimately the top fifty national research universities. The first wave of growth took place among many of the second-tier state col-leges and universities. Then, by the end of the 2000s, for example, North Carolina State University was offering forty-eight online de-grees and ten certificates, and institutions such as Florida State and the University of Nebraska also had a large slate of online credential offerings.[33] Moving up the rankings, Drexel University—which was the only nonprofit to successfully scale its online enterprise in a for-profit subsidiary model—was offering more than fifty online degrees and thirty-five certificates. Northeastern University had built more than sixty online degree programs (including two professional doc-torates) in just a few years, and Boston University, another early inno-vator, had sixteen online degrees and fourteen certificates. Pioneers such as Penn State, the University of Florida, the University of Illi-nois, and the University of Texas system continued to grow rapidly.[34]

The real tipping point in the acceptance of fully online credential offerings was the launch of online degrees by some of the top-ranked universities and the vote of confidence that this brought for academic leaders at other institutions, employers, and students, when many of the more prestigious universities in America were offering and heav-ily marketing online credentials. One of the boldest moves was a 2008 deal signed by the University of Southern California (USC), and a company called 2Tor, now known as 2U. 2U's vision was to bring to-gether the best practices from for-profit higher education (such as marketing and outcome-oriented curriculum design) with the pre-mier brands of nonprofit higher education in a model that aimed for true scale.[35] 2U chose top-ranked universities as its primary focus, and similar contracts would follow in the years ahead with, for exam-ple, the University of North Carolina at Chapel Hill's Kenan–Flagler

Business School; the law school at Washington University in St. Louis; and the School of Information at the University of California, Berkeley.[36] By 2012, 2U's first partner, USC, had as an institution reached 5,500 online students across nine schools, generating more than $100 million in revenue.[37] Meanwhile, operating in models that included in-house online learning units, continuing and professional education schools at institutions such as Northwestern University and Columbia University were now also offering online degrees.[38]

At the same time, less selective private universities such as Southern New Hampshire University and Liberty University had made online degree programs central to their institutional strategy and grew by tens of thousands of students.[39] On the employer side of the equation, a 2010 survey of employers conducted by the Society for Human Resource Management (SHRM) found that 87 percent of human resources leaders agreed that online degrees were viewed more favorably compared to five years prior—although 60 percent of employers still preferred to hire job applicants with traditional degrees, assuming all other factors were equal.[40]

## Business Models Align

Indeed, with exponentially lower technology costs and shifts in how education firms were being capitalized, the process of starting up and offering online programs was also becoming much easier as a market of "online enablement" firms was rising to provide course design, technology infrastructure, and marketing services in a turnkey fashion. A college could sign a contract with these companies and be up and running within a year. This approach was very different from needing to build out an in-house online infrastructure. In the early years, the companies that drove institutions' growth in online education had included IBM and PWC through the eArmyU initiative; Deltak; and companies such as eCollege, Compass Knowledge, and Embanet.

Today institutions are still mastering the recipe for starting and delivering an online credential program. Creating a new degree or converting a degree to an online format requires funding and investment capital up front, including the marketing and advertising funds to build awareness and generate applicants. Front-end market research and product development are important, followed by perhaps the most substantial activity, instructional design and course development. Assuming the program is offered in other states or if it involves a licensed credential of some sort or a clinical placement (such as in health care or teaching), universities need to secure and manage regulatory approvals. Work also includes training faculty to teach online; teaching the courses; developing appropriate approaches for academic advising and student services; and managing registration, financial aid, and billing. Of course, universities tend to be expert and experienced in many of these activities, but they need to adapt approaches and systems for an online market. Plus, the online experience needs to run on a learning management system and IT infrastructure, and potentially be supported by a 24/7 help desk. Jeff Seaman of the Sloan Consortium, recollects: "Something we were always tracking was when you went from zero to one fully online student, you had to think through all of the aspects with how do you deal with a student online, register them, give them grades, take exams, etc. That was a mighty step—going from online as a special case to online at scale."[41]

Online enablement firms specialized in these services and processes and primarily contracted with universities under a low-risk revenue sharing business model. The company would provide the up-front investment, often $1-2 million per program—a substantial amount, but compare this to $1 million *per course* spent at UNext years prior—and take a 50 to 80 percent cut of the gross tuition revenue.[42] Contracts would generally run five to ten years, with the enablement firm running losses early but making its profit in the later years of the multiyear contract.[43] By 2011, these companies were netting an estimated $250 million in annual revenue, and more were entering or making new investments in the market each month. In addition to those named earlier, companies included Altius, Everspring, Orbis Education, Academic Partnerships, Learning House, and Colloquy.[44]

Although many institutions engaged in university- or systemwide online education strategies, college or school deans often drove decisions about online degree offerings, with the blessing of their provosts or presidents. Deans had autonomy within their institutions and often had the ability to steer their academic unit's credentials in the direction that they wished. This was especially the case not only with professionally focused business schools and engineering schools, but also autonomous schools and colleges of professional education that had their own faculty and/or degree-granting authority. Now accepted within mainstream and top-ranked institutions, online university credentials had gone from being novel and a higher-risk business undertaking to being established and in demand.

## A MATURE ONLINE DEGREE MARKET AND ITS LESSONS

In the ten-year period following the bursting of the dot-com bubble, online degrees moved from the fringes of higher education to a mainstream growth driver. An era that began with disillusionment ended with even the elite universities embracing and succeeding with the online delivery of credentials—and in the intervening time, saw the rise and decline of for-profit universities. Notably, nonprofit universities—both on their own and through enablement firms—successfully coopted the strategies, methods, and tools of for-profit universities. As market conditions changed and for-profit universities fell out of favor in the regulatory environment and investment community, online enablement firms became the preferred vehicle in which to deploy both investment capital and also the human capital and talent of the online education industry. Enablement firms, working on behalf of nonprofit universities, were fueled by the same investors that funded for-profit universities, and they were cross-pollinated with executive teams that often came from for-profit higher education. For-profit universities such as the University of Phoenix could be considered as classic cases of first-mover advantage, pioneering the online degree market by filling a gap with a novel offering, but later declining when incumbents embraced this same approach. With measured approaches and attention to best practices, nonprofit universities later harvested the wheat that the for-profits had sowed. Between 2012 and 2014, for instance, exclusively distance education enrollment at private, nonprofit institutions surged 22 percent, compared to an 11 percent decline at for-profit institutions, according to federal data.[45]

Our review of the online degree market's evolution also illustrates how innovation can take time but ultimately arrives in higher education: credentialing innovation entails a significant amount of difficult *cultural* change across a complicated ecosystem. Universities' traditions and governance procedures, state and federal regulations, and employers' hiring practices all have long traditions and deeply embedded practices. Credentials are among the core products of universities and are at the backbone of the financial aid, accreditation, and state higher education regulation system. Additionally, for individuals, university credentials such as a degrees are qualifications that people hold and invest years to obtain; they become a part of individual identity. Thus, these systems, products, and norms don't get disrupted overnight; rather, they tend to experience iterative evolution, as we see with the online degree market, and this is perhaps par for the course in a complex, regulated market.

The story of online education's growth and mainstreaming also shows, not surprisingly, how significant peer effects can be in higher education—and how comfortable with experimentation institutions can become when other institutions they respect make bold moves. This pattern was present in the growth of online degrees, repeated itself with the recent arrival of MOOCs (as detailed later), and will likely continue with various microcredentials and new types of certificates, as also discussed later in this chapter. Additionally, the growth of the online degree market shows us that innovation can and does often occur at an institutional level, but given the diversified nature of higher education institutions and their units, innovations often bubble up from experiments by individual programs and colleges and schools, and are also often catalyzed by outside organizations.

The maturing of the online degree market is another illustration of the role of private capital in the evolution of higher education and credentials, insofar as various technology vendors and entirely new universities were fueled by private investment in the expensive, multiyear undertaking that is developing and launching new credential programs. Private capital in the philanthropic sense has been another clear market driver, from the Sloan Foundation's ALN grants, to the significant funding being deployed by the Gates and Lumina Foundations more recently. The initial bubble and overabundance of capital compared to its later absence not only shaped the market, but also led to new realities and reflection on mission. Mike Offerman, formerly of Capella University and the University of Wisconsin, remarks: "You could see higher ed's version of the dot-com bubble developing. It was amazing, the parade of investors that were coming to visit us at a public university. When the bubble burst, it was a very important sobering. Aside from the obvious downsides, it had a positive effect for online learning as a movement: it forced everybody to step back and become more mature as we went forward and to think more about quality and students than about billions of dollars."[46]

The pattern through which the US online degree market developed also illustrates the interplay between university strategies, consumer (student) and employer receptivity to new forms of credentials, private companies and investors, and the regulatory environment. Within this ecosystem, it can be argued that as the owners of credentials, the higher education *institutions* are in the driver's seat, leading the innovation process through experimentation with new offerings within existing regulatory and quality assurance constructs. It takes many years for consumers and employers to respond to the quality of these programs and their graduates, and the regulatory framework eventually catches up due to stakeholder interest or institutional lobbying.

Given that colleges and universities are often defined by place and physical presence, offering online degrees was a bold enough evolution in a centuries-old business model. However, the growth of the online degree market consisted largely of porting traditional credentials and their historical constructs into an online format. With that door open and the digital delivery of credentials now accepted, the stage was set for more significant innovations connected to credentialing.

## MASSIVE OPEN ONLINE COURSES AND ONLINE EDUCATION'S FOURTH STAGE OF EVOLUTION

Stanford University is at the epicenter of the global start-up ecosystem, so perhaps it is no surprise that it was there in 2011 that computer science professor Sebastian Thrun founded Udacity, one of the modern MOOC progenitors, following his experience teaching a large-scale artificial intelligence course with more than 100,000 students.[47] In 2012, fellow Stanford computer science professors Daphne Koller and Andrew Ng founded Coursera with a $16 million funding round from some of Silicon Valley's premier venture capital firms.[48] Not to be outdone, the Massachusetts Institute of Technology (MIT) built on the heritage of its decade-old MIT OpenCourseWare initiative in launching MITx, a next generation online learning platform at the end of 2011—later teaming up with Harvard University in 2012 to create the nonprofit MOOC platform provider EdX.[49]

A fourth stage in the evolution of online education had arrived with MOOCs—a concept originally pioneered by Canadian educators George Siemens and Stephen Downes in 2008.[50] Compared to traditional online education programs such as those covered here and in the preceding chapters, MOOCs were unique in their large-scale enrollment (tens of thousands of students or more per course section) and open-to-all approach. MOOCs were characterized by not being closed, instructor-led courses, and existing as noncredit offerings unconnected to a credential-based program. Most MOOCs were free, video-based, one-to-many streaming lectures powered by various automated features—a model that is arguably driven by the ethos and tools of computer scientists and "freemium" Internet start-up business models more than pedagogy. Following the launch of organizations such as Udacity, Coursera, and EdX, a frenzy ensued as universities such as Johns Hopkins, the California Institute of Technology, the University of Washington, the University of Texas, and countless other large-scale, top-ranked institutions joined the MOOC movement.[51] The *New York Times* declared 2012 "The Year of the MOOC," while the *Atlantic* called MOOCs "the single most important experiment in higher education."[52] An entire book could be written about the MOOC craze and its aftershocks, but our focus here is on the perception of online education and various emerging forms of credentials in employers' hiring activities.

One of the initial revenue generation models pursued by MOOC firms was the concept that large-scale courses could serve as talent pipelines and screening mechanisms for employers, especially technology firms. The MOOC companies were squarely targeting the recruitment and hiring process at the core of our earlier discussion.[53] In this way, courses would be free to the consumer, but employers would pay based on their interest in acquiring student talent on the back end of the completed course. Coursera's approach was thus described in a December 2012 *Chronicle of Higher Education* article:

> A participating employer is given a list of students who meet its requirements, usually the best-performing students in a certain geographic area. If the company is interested in one of those students, then Coursera sends an e-mail to the student asking whether he or she would be interested in being introduced to that company. The company pays a flat fee to Coursera for each introduction, and the college offering the course gets a percentage of the revenue, typically between 6 and 15 percent. Mr. Ng noted that Coursera might try other types of matchmaking arrangements in the future, depending on how well the current model works for students and employers.[54]

MOOCs were envisioned as disrupting the degree's status as the gold standard in hiring. The problem? Employers prefer degrees, and they still do not trust the outcomes of self-paced, non-instructor-led online education, an important distinction between modern online degree programs and MOOCs. In 2013, the *Chronicle of Higher Education* reported that EdX was abandoning plans to link MOOC students with employers, following a pilot project in which of 868 students who completed a course, only 3 were granted job interviews and 0 were hired.[55] EdX's conclusion was that corporate HR functions preferred traditional degrees in hiring and filtered out nontraditional candidates and credentials—a finding consistent with our earlier examination of employers' hiring practices and a theme we will continue to explore here.[56]

## Employers' Current Perception of Online Education and the Unbundling of the Degree into Shorter-Form Credentials

Rather than disrupting higher education or employer hiring practices, the explosion of MOOCs onto the scene did disrupt something: the relatively stable notion of what university-based online education entailed. The MOOC era is a demarcation point and a new chapter in online education's history. Today, online university courses and credentials are no longer just traditional courses and programs mediated through technology—but much more experimental, more granular or modular, and more tightly aligned with industry interests. The history of the online degree market was one of steady growth and acceptance. From the year 2000 onward, perhaps ten to fifteen million Americans had directly experienced an online degree program. These programs were serious and instructor-led undertakings, typically involving an admissions process, grades and assessments, multiyear commitments to completion, and accredited credentials at the end of the process. With MOOCs, suddenly tens of millions of individuals (an estimated thirty-five million people globally took at least one MOOC in 2015) were experimenting with an open online course affiliated with a university, and the experiences—given the speed at which MOOCs moved and the early lack of attention to instructional design—were often mixed.[57]

In 2013, Northeastern University in partnership with FTI Consulting conducted a national telephone opinion poll of business leaders and consumers, part of an ongoing annual initiative focused on understanding innovations in higher education.[58] This research effort asked specifically about MOOCs, and among both business leaders and the general public at this time, only 27 to 28 percent agreed "MOOCs provide the same quality of education as in-person classes." However, more than half of those polled believed that MOOCs would fundamentally transform education and that MOOCs should be articulable into degrees for credit. Clearly, MOOCs were perceived as holding promise.[59] In my own survey and focus group work with employers and prospective graduate students around North America around this same time, MOOCs were spawning entirely new questions about online education. Many employers and prospective students were concerned about the level of faculty interaction and engagement, the relationship between quality and price, and the utility of courses that don't lead to recognized credentials—issues that were nonexistent or much less present in the online degree market.[60] MOOCs were accelerating the attention given to online education but also confusing the still nascent notions of quality and outcomes.

Despite continued growth, it is still relatively early in many employers' understanding of online education. Tom Hanna, staffing manager at Robert Bosch Tool Corporation, notes: "Opinion has shifted over the years. With the University of Phoenixes (of the world), originally there might have been some doubt cast about online programs, skepticism that you'd get the same value from that program versus being in the university setting. But with distance learning becoming more common and new educational models, online is something as a business structure we have to accept, realizing that it's changing. And we have to figure out how we can evaluate those programs in a more effective way. We're still at the early stages of understanding all of this."[61]

Dynamics within employers' own businesses are contributing to the growing credibility of online education. First, the nature of work itself is increasingly distributed and conducted virtually and at a distance. As described by Tom Mathews of Cree: "Many of these people are working with remote teams, and if you haven't been comanaging someone in Brazil, China, India, or Canada along with a local domestic team, it might have been valuable to have done this online, where you had that type of group work where no one's in the same place or time zone."[62] Perhaps even more significantly, a major share of employers' own internal learning and development is now conducted online. In 2014, more than 50 percent of US-based corporations' total training hours were delivered through blended, online, or computer-based methods.[63] Adrienne Alberts of the American Red Cross explains, "Now we're using online education much more ourselves to provide education and training for our workforce—almost exclusively. Nearly all of the delivery of skill improvement that we use as an organization is online. So hiring managers and leaders see and embrace and utilize that in our building of the workforce."[64]

Beyond just representing an evolution in online learning, MOOCs burst onto the higher education scene at a moment of concern about cost, outcomes and transparency, the sustainability of the traditional university business model, the potential impact of technology, and globalization. As a result, MOOCs brought even greater attention to the value of lifelong learning and professional development and the role of educational credentials in the job market. In this way MOOCs have also accelerated a relatively new and percolating discussion about the unbundling of the degree and faculty roles.

## The Unbundling of Degrees into Shorter-Form Digital Credentials and Certificates

Influenced by the rise of MOOCs and the dialogue they spawned, the American Council on Education (ACE), one of the country's preeminent higher education associations, in 2013 launched a Presidential Innovation Lab consisting of fourteen participating CEOs from a wide range of colleges and universities.[65] This special working group's charge was to study trends in new educational models and technologies and their potential impact on access. This effort resulted in the publication of a series of papers documenting conclusions including that traditional university credentials were threatened by alternatives, that an increasingly wider array of credentials and certificates would need to be monitored and presented opportunity, and that instruction and faculty roles were becoming unbundled from traditional structures.[66]

Given that the value of education in the marketplace largely lies in credentials, the MOOC movement has come together with the interests of the completion agenda and the general trend toward work-oriented lifelong learning to create a groundswell of activity focused on new, shorter forms of credentials and certificates that unbundle, or break apart, the constructs of the traditional degree. Yet, most of the alternative credentials so often discussed in the media and in boardrooms are, at this point, issued by independent companies rather than universities. Examples include new types of certificates: verified certificates, nanodegrees, micromasters, and credentials of readiness, among other terminologies.

Our concern here is how employers perceive the proliferation of new types of online credentials and their semantics. Across my many employer interviews and prior research, it is apparent that sorting through the diversity of new credentials is difficult for hiring executives, and while we are still early in this trend, this is reminiscent of the latter stages of the late 1990s IT certification boom. And, in many cases, employers have little or no familiarity with certain new types of credentials; in others, curiosity or confusion. Tom Mathews of Cree describes some of these dynamics:

> There's definitely confusion . . . it's one of the things I talk about with my recruitment team as they get in discussions with their hiring managers. It's changing so rapidly, there are so many different variations and flavors . . . with a lot of these things, I'd have to say there's skepticism at this point. Is that [a given credential] really valuable? Micro-this, mini-that—it sounds like less and smaller? What's that mean?

We as employers—unless we're deep in the space—we don't really know what you're getting for a given credential. That's why there's uncertainty and skepticism: we need to be educated here, there needs to be a playbook here.[67]

Similarly, Adrienne Alberts of the American Red Cross offers the following on MOOCs and alternative online credentials as tools in hiring: "Our leaders have given them very little credibility—they're just not talking about it, it's not registering for them. I have had a number of conversations with my colleagues about how is this going to work in the educational field. Will this displace higher education in some way? Will it give us a more even playing field? You can get some Ivy League exposure online, but is that building a real credential? I love the opportunity behind the idea, but I have not seen it show up in the workplace in that way. It hasn't moved into the mainstream enough quite yet."[68] Indeed, hiring leaders do appear to have a strong preference for traditional credentials, even if they are earned online. As Gail Jacobs, senior director of talent acquisition and HR operations at risk management firm RMS, explains, for example:

Years ago when the University of Phoenix was starting to become popular, most hiring managers and recruiters would look at it and say these are worthless because it hadn't caught on, and they were so skeptical of the online schools. Today most people know MIT puts their curriculum online and most of the big schools are offering online curriculum now. But when somebody comes in and says I have my "microdegree" . . . we're not trusting that yet as a credential that's worthy . . . Most of the UNC Chapel Hill– or Stanford-type MBAs that are done online are acceptable—but ten years ago, with those we would have said if you're not in the classroom, you're not learning. So there's been a culture shift over the last few years.[69]

Even the growth of more traditional certificates creates difficulty for employers sorting through what credentials mean, given the wide variety of forms and lack of standardization. The fact that a certificate on a resume can signal anything from completing a single course or executive education program to a near degree-length experience is problematic as a signal. As the head of talent at a large publicly traded company explains: "The danger with a certificate is . . . what did it take to get the certificate—and was it a series of 3-day seminars, or is it a collection of 5 credit-bearing classes? What is behind that certification that's there?"[70] The last part of this quote also serves as a reminder that the market continues to conflate the term *certification* with *certificate*. In fact, when asked about university certificate programs, many corporate leaders begin to share their views on popular occupational certifications in fields such as IT, project management, and supply chain.

Many employers appear to think dichotomously, with one category consisting of university-issued *degrees* as a key job qualification based on their breadth and depth; and certificates, individual courses, and new microcredentials in another group representing continuing education and skill acquisition more than a job qualification. Udacity's "nanodegrees" and Coursera's "specializations"—in areas such as iOS development, data science, and so on—are, in effect, IT certifications focused on specific skillsets. By contrast, degrees are clearly distinguished by employers as more substantive job qualifications that represent a greater level of commitment, depth, achievement, and perseverance. As described by an HR leader for a consumer products company: "Degrees are more—it's more solid as far as a result to look at on your resume. It took 18 months to get that (master's) and with certificates or any other certification or whatever, it's just not as consistently viewed."[71] Likewise, an executive at a scientific firm comments: "Certificates probably aren't weighed as significantly as someone who's put a year, or year-and-a-half to three years on hold to go after a specific degree."[72]

This said, it is very clear that in hiring, employers value and appreciate short-form credentials and continuing education generally because of the initiative that they show. Employers frequently comment on certificates and online courses demonstrating individuals' commitment to "owning their own development"—an expectation in many organizations in today's training environment—and keeping their skills and knowledge current.[73] As Shelly Holt of Concur Technologies notes, "it shows you're progressing in your development, investing in the development of yourself, and growing as an individual."[74] Similarly, executive search leader Paul Edelman describes: "Online courses can be indicators of initiative and the ability to complete something. They suggest that the candidate has desirable qualities like curiosity, initiative, resourcefulness, and the ability to function with little supervision."[75]

With online degrees fairly well accepted, employers today acknowledge the growth of new types of digital credentials and are monitoring their impact and utility. However, the ability of new forms of credentials to operate as hiring qualifications that substitute for rather than merely complement degrees would require a significant cultural shift within the employer community. Chuck Edward, Microsoft's talent acquisition leader, describes these dynamics related to alternative talent pipelines and credentials: "My current view is that I wouldn't consider any of these things more than a pilot at this point. I haven't had to do it, and I haven't seen a strong desire from many of my hiring managers to expand. For sure, online courses as a proxy, certifications—but in our world the pedigree of a college degree still carries a ton of weight, and the better the school, the more weight, so we're in a culture shift to try alternatives. There's risk in that versus the tried-and-true accreditation (of a degree)."[76]

Of course, in the university credentialing ecosystem, it is not just universities and their programs that are impacted by technological innovation: employers' own hiring practices are evolving in response to new trends and tools. Next, we will look at the trends that are shaping the role of university credentials in hiring, in this era of innovation and digital credentials.

# FIVE

# Credentialing in the Internet Age

*A Brave New World from Digitizing the*
*Credential to Talent Analytics*

Few areas of the economy have been untouched by the reach of technology over the past few years. We are clearly in an unprecedented
period of technology-mediated innovation. Venture capitalist Marc
Andreessen has famously characterized this with his hypothesis that
"software is eating the world"—as now highly mature microproces-
sor, Internet, and software technologies are driving new business
models in sectors as diverse as finance, transportation, and health
care, among others.[1] Following the 2008 financial crisis, investments
into technology companies and their valuations soared, driven by
booms in mobile technology, cloud computing, and social media.[2]
By 2014, venture capital investment topped $48 billion, the highest
level in more than a decade—with $12 billion of that figure going to
Internet-specific firms, the highest share since the dot-com boom
of 2000.[3]

This optimism about technology start-ups has carried over into
the education domain and the emerging educational technology,
or edtech, sector. Since 2011, venture capital investment into edtech
firms has more than quadrupled, from $429 million to more than
$1.8 billion in 2015, with companies focused on higher education
receiving the largest share of that funding.[4] As we have seen, private
capital and the start-up ecosystem can have significant reverberations

in the higher education market. The availability of capital, the evolution of web technologies, and calls for innovation in higher education have come together to spawn a new generation of educational technology companies, a number of them focused on university and professional credentialing.

Additionally, on the employer side of the ecosystem, businesses are making significant new investments into human resources technology. In 2016, many employers find themselves in the middle of a multiyear enterprise system replacement cycle in which they are moving to new, more capability-rich, cloud-based systems for managing their human capital and their recruiting and hiring processes.[5] With this technology cycle comes the need and opportunity to adapt their business processes. And, as in so many other areas of business, data and analytics are just beginning to have a transformative impact within the human resources field: the age of "talent analytics" has arrived. Writing about this particular juncture in a recent *Harvard Business Review* article, HR expert Peter Cappelli asserts, "This is a moment of enormous opportunity. Little has been done in the past few decades to examine the value of widely used practices that are central to how companies operate."[6]

In this chapter, we review some of the key technology trends and players that are shaping the future of the university credentialing ecosystem—from both the higher education and employer sides of the equation.

## EXTENDING AND MODERNIZING CREDENTIALS: E-PORTFOLIOS AND CREDENTIALING MANAGEMENT SYSTEMS

One of the most common complaints about university degrees is that they are blunt instruments lacking in detail about the skill or learning of their holder and existing as static paper documents. In an era in which so many other aspects of business and everyday life have largely been digitized—document exchange, contracts, correspondence—technology is now being leveraged to enhance the utility of the credential and therefore improve the hiring process for employers and the portability and impact of credentials for professionals. Thus, riding the wave of interest that we have established throughout this book in terms of how credentials operate, new types of technology solutions businesses have sprung up around the common themes of documenting credentials digitally, augmenting credentials with additional data and detail, sharing and verifying credentials, and representing and demonstrating skills online in lieu of traditional credentials.

Investor Matt Greenfield of Rethink Education describes the credentialing market as attractive to investors and companies because "it's an area where there's a lot of rapid change, and some of these businesses will be very large."[7] Credentialing technology is also attractive to investors because it presents the opportunity to create a platform business—consider a firm becoming the operating system for credentials—as well as the fact that credentialing technology complements the business model of universities and exists in service of them. Greenfield further explains: "We're very interested in credentialing, but credentialing systems as they interoperate with each other and with existing institutions. Many of the venture capitalists sometimes talk as if history is going to sweep away universities and that they'll be replaced, but we don't think that at all. We think there's a huge opportunity for universities to embrace the full life cycle of learning."[8]

## E-Portfolios and Competency Management Systems

The concept of the *e-portfolio*—a web-based collection of work samples or course outcomes—has been developing in higher education for many years. As far back as 2007 and perhaps earlier, e-portfolios were one of educational technology's next big things. Many institutions experimented with them as ways to augment the traditional resume and present students' skills and accomplishments to employers. Many of these early experiments were even supported by catalytic funding from the federal government and other sources.[9] Leading firms providing e-portfolios include, for example, Digication—which has more than 5,000 institutional clients across all levels of education—and Pathbrite, which was acquired by Cengage Learning in 2015.[10] E-portfolios have continued to receive significant attention from higher education technologists, and they are integrated into many major learning management systems.

There is no doubt that great value could be found in e-portfolios and similar technology solutions that provide greater interactivity and depth about a job candidate's capabilities beyond just a static resume. Hundreds of universities are using e-portfolios, increasingly as a standard offering for students provided by their institutions' career services units. However, employers still have shown relatively little uptake and interest in integrating e-portfolios as currently constructed into their hiring process. According to employers, e-portfolios are "nice to have," but not a game-changer. In a 2008 article in the *EDUCAUSE Quarterly*, Chris Ward and Chris Moser published the results of a survey of more than 5,000 employers under the title, "E-Portfolios as a Hiring Tool: Do Employers Really Care?" They found that many employers at that time were simply unfamiliar with e-portfolios but expected them to emerge as more prominent in the future.[11] Six years later, a 2014 *Wall Street Journal* piece reported that "Giant Resumes Fail to Impress Employers: Colleges Are Pushing Students to Create E-Portfolios, but Hiring Managers Are Skeptical," and this is consistent with my own extensive recent discussions with employers and market monitoring.[12] When asked about the use or potential of e-portfolios in the course of my research, many hiring leaders have surprisingly little to say. Gail Jacobs, senior director of talent acquisition and HR operations for RMS, explains: "The use of a portfolio is still specific to certain areas: for example, the artist or the graphic designer always needed it to show their work. For software developers, that's an area where it's getting more and more common to have some work you can show. But most employers can't handle it with the systems and the processes they have in place; they can't handle portfolio review, and they don't have the applicant tracking systems to screen candidates or attach something that's easy to get to."[13]

Thus, the still muted awareness of and excitement for e-portfolios among employers is an illustration that well-intended technologies originating out of higher education must align with the realities—including the limitations—of employers' existing business process, systems, and culture. Unless it is streamlined or parsed in some form, an e-portfolio is just more extraneous information for employers to cognitively process—and technologically process in their application system—at the first stage of the screening process. Adrienne Alberts, director of talent acquisition for the American Red Cross, describes: "You have to understand that recruiting is a high-volume business. We have to get through it quickly; any additional information that's fed into the process that's not easy to distill probably isn't going to be utilized to make a hiring decision, unless it's much further along in the process with, say, your top two or three candidates. Until e-portfolios can be integrated into applicant tracking system (ATS) technology to be evaluated quickly in massive quantities, I think it's going to be very hard for employers to use those in a meaningful way."[14]

Given this, the greatest potential value for employers, job seekers, and institutions may be less in complements to the resume and more in what thought-leading investor Ryan Craig of University Ventures terms *competency management platforms*—systems that not only showcase competencies, but also allow for better employer/applicant matching, searching, and sorting.[15] In this spirit, we can find a new twist on e-portfolios with Portfolium, a technology company funded by University Ventures that recently announced a three-year agreement with the California State University System to make e-portfolios available to students and alumni across its twenty-three campuses.[16] Portfolium counts more than 2,000 university clients and millions of student users but partners closely with 150 institutions as more of an enterprisewide career services-related portal.[17] The company's value proposition to employers is as "the search engine for college

recruiting," allowing college recruiting leaders at employers to identify talent through search and sorting features built on top of the
rich information aggregated across students' e-portfolios.[18]

Jim Milton, vice president of Customer Development at Portfolium and a veteran of the HR/recruiting technology market, describes
Portfolium's focus as modernizing campus recruiting: "Campus recruiting is stuck in the past. What we provide to employers is a platform that has more than one million students from hundreds of
universities, outfitted with this capability to build a portfolio. We actually score the portfolios, and the huge payoff for the student and
the employer is we can capture and index all this work in a search engine so that employers can find students. That's proactive sourcing,
versus 'posting and praying.' The things recruiters have been doing
on LinkedIn for experienced hires, we're doing with students. The
data on the competencies of students has been hidden in resume
books."[19] This positions firms like Portfolium in the realm of talent
management systems or professional networks.

## Digitizing, Exchanging, and Verifying Credentials

Another major segment of the technology market that is emerging around credentials consists of firms that allow for documenting, storing, and seamlessly exchanging and verifying credentials in
various ways. Some of these nascent technology efforts have been
catalyzed by philanthropic funding. Recognizing that the credentialing ecosystem is key to innovation in higher education, the Lumina
Foundation has since 2013 made more than $35 million in grants
dedicated to "creating new credentialing systems."[20] This includes,
for example, a $2.25 million grant to George Washington University
and two partner organizations to create a unique credential registry
for use by employers, colleges, and other stakeholders.[21]

Parchment is a notable firm focused on the secure online sending
and receiving of credentials—serving students, educators, employers, and associations across K–12 education (that is, high school
to college transcript transfer and college matching), higher educa-

tion, and the professional world.[22] Parchment has raised more than $50 million in venture capital funding and has actively positioned itself as a thought leader in the future of credentialing.[23] Parchment CEO Matthew Pittinsky has a unique perspective on the opportunities in credentialing technology, as he is also a PhD-trained sociologist of education and a cofounder of Blackboard, one of the most successful educational technology firms of recent years.[24] Pittinsky describes Parchment's platform as "a credential management system: our job is to allow credential issuers, mainly universities, with their diplomas, transcripts, and degrees, to migrate or reinvent them in digital form. That ranges from as simple as making the credential available online in a digital form, to embedding structured data, to expanding the content and detail, to rethinking the visual presentation to be more insightful to the employer . . . doing what digital can do that paper can't."[25] As Pittinsky notes, "The challenge with scaling this (innovating credentialing) is it's like online education, it's hard. Most institutions don't have the information systems that track and record the kinds of content they'd like to extend their credential with. Most institutions don't really have a clear institutional owner for rethinking the form and function of credentials, so there's an issue of leadership, there's a lack of systems, and it takes time."[26]

Accreditrust is another example of a credentialing technology company. It is focused on credential processing and verification in both education and industry, with application programming interfaces (APIs) that work across diplomas, licenses, professional certifications, and even microcredentials such as badges.[27] Eric Korb, Accreditrust's CEO, who has also served as CTO of the American College of Education, offers the following scenario regarding the opportunity for secure credentialing technologies: "Take, for example, a nurse practitioner, who to become employed has to prove that she has a degree, in most cases a master's degree. The labor to produce that information is somewhat automated, but not as automated as it could be. A transcript today could be either printed, e-mailed, or delivered electronically. Most people trust the printed one, but it has to be printed on special paper and in a hermetically sealed envelope and printed with a special kind of ink and signed by someone—that's the dark ages. But that's what most employers still rely on today—is the paper."[28] Korb continues on the efficiency and value of secure digital credentials: "A nurse practitioner needs a drug license, malpractice insurance, an educational credential, and a license. [As an employer] you'd want all four of those things in the same format in your HR system and to be able to query them every time that practitioner logged in to a system or swiped an ID card, to be validated in real time. You can't do that with PDFs, and you can't do that with a paper document."[29]

Various credential registries and security technologies are often positioned as solutions to the problem of fraud. The fact that a credential is digital and verifiable online makes it more reliable; and there is certainly significant value in this. Obviously, credential fraud and diploma mills are a serious concern for higher education. Sociologist David Baker points out that the primacy of educational credentials in our society is illustrated by high-profile cases of individuals falsely claiming degrees and the diploma mill industry.[30] However, in terms of a use case for new technologies, most employers do not put credential verification high on their list of burning issues. As Gail Jacobs of RMS describes, "We do background checks on all of our hires, so it's not a problem for us to go verify if they have a degree. When you're screening candidates and going through that process, someone might make it through who has lied about a degree, but we're going to nab them as soon as they start or after the offer is accepted."[31] Many employers outsource credential verification to specialized companies. In a globalizing market, however, with hiring increasingly moving outside the United States, new challenges are emerging. Steve Knox, global talent acquisition leader at General Electric, speaks to this challenge: "Our partners around the world [external degree verification vendors] certainly help, but sometimes we struggle with, Is this an authentic, genuine institution? Certainly in some emerging markets around the world—like Africa—do we know if our vendor is following the right process?"[32]

On the more consumer-facing side of the market are companies such as Degreed, which was founded in San Francisco in 2012. Degreed positions itself as a lifelong learning platform with the mission to "jailbreak the degree" on the premise that learning occurs in a variety of settings and the college degree needn't be the principal credential that employers need to rely on in hiring.[33] In essence, Degreed is aiming for the data in its platform to be a substitute for a degree. The Degreed platform collates and organizes an online record of an individual's learning—both formal and informal educational credentials—whether that learning took place through a MOOC, a YouTube video, an IT boot camp, or an educational institution.[34] In January 2016, Degreed secured a $21 million funding round, announcing that it had grown from three to nearly one hundred clients in the previous year.[35] It appears that in addition to targeting the consumer market, Degreed's employer-facing services are about documenting organizations' own learning and development as much as hiring or recognizing outside credentials.

Companies like Parchment, Accreditrust, Degreed, and a number of others have chosen to organize their businesses around the problems and opportunities of credentials in the job market. It thus appears the ultimate market opportunity for credentialing technologies is not simply sharing and verifying credentials, but in interpreting them, mapping them to competencies, and advancing their utility for employers through the power of dynamic data.

## EMPLOYER-SIDE GAME CHANGERS: TALENT ANALYTICS, PREHIRE ASSESSMENTS, PROFESSIONAL NETWORKS, AND COMPETENCY-BASED HIRING

The technology-driven innovations shaping the university credentialing ecosystem are, of course, not limited to higher education. It is critical for higher education leaders to understand the transformations in the tools and practices of the HR field. Here, the impact of data, analytics, and evidence-based changes to long-standing practices is the common theme.

## Talent Analytics: From Signals and Anecdotes to Hard Data and Evolved Strategy

Similar to many other business functions and sectors, taking advantage of analytics and big data is at the top of the priority list for HR leaders today. The momentum for talent analytics (sometimes referred to as people analytics) is significant. According to research by leading HR consultancy Bersin by Deloitte, 78 percent of large companies rate talent analytics as urgent or important, making talent analytics one of the top three areas of importance to HR.[36] Part of this urgency is the desire to catch up. As we established earlier, detailed analysis of hiring strategies and linkages to educational credentials has been rare for employers, and Bersin's research finds that a stunning 86 percent of employers report *no* analytics capability in their HR function—compared to much higher utilization rates for analytics in finance, operations, sales, and marketing.[37]

Shelly Holt of Concur Technologies comments: "Traditionally, HR systems have been behind the times. It's only been the last few years that we've started to see much more investment, new companies entering the market, and overlaying analytics to put on top of all your existing systems. Those are primarily looking at existing trends and not predicting the future. That's the next trend—predictive versus historical analytics, and it's just starting now."[38] Expert Josh Bersin, the founder of Bersin by Deloitte, has been following the growth of talent analytics closely, and remarks: "The people analytics market is really starting to pick up. Our data shows that last year only 4 percent of companies we studied have a predictive analytics team or real solutions they're using. This year that's grown to 8 percent, so it's doubled, but it's very small—yet it's growing very fast. Most of the vendors are selling much more integrated talent software."[39]

As Shelly Holt further describes the power of predictive analytics in HR, "You get a more holistic integrated picture of your talent. What talent are you recruiting through the door? Who are you promoting? What roles are open in the organization that you'd like to fill internally but don't have the skillset to do? What roles are critical for succession planning? One of the big things we're trying to do is identify those types of gaps, where to add more training, send people out on assignments, get them certifications or degrees."[40]

It is important to note that the talent analytics movement is driven not only by software, but also often by bespoke analyses conducted by human analysts dedicated to investigating patterns in hiring and human resources themes. According to Michael Piwoni, HR director at Stanley Infrastructure, "We [in HR] really underutilize a few really important disciplines—and those are economists and statisticians. Having people in-house who could help sort through data."[41] Tom Mathews of Cree explains: "Companies with scale have the resources to put against it. Some have three to four people who do nothing but HR analytics work. I could study things like, How long does it take for a call center rep or inside sales rep to get to full proficiency? Do engineers from a certain school perform for us? We could go in and look at how long they stick around, their performance review levels assuming that's captured, and might find, wow, more of our University of North Carolina hires are categorized as 'A players' and are listed as successors to executives compared to either Duke University or North Carolina State. That would dictate your college hiring strategy."[42]

Indeed, for many employers, this type of historical and predictive analysis that evaluates job performance against educational credentials or hiring source is increasingly common, and is referred to as *quality of hire analysis*. Quality of hire analysis compares measures from the hiring process—such as the sourcing channel, assessment scores, and new hire attrition—with posthire performance—such as productivity, peer ranking, performance review results, and employee engagement.[43] Chuck Edward of Microsoft, a leading organization in this type of analysis, explains: "There are two primary ways we're going after quality of hire analysis. One is survey-based, asking hiring managers, employees, and teams questions about hire quality. The other is one to three years out, assessing: how did people perform? For example, a former intern is our top quality of hire source—and we can prove it. It's a strategic shift in talent and technology: there's more and more data available. It's a mindset as much as it is a tool."[44]

Notably, as employers deploy this type of historical and predictive analysis, changes to hiring strategy follow—such as refining the list of schools at which employers actively recruit talent or hire from. If it becomes clear that graduates of a given university are not performing particularly well or being retained at the expected rate, then why take a chance on graduates from that institution?

Stephanie Pallante, associate vice president of campus recruiting at Aramark, offers the following example: "Two-and-a-half years ago we implemented a CRM tool that we've integrated with our applicant tracking system, to help us not only capture candidates, but to look deeper at the metrics we're getting associated with each of the universities. And it's really helped us to make good decisions regarding our on-campus strategy—where are we getting the best bang for the buck, and where are our best universities? As an example, in our first year we recruited at sixty-four universities, and now we've reduced to forty universities based on solid data. If not for those analytics, we would never have been able to make those decisions."[45]

Pallante goes on to describe how analytics also shapes selection into the companies' leadership development program: "We use that same technology when the leadership cohort is graduating and moving through the organization. We share those same analytics and scorecards with our executive leaders, to gauge the success of our program. We now know that our leadership program is successful as we only have a 9 percent attrition rate versus a more historical 28 percent rate at the same level in the organization."[46] PepsiCo human resources director Luke Weaver similarly describes an analytics-driven core school model that prioritizes where recruiting efforts will focus.

"In the past we would have gone to any number of local schools, but it's a lot of duplicative work that's not very efficient. Now we've gone to this model where we go to a select set of schools we really know that yield really solid candidates," Weaver said. He continued, "As an organization year over year, you're tasked with being more productive, so you can't continue to go to 140 schools; you need to bring it down to core set of 30 to 40 plus."[47]

At Pepsico, the analytical criteria for this process include alumni success, reputation in certain programs as measured in the *U.S. News & World Report* rankings, geographic proximity, and intangibles such as institutional type or the ability to identify and attract a diverse candidate pool.[48] Weaver notes: "We're looking at three-year retention for graduates. Is it panning out? Is this a good investment long term where we're seeing growth and development from these schools? We also look at short-term and long-term performance, a 'comp index' where we can say, 'Where'd you come from? What's your index score?' and [look] at performance by university. We're also looking at our high potential candidates: Which schools have the highest percentage?"[49] And, as Mark Johnson, director of talent at Fresenius Medical Care underscores, "Companies are putting much more of a process in place to assess the school, the program, the graduates, and the success of the recruiting they've had with those graduates. It's become a very rigorous assessment process that continues to develop."[50]

### LinkedIn and the Economic Graph

No discussion of the data-driven strategic shifts in recruiting would be complete without considering professional social networking goliath LinkedIn—referenced a number of times throughout this book already—which has grown to 400 million registered members globally, 122 million of whom are professionals in the United States.[51] By creating the premier online site that includes resume-like profiles with documentation of experiences, skills, recommendations, and professional connections, the firm is transforming job seeking and hiring through the power and scale of its network, creating a business that public markets value at $15 billion.[52] LinkedIn's talent solutions for employers include recruiting tools and job posting and advertising and branding services, among others—allowing employers to leverage the LinkedIn database to identify passive and active candidates, as well as reach them.[53] LinkedIn's vision is to develop and own the "economic graph" that connects professionals with job opportunities, a vision that has even extended into the provision of education and training itself with the company's $1.5 billion acquisition of online education provider Lynda.com in 2015.[54] LinkedIn has also built out tools and services for higher education with its university pages and college choice analytics for prospective students—increasingly becoming a database that allows users to analyze professional outcomes.[55] All of this activity places LinkedIn in pole position at the intersection of higher education and hiring. LinkedIn is increasingly emerging as an operating system for professional credentialing, and a rankings and outcomes database for colleges and universities.

One of the more prominent features of a LinkedIn profile when it comes to signaling competencies is skill endorsements, which is a one-click method through which professional connections can endorse the skills and strengths of an individual—a microrecommendation of sorts. As LinkedIn describes, "endorsing . . . your colleagues for the skills you've seen them demonstrate . . . helps contribute to the strength of their profile, and increases the likelihood they'll be discovered for opportunities related to the skills their connections know they possess."[56]

However, in my conversations with employers and in countless articles, many HR professionals commonly critique and dismiss the value of endorsements, because anyone can be endorsed for anything, and these measures of skill are not validated in a traditional sense: the LinkedIn system even proactively suggests endorsements (for example, "Does Sean Gallagher know about *Strategic Planning?*"). Michael Piwoni of Stanley Infrastructure describes, "You can vouch for people's skills, but there's no economic value to that because people know that everyone just clicks on things and endorses people. When people I've never met or talked with start to endorse me for things, that completely ruins the value. I would find value if I could trust those endorsements."[57] Endorsements are at least clearly directionally valuable, as Piwoni continues: "It turns to numbers. Sure, person A and person B may have both been endorsed for a skill, but person A was endorsed 375 times and person B 150 times. That tells me people are going out of their way to promote person A, but that needs some kind of validation."[58]

Allen Blue, cofounder of LinkedIn and the company's vice president of Product, explains that the power of LinkedIn's endorsements is that they are socially validated and rely on the scale of the network: "It's very hard to game because they're public and attributed to specific individuals . . . We have outcome-based college rankings, and those are basically going through the data, finding the most competitive jobs, how people got them, and here are the institutions and programs those people went to." Blue compares socially driven skill assessment with traditional credentials in the following way: "The thing that a certification [credential] does really well is it validates technical skills—and how much do you trust the assessment of the training. A *social* assessment basically says I worked with this person and not only can I validate their hard skills, but their proven capabilities for a wide variety of things. Certifications and assessments aren't going away anytime soon. But the technology has the capacity to represent us all with more color and information, because if you're considering someone for employment, you can talk to people who are providing those assessments, in the same way that you ask for a job reference."[59]

Indeed, LinkedIn's ultimate power and impact on university credentialing may be in becoming an operating system that allows for the creation and validation of representations of professional capability. In this way, it essentially becomes a credentialing body or repository in its own right, one that is linked to a set of rich, socially validated data. As Blue explains, "We want to become a platform filled with information that would enable anyone who wants to create a solution for developing skills to do so. For example, we met with some big retailers, and they want to take their internal sales curriculum and make that into a transmittable degree which you can take, come work for us, take the course, and put it into your LinkedIn profile. Then other employers can use it to make a hiring decision."[60] Blue continues with an example of the power of such an approach: "Could you actually create a system where we not only house that information, but we do the kind of reputation work we've done with educational institutions? For example, if you take a training program at company X, then it makes you competitive for all of these other jobs. The individual gets more power in terms of a transmittable, data-represented, socially represented credential—not from a credentialing authority, but from people they worked with as the authority that say you can actually do that and were successful. And this creates an environment for driving innovation in this space. Then anyone who's willing to start a training program can have the same level of visibility of a big institution because they have an environment where they can prove the results of what they're actually doing."[61] In other words, in providing a large-scale, data-rich record of professional outcomes that is socially validated—and perhaps ultimately validated and verified in a more secure traditional sense—LinkedIn could ultimately enable new types of institutions and upstarts to compete with traditional credential issuers. In addition, LinkedIn's analytical capabilities and proprietary understanding of patterns and behaviors—including the relationship between credentials earned, institutions attended, and jobs and skills gained—emerge as immensely valuable.

One of the most notable functions and values of LinkedIn is simply the status it is establishing as the online resume of record. For this reason, it is important to note that LinkedIn is increasingly integrating certifications and credentials from a range of educational providers and professional bodies directly into its system through its

"Add to Profile for Certifications" feature launched in 2014.[62] Currently, the top certification providers using this LinkedIn feature are, not surprisingly, information technology and software development-related. Organizations such as Microsoft, Coursera, Cisco, Lynda.com, Oracle, and IBM are at the top of a list that also includes the American Red Cross, the Project Management Institute, the CFA Institute, and FEMA.[63] However, importantly, these linked certifications are not necessarily verified, but through validation systems, they ultimately could be. Interestingly, according to LinkedIn's data, profiles that include certifications receive six times as many profile views, on average, as those that do not.[64] This is another way that over time LinkedIn is creating value and a leading competitive position as a credential and competency clearinghouse, notable for the power of its analytics capability—and its span across consumers, employers, and institutions/credentialers. As investor Ryan Craig has written in articles with titles such as "LinkedIn Eats the University": "Competency marketplaces (liked LinkedIn) will profile the competencies . . . or capabilities . . . of students and job seekers, allow them to identify the requirements of employers, evaluate the gap, and follow the educational path that gets them to their destination quickly and cost effectively. While this may sound like science fiction, the gap between the demands of labor markets and outputs of our educational system is both a complex sociopolitical challenge and a data problem that software, like LinkedIn, is in the process of solving."[65]

## Prehire Testing and Assessment

Much of our discussion has considered the ways that university credentials operate as evidence, signals, or proxies for intelligence, ability, and skill. We established that US employers have generally shied away from direct ability testing since the 1970s and also that employers can be quite conservative in their determination of when degrees are required versus preferred qualifications, often due to equal employment opportunity law concerns. Yet, online testing capabilities and the power to analyze testing results are leading to prehire assessment becoming much more common, and this is an important trend that bears monitoring due to its potential to substitute for some of the roles played by the university credential in hiring.

Due to the risk-averse approach of human resources leaders and corporate legal counsel when it comes to testing in hiring, companies with pioneering technologies in this area often are challenged to have employers adopt their solutions, but there is clear interest and growth in this area. Dave Balter, currently CEO of Mylestoned and previously head of transactions at Pluralsight, one of the most successful and best funded online education companies, was previously CEO of Smarterer, a skill testing and assessment platform. Smarterer was successfully acquired by Pluralsight for $75 million in 2014.[66] Balter, for example, describes his experience with Smarterer in which he received countless inquiries from employers but often ran into legacy barriers to adoption. "We would get called ten times a week by an employer who said, 'We want to use this in the hiring funnel,'" Balter said. "We'd get three-quarters into that discussion; then someone in the organization, maybe HR or compliance or the CLO, would say 'What about those regulations? And what about bias?' And all of these things are standard assessment practices that have been put in place to ensure a hiring test doesn't cause harm. The interest was high, but the history of hiring was a constant barrier to making it happen . . . yet our algorithms technically solved for bias, and our platform had evolved to where the system naturally understood that."[67] Matt Greenfield, managing partner of Rethink Education, and also one of the investors in Smarterer, adds: "HR is terrified of disparate impact, so right now they're not using it [these technologies] in the HR office . . . it's chilling innovation. But honestly it's not good for diversity to have people use prestige degrees as signals, because if you look at the numbers, there's intelligence to be found everywhere."[68] Indeed, the Society for Human Resource Management (SHRM) does report that the Equal Employment Opportunity Commission (EEOC) is stepping up its enforcement efforts. Retailer Target, for example, paid a $2.8 million settlement in 2015 over tests that were not sufficiently job related or consistent with business necessity and were found to violate the Civil Rights Act.[69]

However, despite regulatory concerns, receptivity to appropriately constructed testing in hiring is beginning to grow in a competitive environment increasingly driven by new technological capabilities and the power of data and algorithms. Incorporating direct assessments of ability in the hiring process is a clear trend among employers.[70] Both Bersin by Deloitte and consultancy RocketHire have sized the prehire talent assessment market at around $1 billion in revenue, and leading firms such as CEB and IBM collectively administer more than sixty-six million assessments per year—and these preemployment tests are increasingly involving simulations.[71] A study from research firm Aberdeen Group in 2015 found that businesses that used prehire assessments were 36 percent more likely to be satisfied with their new hires and experienced a 39 percent lower turnover rate among high-potential employees.[72]

According to Fresenius Medical Care's Mark Johnson, "Assessment is something that's front and center for us right now. We used to use a tool that was more off the shelf. A lot of companies do a boxed approach and do not customize. Now we're putting in an assessment that's customized to the success profiles for these specific roles we're hiring for. We are only one of many, many companies that are doing this—to try to make sure that that assessment sets up people for success. It doesn't diminish the importance of the degree—that's still a requirement, a necessity—but it's an additional piece of the interview and assessment process to ensure you're getting the right candidate."[73]

Kevin Oakes is a thought leader on talent management issues and CEO of the Institute for Corporate Productivity (i4cp), a membership-based best practices organization that researches the people practices in high-performance organizations, and includes many brand-name employers. On the trend toward testing, Oakes reflects that "it's a huge trend; every day it seems there are more and more assessments being applied to new candidates coming in. But there's a new thinking that—as opposed to relying on generic assessments to indicate what might make for a good employee in your organization—it makes more sense to fingerprint and tailor questions to the unique culture of the organization and what success has been in specific jobs, roles, departments, and divisions." However, Oakes cautions that "while assessments can provide additional valuable information, they aren't a cure-all: if you expect them to work 100 percent of the time, you are guaranteed to be disappointed."[74]

As much as legitimate concerns exist about the legal pitfalls of testing job applicants and risk aversion among employers, testing is possible—as long as it is clearly job related, solidly validated, or does not have a significant adverse impact. Attorneys Lawrence Ashe Jr., senior counsel, and Paul Barsness, associate, are legal experts in this area with the law firm Parker Hudson Rainer & Dobbs in Atlanta. As Lawrence Ashe notes, "Keyed to the requirements of the job and the material that people need to read or do on the job, testing is easier to defend and less likely to produce complaints. Being job-related is key. Take the example of a common test for firefighters that was thrown out: running two miles in sixteen minutes or less. But how often do they do that on the job? Never! Instead, you should be testing for job tasks such as holding weight, or going up and down a ladder. Too frequently people making decisions about job selection don't know what the requirements of the job are."[75] Gail Jacobs of RMS describes that the key to effective testing is that tests map to specific job skills and notes that custom tests can be expensive to develop yet aren't always perfect: "Skills-based tests are really expensive to develop. Most companies don't have the desire to potentially get into that legal hot water, but need to invest $20,000 to $30,000 to do an assessment that they're not even sure is going to work."[76]

Paul Barsness of Parker Hudson Rainer & Dobbs further describes, "As the technology grows, employers see tests more and more as a way to really do better at selection, rather than just relying on resumes, interviews, and things like that. For example, now we have simulations. With testing you can open up where the qualified candidates are coming from, reach a broader group of candidates, submit them to simulations and situations that mirror what it is actually like to do the job, and see how people perform. It is a neutral screen, and it's not something where an interviewer is looking at what schools people went to, do they live in a certain town, and what does their name sound like."[77] David Lucey, of Epsilon, notes: "We've had a lot of guidance and counsel from our employment legal experts, because we do utilize online independent testing as a hiring criterion for a number of our jobs. There's a place for it, but it's not the ultimate hiring criterion for us. It's a part of the evaluation, especially for a technical job, or even for a clerical job where, for example, Microsoft Office or Excel is really a core part of the role. Our philosophy at least is using a test as a gauge to see how far do they need to come to get to the level where we need them—but we can't and would never use the testing as the number-one decision maker."[78]

Appropriately sensitive to the potential legal and other issues related to prehire assessment, employers are increasingly recognizing its potential and moving in this direction. Perhaps not surprisingly, testing appears to be most common in computer science and software development, given that field's practical, skills-oriented focus—and the ability of online tests and simulations to duplicate the actual work performed in writing software code, for instance. It is for this reason that some of the early computer-science-focused MOOCs—which consisted of automated assessments that could gauge the integrity or correctness of software coding exercises—were seen as potentially transformative to employers' hiring process. Firms specializing in the prehire assessment domain in computer science include HackerRank, which ranks software engineers based on their performance in coding challenges and allows employers to source, screen, and interview top talent; and Codility, a recruiting platform that tests and filters programming candidates based on automated online tests.[79]

Prehire assessments that are higher quality, customized, better validated, and cheaper should increasingly chip away at some of the roles of educational credentials in the employee screening process, should they continue to be embraced and gain momentum. However, testing is not a panacea, and hiring done right will always involve a human and behavioral element. Michael Piwoni of Stanley Infrastructure, who has spent a significant portion of his career deploying and studying selection tools, ties together the challenges of testing with the push toward objective, data-driven talent analytics: "My research has always turned up that no matter what you do right now with tools that are available, including testing, you can never be more than 60 percent accurate with your hiring—meaning there's still a 40 percent chance the person is not a fit for your organization . . . it's exactly like *Moneyball*. People are always going to think they're better than a robot at figuring out where talent is. But the problem with a lot of these tests is they don't capture everything. Tests can capture things related to skillsets and background and maybe even personality, but what about people who can think their way out of problems and have an entrepreneurial spirit? I don't know that we have algorithms right now that are going to be able to select those people. It's also about thought process."[80]

## Success Profiles and Competency-Based Hiring

Ultimately, talent analytics, quality of hire analysis, and assessments are among the factors leading toward employers' development and implementation of proprietary, internal *success profiles* in which organizations match up the most successful internal performers against the credentials and background of job applicants. The first step in this process is having accurate job descriptions that reflect the competencies and skills required for various roles, as well as strong and reliable data on employee performance—both of which can be wildcards for many employers. It is then that the traits of high performers can be mapped against profiles of applicants and candidates. Mark Johnson of Fresenius Medical Care explains: "Along with your degree, employers are going to match a candidate up against a profile. Companies, mostly large companies who take their assessments seriously, are going to match that candidate and, regardless of the position, against a profile . . . and a lot of it's what are called 'success profiles'—usually done by outside organizations that specialize in these assessments. They do a profile of that position and what makes that person successful: the internal incumbents in those roles, from a performance standpoint."[81]

Although this success profile approach can yield tremendous results when properly executed, leaders such as Adrienne Alberts of the American Red Cross caution about some of the unintended consequences and the risks of homogeneity: "As we start to embrace big data, it makes it easier for us to find trends and talent, to evaluate where top performers are in our organization, what competencies they have, what backgrounds they come from, what degrees they have. We can direct our activity to find good candidates quickly. The problem is it can lead us to a very homogeneous population. Diverse organizations are more resilient. The trend toward coalescing all of the data quickly to target and find proven talent quickly could negatively impact our ability to be very unique in the individuals we bring into an organization."[82]

The notion of developing success profiles is part of the movement toward *competency-based hiring*—the careful mapping of the competencies, skillsets, attributes, and experience required for a role to the hiring and assessment process.[83] One would think that this is a foundational element of employers' hiring process, but a theme throughout this book is that employers' approach to hiring is not necessarily as rigorous or analytical as might be expected, given the stakes. Indeed, to truly optimize how educational credentials are used in hiring, employers first need to make their hiring processes, articulation of job responsibilities, and tracking of performance more rigorous.

This change is beginning to happen, aided by technology and necessitated by the competitive environment, changing trends in employee turnover, demographics, and other factors. Aramark's Stephanie Pallante describes: "More and more companies are moving toward a competency-based model of hiring. Traditionally, people tended to look at a job description, and unless you had that experience, you were not considered. Versus if you look at a candidate from a competency model, people are grouped into quadrants of competencies such as service, leadership, individual, and team—and we're talking about fairly basic competencies . . . and throughout the course of our behavioral-based interviews, we probe with our questions on those elements."[84] Steve Knox, global talent acquisition leader at General Electric (GE), notes, "When a line manager posts a role, do they really understand what they're looking for and what are the competencies and skillsets? There may be a disconnect across the business: the line manager thinks we need X; the HR manager thinks we need Y; and the unit leader things we need A, B, C. We need to map out what are the true competencies and how do we assess for them. In the past it was, Where did you go to school, where'd you work, what titles did you have? But we're now realizing we need a competency-based approach to hiring."[85] As employers themselves enhance their screening and interviewing process and move toward competency-based hiring, this may in fact reveal greater value for competency-based education approaches and more detailed transcripts, digital and otherwise.

## AN EVOLVING ENVIRONMENT

In this chapter we have covered the ways in which various technologies and start-up organizations are impacting the credentialing ecosystem, and perhaps most significantly, how employers' hiring practices are beginning to change in ways that could reshape the functioning of university credentials as job qualifications. Private capital continues to fund both credentialing enablers and credential substitutes: which firms emerge as leaders or consolidators will be important to monitor, particularly in the case of credentialing management systems and networks that could become the operating system for digital credential documentation and exchange. It is hard to envision why all university credentials shouldn't be available in an extended digital format if sound technology standards emerge, but this will require interoperability of systems and coordination between firms, universities, employers, and government. Insofar as we live in an age of proliferating credentials, the wider range *and* greater volume of credentials being produced mean that there is significant importance and value in the technology platforms to sort through, organize, and present credentials—as we leave the era of a framed piece of parchment on a wall and paper transcripts in a sealed envelope.

Employers' interest in talent analytics and online prehire assessments represents the most significant risk and opportunity for how university credentials work in the job market today, as these significant changes in practice could over time fundamentally remake the hiring process. As Josh Bersin writes with respect to how early it still is for talent analytics, comparing this movement to how long it took for marketing analytics to become commonplace: "Marketing analytics took about 20 years to mature—and today you can buy off the shelf analytics solutions that rival hugely expensive custom customer data warehouse projects of only 10 years ago."[86] To realize the full potential of talent analytics, employers will need to reevaluate many aspects of their hiring process and culture. And interestingly, as much as higher education is critiqued for its slow pace of change, the human resources function and employers' hiring practices have their own codified traditions and technology-driven change management opportunities that are currently being worked through. With carefully validated, customized assessments and the ability to leverage powerful online networks or competency marketplaces, the hiring environment of the future is a dynamic and perhaps more optimized one.

Next, we will turn our attention to the new approaches universities and other entities are taking to develop new types of credentials that map to the needs of the job market.

# SIX

# Innovative Directions in University Credentials

So far, we have developed a solid understanding of the history and evolution of university credentials and how they work in the job market. We have also established the directions that employers, universities, and technology providers are moving in—particularly with respect to online, or digital, credentials—as well as the interplay between these parties. Throughout the course of this book, we have seen how employers highly value the university *degree* and how it is still dominant in its share and impact. Yet, as much as the future of university credentials certainly must be about degrees—their structure, curriculum, outcomes, delivery, and so on—the central question in the future of university credentials is what truly *new* forms of credentials will emerge as valued in the market.

As of 2016, universities are developing and launching relatively few new and transformative credentials (in both a semantic and structural sense). Headline-grabbing credential constructs such as nanodegrees, badges, and so on are today products of technology firms more than they are of accredited universities. Most contemporary innovations related to university-issued credentials relate to new modes, formats, and approaches to delivery, rather than an entirely new credential framework. However, as we have established, a convergence is occurring between the university credentialing environment and the professional credentialing realm, aided by many of the

137

technology trends covered previously. Additionally, both bottom-up innovation in credentialing and top-down policy mandates for it are certainly occurring at a much greater rate than in the past.

In this chapter, we review a number of selected examples of new forms of credentials and paths to credentials as illustrations of what the future may hold. While focusing principally on what is being offered *by universities,* we also cover some of the adjacent, noninstitutional credentials and credential pathways that are emerging, focusing on how they intersect with, complement, or substitute for traditional university credentials. Some of these new forms of credentialing are quite novel, many of them are incremental evolutions, and others could be true game-changers depending on employers' and consumers' ultimate receptivity to them.

First, we begin by establishing how the regulatory and quality assurance environment within the university credentialing ecosystem is reacting and opening up to innovation in credentialing.

## AN EVOLVING QUALITY ASSURANCE AND REGULATORY FRAMEWORK

The voluntary accreditation system and state and federal regulation provide the authority through which universities award degrees and that these credentials are recognized in the marketplace as legitimate.[1] As a result, this regulatory and quality assurance system's standards—such as definitions of the credit hour and seat time, what constitutes a given credential, the role of faculty, the nature of distance education, and so on—shape the bounds within which university-awarded credentials operate. There is a perception that accreditation and various levels of government regulation inhibit innovation, and there certainly are standards and protocols that many would consider restrictive, archaic, or not responsive enough to the pace of change in the market. As referenced earlier, the accreditation system as it exists today has been under fire in recent years. In late 2015, this situation began to escalate further as the US Department of Education announced plans for new requirements on accreditors through executive (presidential) actions—even as the US Congress simultaneously continues to consider changes to the role of accreditation within the current legislative dialogue regarding the reauthorization of the Higher Education Act.[2]

Against this backdrop, quality assurance and regulatory bodies are responding to the experimentation occurring in the ecosystem, and the strong demand and calls for more professionally aligned and flexible higher education. The challenge for accreditation is that it focuses on *institutions* rather than individual programs and credentials, and it also tends to work on long time scales such as five- and ten-year cycles. In addition, much of the innovation in credentialing is occurring in partnership with entities that are not traditional higher education institutions, and the boundaries between the professional space and academia are blurring. Barbara Brittingham is president of the Commission on Institutions of Higher Education for the New England Association of Schools and Colleges (CIHE of NEASC), one of the most significant regional accreditors. Brittingham notes: "There are these non-higher-education, noninstitutional providers coming along, and it's hard to know how enduring they are. Part of what accreditation does look at is, Does the institution endure? Its durability and its systems . . . When people talk about these new credentials, they want to get very specific about the quality of the individual offering—something like program accreditation."[3] Brittingham continues, commenting on the need for a common vernacular in a world of proliferating credentials: "It's all getting more complicated . . . I think part of it is we're just learning how to talk about these offerings and figure out what the right metaphors are and how they serve people."[4]

An accreditation expert, Judith Eaton is president of the Council for Higher Education Accreditation (CHEA), a Washington, DC–based recognition body for sixty institutional and programmatic accrediting organizations and an association of 3,000 degree-granting institutions, and serves as a national voice of accreditation in the

United States.[5] As Eaton describes it, there are two dynamics characterizing the situation in 2016: "One, it's clear from Congress and the Department of Education right now that some form of quality review of new, innovative providers and their credentialing or educational experiences would be desirable . . . Two, the Department of Education experimental sites for partnerships between degree granting institutions and new providers is calling for new 'quality assurance entities' (QAEs) and provides an opportunity to explore both how these innovative providers can be effective, along with the QAEs."[6]

Seeking to raise visibility of these issues, CHEA has piloted its own experimental "quality platform," because, according to Eaton, "we think this universe of new providers is going to grow and someone needs to look at it to protect students and society."[7] The CHEA quality platform—essentially a set of standards particularly focused on evaluating noninstitutional providers through outcomes-based external review—seeks to account for learning that occurs through new approaches to online learning, certificates, badges, and so on.[8] Recognizing the growing need for more nimble and program-focused quality assurance, various independent entities and companies outside of traditional accreditation are proposing new quality assurance frameworks.[9] It appears clear that new structures and frameworks will be needed to ensure quality and consumer protection for noninstitutional training and credentialing, that the historical accreditation process must evolve to become more nimble and responsive to the pace at which today's market is moving, and that there should be ways to evaluate activity that is happening at the juncture of the two spaces.

On this front, at the federal level, the US Department of Education has been increasingly active in encouraging and enabling innovation in university credentialing. Writing in July 2015, Under Secretary of Education Ted Mitchell emphasized that the quality assurance system in the United States was not built for this environment of nontraditional programs and providers: "The problem is that we have few tools to differentiate the high-quality programs from the poor-quality ones. The normal mechanism we use to assess quality in higher education, accreditation, was not built to assess these kinds of providers . . . The U.S. Department of Education (ED) is interested in accelerating and focusing the ongoing conversations about what quality assurance might look like in the era of rapidly expanding educational options that are not traditional institutions of higher education. We are particularly interested in thinking about quality assurance through the lens of measurable student outcomes and competencies."[10]

In this spirit, in October 2015, the Department of Education announced the Educational Quality through Innovative Partnerships program (EQUIP), an experimental sites initiative similar to the Distance Education Demonstration program.[11] By waiving certain statutory and regulatory requirements, this experimental sites initiative will provide a small set of higher education institutions and their partners with the ability to offer federal financial aid for programs such as boot camps, MOOCs, novel types of certificates, and so on that would not otherwise be eligible.[12] Thus, these experiments will represent a measured pilot to study and seed innovation. Perhaps most interestingly for the future of higher education and its credentials, EQUIP appears designed to encourage innovation not only in credentialing but also in quality assurance—by calling for new, highly outcomes-focused Quality Assurance Entities (QAEs) such as those referenced by Judith Eaton earlier. The role of the independent QAE is to review, monitor, and report on each individual program and its quality—in essence, emerging an alternative to traditional accreditation.[13]

David Soo, senior policy advisor in the US Department of Education, has been a leader in many of these efforts, including EQUIP. As Soo describes, "We see it as an opportunity to stimulate innovation and new thinking in the quality assurance space, and to inform the policy changes going forward."[14] On what this means for the future of credentials, Soo adds: "There are many new credentials being developed, which their creators hope will complement or replace degrees. Our hope is that they are much more outcomes-oriented, so instead of saying, 'Here's a given degree,' the credential will also tell what competencies or proficiencies are within it. What are the claims this credential is making? What's the evidence? What are the outcomes?"[15] As of this book's writing, the EQUIP initiative is still in the early phase of its development, but it is a key example of how market forces, government policy, and various parties in the ecosystem are aligning to support credentialing innovation.

Having established some of the themes in the regulatory and quality assurance architecture that underlies the future of university credentials, we now turn our attention to a series of notable new approaches to university-delivered credentials and adjacent forms of credentialing.

## DIGITAL BADGES: INTERESTING POTENTIAL BUT LITTLE EVIDENCE OF UPTAKE OR IMPACT

Online credentials are becoming more bite-sized and disaggregated from degrees. In this vein, digital badges have received a great deal of attention as an emerging and alternative form of credential that many expect might disrupt the degree. As higher education analyst and champion of digital higher education Kevin Carey aptly defines them, "badges indicate specific skills and knowledge, backed by links to electronic evidence of how and why, exactly, the badge was earned."[16] Strictly speaking, badges are not necessarily credentials in and of themselves: badges are typically microlevel online representations of skills or competencies, or online representations of an actual traditional credential. Badges represent the unbundling or atomization of credentials, curriculum, competencies, and skills taken to its extreme, and badges seem best suited for recognizing informal and lifelong learning.

The badging movement's origins are largely in youth activities, K–12 education, and the video game industry. As experiments with digital badges gained momentum in other sectors of education and professional development, they came to be championed by technologists and considered by higher education. Alongside other innovative types of skill demonstration, badges have been central in the discussion about credentialing innovation, which is why we review them here. For example, in late 2011 at a MacArthur Foundation event, speaking to education at all levels, US Secretary of Education Arne Duncan had remarked: "Badges can help engage students in learning, and broaden the avenues for learners of all ages to acquire and demonstrate—as well as document and display—their skills. Badges can help speed the shift from credentials that simply measure seat time, to ones that more accurately measure competency. We must accelerate that transition."[17] The headline of a 2012 *Chronicle of Higher Education* article declared, "Badges Earned Online Pose Challenge to Traditional College Diplomas," and this type of rhetoric has been common among those analyzing the potential of alternative credentials.[18]

The recent growth in attention and capability for badges traces to the Open Badges technology framework, which was established in 2011 by the Mozilla Foundation (a spin-off of Netscape) and Peer 2 Peer University, in partnership with the MacArthur Foundation.[19] This effort created a free and open technical standard for digital badges that is information-rich, portable, and secure.[20] In addition, in 2015 the IMS Global Learning Consortium—an entity with participation from key technology vendors, educational institutions, and others that is focused on interoperable technology standards in education—announced a partnership with the Mozilla Foundation, called the IMS Digital Credentialing Initiative, an important effort that aims to accelerate the adoption and interoperability of digital badges.[21] Badging systems allow for secure identity management, verification, validation, and lifelong hosting and ongoing management of these credentials.[22] With the Mozilla Foundation's Open Badges framework as the key standard, companies such as Credly (a start-up badge platform) and Pearson Education have been active in these technologies; support for badges has also been added to popular Learning Management Systems such as Blackboard and Canvas.

Despite promise and great hype, it is still quite rare in 2016 to find examples of accredited higher education institutions issuing badges, which are more commonly issued by industry groups, non-traditional education providers, and other entities. The University of California at San Diego's Extension unit has integrated badges into its precollegiate programs, using them as microcredentials that are focused on single skills and competencies, based on careful assessment, documented on the transcript, and able to be showcased via social media.[23] The University of California at Davis has experimented with badges as an add-on to a traditional degree program to certify the skills of traditional graduates.[24] The University of Illinois has used badges to certify the skills of its IT employees and student workers.[25] Seton Hall University and Michigan State University are among institutions using badges for students to show participation in campus events.[26] Not surprisingly, badges appear to have the greatest momentum among community colleges and in continuing education and workforce development. Examples include Harper College in Illinois, which offers badges for career development program completion and job training; and Santa Barbara City College in California, which issues badges in connection with certificates in its Career Skills Institute, in areas such as web design, sales, and digital marketing.[27] However, cases of badges issued by higher education institutions (especially four-year universities) as complements or substitutes to traditional educational credentials are—despite the hype—exceedingly rare.[28]

Pearson offers a badging product called Acclaim, which is based on the Mozilla Open Badges framework and provides interested higher education institutions and others with a system to issue and make badges accessible as well as gather trend data. The company's scale and established client base give it an important window into trends in the badging landscape.[29] Peter Janzow is senior director of business and market development for Acclaim. As Janzow explains:

"The distinction you need to make when talking about badges is it's not a new form of credential; it's just a new form to represent an existing credential. There are some people who want to innovate with new forms of microcredentials, but of the millions of credentials in the Acclaim platform, 95 percent are just a digital form of an existing credential, everything from the GED to continuing education certificates and professional certification programs."[30] To date, badging players have been focusing on getting academic institutions, credentialing organizations, and professional bodies to issue badges, meaning relatively little awareness has been built downstream, among employers. Also, of all the badges that are earned and issued, fewer than half of them are claimed or used, according to Pearson's metrics.[31] As Janzow continues, "The first step was to educate issuing organizations around what they could issue badges for, and develop best practice so that they're high-impact badges. The next goal is once you issue a badge, it has to be valuable enough for the earner to claim it and then be useful enough that the earner would share it with someone who wanted to view it—an employer, a learning organization, a college. The next logical phase that's beginning to happen now in 2016 is that employer awareness is beginning; that's the focal point for the near future."[32]

Throughout my many interviews with hiring leaders at employers, they rarely mentioned badges. When asked to comment on badges, most leaders at employer organizations were either unaware of them or considered them not yet relevant as educational or professional qualifications in hiring. Nicola Soares, vice president and managing director for product strategy at Kelly Services, a Fortune 500 staffing agency that works across a significant global client base, remarks: "Badges are not resonating right now; it's not on the horizon for corporate clients or workforce staffing companies. At this point in time, it's not relevant at all. From a development perspective, badges are in their infant stages. In terms of how recruitment works, the methodologies, and the ways companies source candidates—that's all dramatically different from badges, which haven't caught on yet."[33] And, as Matthew Pittinsky, Parchment's CEO, summarizes, "The least interesting element [of badges] is being a new credential; I don't think the term will survive like the diploma. *Certificate* works perfectly well. The fact that companies are asserting themselves as credential issuers, that's the real trend—not the badging format, but awakening a whole set of organizations into the role of credential issuer and broadening the types of credentials people realize they can present to employers and others."[34]

In this sense it is interesting to consider the example of companies like IBM, which has created an Open Badge Program to attract, recognize, and contribute to the career progression of professionals across the company's ecosystem, in areas such as cloud computing, big data, and software development.[35] In this way, IBM's program—which has touched 120 countries across dozens of different badge areas in its first year—is a twist on classic vendor-sponsored IT certifications, but in a more open way and at a much more micro level. David Leaser, senior program manager for innovation and growth initiatives at IBM, explains that based on the badge initiative: "We've built a skills program where we can start getting students in colleges taking online courses with IBM or our partners, issuing badges for them, and starting to create a skills registry for all of those students, and progress them, for example, to find jobs and careers which match their skills and desires . . . The college degree is here to stay, just like certifications, but badges show at the nano- or microlevel what happened within that college experience: if I'm able to catalog all of those microlevel skills, then we at IBM can really understand where a person can fit into the workforce."[36] The initiative also includes a significant focus on IBM's own employee learning and development. It is worth higher education monitoring the potential trend of large-scale companies becoming educators, certifiers of skill, and managers of their own talent pipeline.

Perhaps the promise of badges will be realized as a framework for documenting corporations' own learning and development, and individuals' various continuing education and training experiences—ultimately mapping into a system like LinkedIn. The highly specialized and micro nature of badges certainly makes them theoretically useful as signals of specific skills and capabilities. However, this also places them at the *opposite* end of the credential spectrum versus degrees when it comes to representing a substantive and coherent package of outcomes—something employers value far more than a potpourri of skills or competencies. With nearly any type of organization able to issue a badge, it will be difficult for employers to truly understand what a given badge entails from tens of thousands of options. There is also the question of when a given amount of learning or skill rises to the level of a badge, or when a badge or series of badges graduates to a certificate or something else. With badges issued for everything from attending an event to completing a single hour-long class, many organizations involved in badging are careful to note that their efforts or platforms focus on resume-worthy achievements, and where that line lies is an open question and very important in the potential utility of badges as a signal or screening device in the employer hiring process. Badges can certainly be useful add-ons to degrees, particularly as a part of competency-based education framework, but no evidence yet exists that badges will be able to replace or truly compete with degrees in job attainment in the ways that many advocates of badging claim.

## THE RISE OF THE BOOT CAMPS AND THE POTENTIAL OF HYBRID EXPERIENCE-BASED CREDENTIALS

In the technology-driven economy of the past five years, a new class of IT-focused postsecondary education organizations has emerged: boot camps. These intensive, short-term programs train individuals—often with no prior experience—for high-demand careers in everything from software and web development to digital marketing, data science, and mobile development. Course Report, an organization that tracks this market, estimates that boot camps such as General Assembly, Coding Dojo, Metis, Flatiron School, and Dev

Bootcamp (to name just a few) were on track to graduate 16,000 students in 2015, up from just 2,100 in 2013, and generated nearly $200 million in revenue.[37] The typical boot camp lasts ten weeks and costs $10,000.[38] At the end of these programs, students are placed in jobs that average $76,000, with 75 percent placement rates in jobs requiring skills learned in the boot camp, based on Course Report's studies on student demographics and outcomes.[39]

We have referred to boot camp models throughout this book, and given their explosive growth and job placement success, boot camps have attracted significant attention from the media, investors, higher education leaders, and government and policy leaders at the highest level. On the surface, boot camps appear to be working as a uniquely well-functioning alternative to university credentials as a pathway to lucrative and in-demand professional jobs—similar in many ways to the IT certification paths of the 1990s. As President Obama remarked in 2015: "While four-year degrees in engineering and computer science are still important, we have the opportunity to promote programs that we call, for example, coding boot camp— or online courses that have pioneered new ways to teach tech skills in a fraction of the time and the costs. And these new models have the potential to reach underserved communities . . . Understand, within the tech sector, there are going to be tiers of jobs, all of which are tech but they're not all the same. There's still going to be the place—we still have to produce more engineers and advanced degrees in computer science at the upper tier, but there's all kinds of stuff that's being done within companies at different sectors that can create great careers."[40]

Thus, the success of boot camps in placing graduates in jobs is one of the reasons that the US Department of Education has launched experiments like EQUIP: to connect these educational experiences with broader and more lasting educational credentials. However, quite notably, according to Course Report's survey data, 89 percent of boot camp students already have a bachelor's degree or above. It therefore appears that today's boot camps are less of a substitute

for a bachelor's degree and more of a high-value postbaccalaureate continuing education experience or alternative to a specialized
master's degree or certificate. Increasingly, there is recognition that
the boot camp model may not be as high impact if it remains independent of recognized credentials and outside of an accreditation-
like quality assurance and consumer protection process. Although
boot camp firms are the poster children in the discussion of alternatives to the degree, rarely if ever are any credentials—university or
otherwise—attached, with a growing number of notable exceptions
that we address later. It is important to understand how employers
view boot camps relative to degrees and more traditional university credentials and how boot camps may present an opportunity
for universities.

Among employers, boot camps appear to have much greater awareness and appreciation as an emerging alternative pipeline for talent,
as compared to various alternative credentials such as badges or mi-
crodegrees. Many employers whom I interviewed for this book were
able to speak to the boot camp value proposition in detail or proactively raised the topic. They note, however, that the jury is still out, as
boot camps' credibility is being tested among hiring managers, many
of whom are still reliant on prestige and certainly prefer degrees, all
other things being equal.

David Lucey, Epsilon's vice president of talent acquisition, points
out: "Some hiring managers would look at something like this and
ask, 'How does a ten-month program prepare you for this kind of
job?' An undergrad might possess more well-rounded soft skills,
thinking critically, etc. Someone coming out of a coding school
might know how to write code in Python, but do they have the other
skills?"[41] Chuck Edward, Microsoft's global talent leader, remarks:
"This new system of up-skilling—that is not full-fledged college degrees . . . leaders come to me and say, 'Why are you not going to alternative sources?' I'm open to that, but we're not sure what our hit
rates will be . . . with the pressure we're under, we need to have more
hits than misses fast, so the degree becomes useful shorthand."[42]

Similarly, Gail Jacobs of RMS offers: "We hire software developers who don't have degrees, and we hire software developers who have come through boot camps, but it's few and far between. The media seems to make it out as this is the way of the future, but a college degree, especially for a younger person in the field, it's a much harder road to get your foot in the door if you don't have a degree."[43] Jacobs also notes that just as with traditional university credentials, the credibility of these boot camp models comes over time and through direct experience with graduates: "Take Flatiron School, for instance. I've done a lot of work with them personally. In their first graduating classes, I never would have taken a look at them, but then we took in an intern who we found was competent and thought maybe we'll look into this; then the manager likes them and we decide, let's hire them. But if another school opened up doing the same thing, I'd give it a year or two to see if it's going to survive—and that would be the same for any online program or certification that comes up."[44]

One notable market opportunity is for accredited universities—with their reputations, resources, and understanding of education—to get into the boot camp game, connecting boot camps' accelerated and job-focused modes of learning with new or existing types of university credentials. As we saw with online education and even IT certifications, might traditional nonprofit institutions, whether in-house or in partnership with enabling entities, co-opt the innovation of the boot camp? A number of universities are experimenting in this direction, through partnerships or on their own. This represents another area in which the world of noninstitutional professional training and outside firms is blending with traditional higher education and its credentials.

Galvanize, a boot camp firm founded in 2012, has six campuses across the United States and offers programs in software development, data science, and data engineering.[45] In Fall 2014, the University of New Haven partnered with the firm to launch a master of science in data science in which instructors appointed by the University of New Haven will teach the program at Galvanize's San

Francisco campus, building on the Galvanize data science curriculum.[46] The program is an intensive, full-time, one-year program costing $48,000.[47] In a novel twist on the classic study abroad model, in Fall 2015, market-leading boot camp provider General Assembly announced a partnership with Florida's Lynn University, in which the university will award fifteen credits—a semester's worth—to undergraduates who complete a sixteen-week General Assembly boot camp program that will cost $14,000 in tuition and $8,300 for housing.[48] Lynn University students will be able to study at General Assembly campuses in New York, London, San Francisco, or Sydney.[49] In a similar blending of undergraduate education and boot camps, in Fall 2015 Southern New Hampshire University announced a partnership with Flatiron School that includes a "3+1" program that tops off a Southern New Hampshire degree with a six-month Flatiron boot camp experience.[50] In each of these models, the university is augmenting or building its own traditional credentials around the capability and career-focused value proposition of the boot camp.

Other universities are stepping into the boot camp market with their own offerings, building on the long heritage of noncredit professional development workshops and seminars offered by university continuing education units.

Rutgers University began its own twenty-four-week boot camp in web development in January 2016.[51] Graduates receive a certificate of completion from Rutgers' Division of Continuing Studies. The program is positioned as distinct from competing boot camps—many of them based in New York City—due its part-time model for working professionals, access to the Rutgers corporate partner network, and a credential from New Jersey's top public institution.[52] In Fall 2015, Northeastern University launched Level, an eight-week, $8,000 analytics boot camp that trains students to become data analysts.[53] (I played a minor role in assisting in the development of Level at Northeastern.) The program is built around experiential projects, highly qualified instructors, a noncredit Northeastern University certificate credential, and participation from early corporate partners such as

Starbucks, Wayfair, and Care.com.[54] Following the 2015 pilot class in Boston, the program was rolled out to Northeastern's Silicon Valley, Seattle, and Charlotte campuses in 2016. According to Level's creator, Northeastern's vice president for new ventures, Nick Ducoff, the program is notable because "while students graduating from Level receive a noncredit certificate of completion, what they primarily value is Northeastern University's network and the relationships they cultivate throughout the experiential program with employers through guest lectures, panels, and micro-capstone projects."[55]

## VARIATIONS ON THE CLASSIC CERTIFICATE

We have covered the diversity of higher education certificates at various times throughout this book, and certificates represent an established experimentation zone for many traditional universities. New approaches to certificates build on both an established nomenclature and a baseline of acceptance in the job market.

### MOOC-Based Certificates

Following the first few years of experimentation with free online courses, in 2015, MOOC providers began to find a revenue stream and a potentially sustainable business model in offering for-fee certificate programs, recognizing that credentials carry far more value than stand-alone courses as a currency in the job market. MOOC platforms have moved away from free, unverified certificates of completion and are now charging for a more reliable certificate that also represents the completion of a truer curriculum: the demonstration of skill in certain areas of specialization based on the successful completion of a collection of courses. Other than the MOOC-based foundation, there is conceptually no difference between these certificates and classic noncredit certificate programs offered by universities. However, MOOC-based certificates are distinguished by the fact that they are awarded by the MOOC provider in affiliation with rather than by the university; the fact that they are shorter and far less expensive than traditional certificate programs; and that many of them have been designed in partnership with industry-leading firms and include work-related capstone projects.

Udacity was one of the first MOOC companies to embrace a credential-driven business model, which investor Ryan Craig estimates generated perhaps $20 million in revenue in 2015.[56] However, most of Udacity's business activity is not in affiliation with universities, but rather operates as an independent online training and skills provider. Udacity offers programs such as nanodegrees—or industry certificates that are "built in partnership with industry leaders" such as Google and Facebook—in areas ranging from Android and iOS software development to data analysis and programming.[57] Udacity's nanodegrees typically cost around $2,000 and take six to twelve months to complete. In early 2016, the firm announced a job placement or money-back guarantee for students who met certain conditions and paid a higher fee.[58]

Coursera's specialization certificates, launched in 2015, represent a more university-related model.[59] For example, the University of Pennsylvania's Wharton School offers a Business Foundations certificate via Coursera that consists of the completion of four courses in accounting, finance, marketing, and operations management, plus a capstone project, for a cost of $595.[60] In an earlier incarnation of this certificate program, 25,000 students had earned certificates.[61] Interestingly, Wharton is using this program as an admissions pipeline for traditional programs by inviting the top fifty certificate completers to apply to its traditional MBA program and offering up to five $20,000 scholarships.[62]

Another notable example is Coursera's Data Science specialization certificate in partnership with Johns Hopkins University. It consists of completing ten courses for $470 (up from $250 in 2014) and is typically completed in three to six months.[63] Millions of students have enrolled in these high-demand courses, launched in 2014, and tens of thousands have completed a version of the certificate.[64] In 2014, Johns Hopkins announced that the specialization certificate would include a collaboration with London-based keyboard and language prediction technology company SwiftKey, by bringing SwiftKey's real-world text prediction data into the course exercises.[65]

Harvard Business School's HBX CORe, or "credential of readiness," is an even more robust example of a new online credential program and represents Harvard Business School's first online offering.[66] The ten- to eighteen-week, $1,800 online program is essentially a pre-MBA curriculum focused on understanding business fundamentals via Harvard Business School's case-study-based pedagogy, taking 120–150 hours to complete.[67] HBX CORe courses are graded, and the university understands the value and questions associated with this new type of credential, explaining: "We understand that in order for a credential to be meaningful, it has to be more than a piece of paper you can hang on a wall. It has to signal to the world that we're prepared to put our credibility behind your achievement in a substantial, longstanding way."[68] Following a very successful pilot, Harvard was forecasting a few thousand student enrollments in cohorts of 300–500 each in 2015, and even began marketing the program to admitted MBA students at rival business schools as a primer on business basics.[69] The HBX CORe offering is also unique in now having a pathway to degree credit, via a partnership between Harvard Business School and Harvard Extension School that will award eight undergraduate credits for the completion of a $3,600 for-credit version of CORe.[70]

### New York University's Industry-Focused Professional Diplomas

While online programs and MOOCs are attracting attention, some universities are evolving their more traditional certificate offerings in fundamental ways. New York University's School of Professional Studies (SPS) has long had one of the largest industry-focused non-credit professional development and certificate businesses among major universities. However, changes in the job market and new online and other competitors had begun to erode that business, according to Dean Dennis Di Lorenzo, who has been with NYU SPS for twenty-three years.[71] NYU SPS's noncredit credential programs didn't seem to have the same appeal and resonance in the consumer market and among employers as they once did. One of Di Lorenzo's explanations for this was "the term *certificate* began to mean less in the job market." According to Di Lorenzo, "We offered 189 certificate credentials that were pieces of paper reflective of only a few courses in our 1,500 course catalog. Very few students were earning these credentials, yet many students were presenting themselves as having attained them. We realized the term, and the credential itself, had become diluted and devalued. Hiring managers became aware of this as well. It was no longer enough for someone who may have completed a number of courses but who had never been assessed for the work they had done to present to a hiring manager a certificate in digital marketing or any other subject. In our previous certificate model, any student could register for any course regardless of their professional background and educational level—however, for hiring managers, these things matter. We needed to become more transparent to the marketplace."[72] Thus, NYU SPS decided to eliminate its noncredit certificates and introduce a new offering under a new moniker: a series of job-focused *diplomas*, which are more rigorous and more affordable one- to two-semester programs with clearly articulated and validated learning outcomes and skill acquisition, as well as wraparound career development services.[73]

Importantly, the new diploma offerings are segmented into three tiers based on level of education and work experience, and, as part of SPS's access-focused mission, tailored to audiences such as career changers and the under- and unemployed. Di Lorenzo explains the difference between NYU's prior noncredit certificate model and the diploma programs' segmentation by prior educational experience: "A basic diploma, which costs $1,750, is designed is for someone who has earned a high school diploma. They have been developed in industries that hire students at an entry level—from service management and restaurant operations to construction administration and bookkeeping." A "professional" diploma, which costs $2,250, requires some college credit and/or work experience and includes programs in customer intelligence analytics and meeting and convention management, among other areas.[74] "For those with a greater level of education and professional experience, we saw a huge demand for postbaccalaureate training. The 'advanced' diplomas are targeted toward those postbaccalaureate millennials, and focus on developing advanced skill sets in complex disciplines such as energy finance, certified financial planning, project management, and health informatics."[75] An "advanced" diploma requires a bachelor's degree and costs $2,750.[76] As Di Lorenzo notes, "We're finding it's much easier for our students to manage $1,750 for a job training diploma, compared with two years of tuition at a community college."[77] In this way, the value proposition is similar to a boot camp, but with an NYU credential attached. The diploma programs also include a strong career development component, covering, for example, the basics of how to engage in a job search, as well as interviewing and resume writing techniques. NYU also opened up access to its career services network for these students, something that had not been done for prior noncredit programs.[78]

Di Lorenzo explains some of the decision making related to the semantics of the term *diploma*: "The only reason we used the word *diploma* was for lack of a better term. We didn't want to use the word *certificate* because the old NYU SPS certificates were so widely known in the field; we knew we had to sunset the old and introduce the new. On the other hand, because this was a noncredit credential, we didn't want to allude to a degree or something like a nanocredential," reasoned Di Lorenzo.[79] Di Lorenzo notes that with the new diploma construct, "we felt we needed to stop thinking about the noncredit credentialing as a market construct, and start thinking about credentialing in the noncredit space as a true educational construct. We needed more transparency."

NYU's diploma programs were only recently launched in Fall 2015 and at that time had reached their initial enrollment goal of fifty students. Enrollments for Spring 2016 are triple that number.

Going forward, Di Lorenzo says, "This is also about partnership. I've reached out to all of the school's many industry partners to talk about these new credentials and they're very excited. We're also in conversations with local and regional government agencies and are working with the NYC Mayor's Office of Workforce Development to pilot a diploma in construction management for which the city would bring its industry partners to the table, and students would engage in a learning experience that would allow them to work in the field during the semester, gaining invaluable hands-on experience."[80]

While perhaps modest in the scheme of many bolder and often digitally driven credentialing innovations, NYU's diplomas provide an example of a traditional institution that has embraced a job training and career advancement mission and was willing to reboot and even put at risk its existing portfolio based on the evolving needs of employers and professionals. It did so via a short-form credential that is carefully segmented, industry focused, outcome oriented, lower cost, and competency and career development heavy.

## EVOLVED DEGREES: BUILDING ON NEW ONLINE AND COMPETENCY-BASED EDUCATION FOUNDATIONS

A number of job-market-focused innovations occurring in the market relate to the traditional degree, and many of these approaches are built on top of MOOCs or competency-based education models. These new programs often aim to be more accessible to professionals, modular, and lower cost.

### MOOC-Based Foundations for Credentials

The Georgia Institute of Technology's Online Master of Science in Computer Science (OMS CS) is one of the most watched experiments in new approaches to delivering a university credential. In 2013, Georgia Tech made headlines with its launch of this roughly $7,000 program in partnership with Udacity and AT&T.[81] This effort was notable as a hybrid between a traditional master's degree and a MOOC, plus the direct involvement of a major employer, AT&T, which provided $3.5 million in financial and curriculum support.[82] According to Georgia Tech officials, the goal of this program, still in it early years, is specifically to test whether high-quality education can be delivered at a lower price point.[83] By late 2015, the program had reached enrollment of nearly 2,800 students and was attracting more than 1,300 applicants for each new term.[84] Georgia Tech officials hope to scale the program to many thousands of students.

A somewhat similar initiative is the University of Illinois at Urbana–Champaign's iMBA in partnership with Coursera, launched in the spring 2016 semester.[85] Built on University of Illinois course content that is offered free on Coursera, the iMBA is described as the equivalent of a University of Illinois MBA and available for a total cost of approximately $20,000 to students who complete a traditional admissions process that includes a 3.0 or higher undergraduate GPA, three years of professional experience, an essay, and optional test scores.[86] Compared to simply an aggregation of MOOC courses, the iMBA is importantly distinguished by the involvement of live faculty, additional case studies, projects, discussions, and graded assessments.[87] The iMBA is interesting in being a stackable credential that can be achieved by completing eight distinct Coursera specializations (such as accounting and finance) that add up to the degree.[88]

Another notable credential built on a MOOC-based foundation is the Massachusetts Institute of Technology's (MIT) MicroMasters program, announced in Fall 2015 as an experimental pilot within MITx.[89] In coining the term *MicroMasters*, MIT explicitly hopes that "the MicroMaster's credential becomes a new unit of currency in higher education," and that "if other universities wish to adopt this terminology for programs that are master's-level, we will welcome that enthusiastically."[90] The MicroMasters in supply chain management—which is open to anyone—stands on its own, and students who complete one semester's worth of online courses and complete an examination can earn this credential.[91] This microcredential then relates to MIT's traditional, selective, ten-month-long, on-campus supply chain management degree by serving as an "inverted" admissions vehicle for it: the best students who have completed the Micro-Masters will be considered for admission to the traditional program based on their performance in the online courses.[92] While experimental, this is another example of the blurring of boundaries between MOOCs and traditional on-campus delivery, traditional and digital credentials, and large-scale free online course markets and elite traditional programs. MIT's online education strategy continues to be about impacting traditional programs and residential education as much as opening up new markets.[93]

## Competency-Based Programs

Competency-based education (CBE) is an educational approach that relies on the demonstration of skills rather than seat time, and has existed in one form or another for forty years.[94] CBE models have received particular attention over the past few years, with hundreds of institutions reported to be experimenting with CBE approaches, and these approaches are often bundled into discussions about alternative credentials.[95] The attention for CBE increased dramatically following the US Department of Education's 2013 endorsement of competency-based models that rely on direct assessment of student competencies without linkages to the traditional credit hour as being eligible for federal aid.[96] This is significant because it opens up the opportunity for individuals to earn credentials based on what they know or can do, rather than unnecessary time in an academic setting. Therefore, CBE is seen as a key vehicle in educational attainment goals and the completion agenda because of the opportunity for individuals in the workforce to more efficiently earn credentials, and done at scale, this approach could significantly improve economic opportunity.

Because of CBE's focus on competencies, the approach is certainly at the epicenter of the dialogue about greater alignment between higher education (and its outcomes and business model) and employment. It is important to note the potential alignment between competency-based education (what can a graduate do) against the competency-based hiring trend highlighted earlier (what does an employer need). Yet, if many employers have not yet understood their talent requirements or been rigorous about job descriptions and competency-based approaches to hiring, how might they best utilize competency-based educational credentials? A 2015 national survey of nearly five hundred hiring managers by consultancy Parthenon-EY found that "employers remain generally unable to articulate discrete needs as competencies; they rely instead on hiring generalizations grounded in the traditional idea of 'fit' that lack the specificity needed to create an effective competency map."[97] This is, of course, consistent with my own research and that of scholars such as Lauren Rivera.[98] Perhaps even more importantly, this Parthenon-EY survey found that only 9 percent of employers had a strong understanding of what competency-based education was—and more than half had never heard of it or couldn't explain what it was.[99] Interestingly, even within higher education, competency-based education has a wide range of disparate definitions. Thus, while this approach is promising, we are still in the early days of employer awareness and acceptance—and likely far from the transformative revolution that many foresee. CBE also has a long way to go in terms of acceptance among university chief academic officers, according to an early 2016 national survey by *Inside Higher Ed* that found growing experimentation but significant pockets of skepticism.[100]

A thoughtful analysis by Robert Kelchen, assistant professor of higher education at Seton Hall University, surveyed the landscape of competency-based education programs in 2014 and estimated that more than fifty institutions were offering competency-based programs. More recent anecdotal estimates suggest this number has grown to hundreds of institutions, enrolling tens of thousands of students.[101] Adult-learning-focused pioneers such as Western Governors University and Excelsior College have been successfully offering competency-based degree programs at scale for many years. What is changing in the current environment is that the model is spreading to more traditional institutions such as Colorado State University, the University of Wisconsin, and Indiana University, among many others.[102] Like online education, most of today's competency-based programs represent new modes through which a traditional credential (such as a degree) can be earned, rather than resulting in truly new types of credentials. However, CBE is notable in its recognition that an educational credential is a demonstration of capability or skill that can be fairly independent of the process through which the skills and knowledge were acquired, and in this way, it opens up a pathway to much more job-market-relevant professional credentials.

Southern New Hampshire University's pioneering College for America program is a competency-based associate and bachelor's degree program, and this effort was the first to receive US Department of Education approval to be eligible for Title IV financial aid in a direct assessment model.[103] Students earn 120 competencies in nine key areas such as communication, quantitative skills, and ethics and social responsibility.[104] The program costs only $2,500 per year, and can be completed over many years or just a matter of months, depending on professionals' mastery of various concepts.[105] College for America is also notable for its business-to-business (B2B) model focused on employer partnership—with organizations such as Anthem Blue Cross and Goodwill—rather than a direct-to-consumer focus. As of 2016, the program enrolled more than 3,000 students across seventy employers, with students reporting very high levels of engagement and satisfaction.[106] Competency-based education is also increasingly taking hold in professional graduate programs. Michigan State University's competency-based Master of Health Professions Education program is an example of this—a program with no traditional classes, evaluation by a competency assessment panel, and a summative assessment based on a learning portfolio.[107] Another example lies in adult-learner-focused University Maryland University College, which is transitioning its entire portfolio of degree programs in its graduate school—twenty-five master's and two doctoral degrees—to a competency-based model.[108]

## STILL EARLY DAYS FOR NEW UNIVERSITY CREDENTIALS

There is clear momentum for new types of university credentials, and even more momentum for new approaches to the delivery of traditional credentials such as certificates and degrees. However, few examples of new credentials being offered by universities exist, and certainly very few are at scale. Georgia Tech's and Southern New Hampshire University's new approaches, both begun a few years ago, have already enrolled thousands of students and are clearly meaningful new models. However, as it concerns new constructs for university credentials, both of these efforts result in a traditional credential such as an associate, bachelor's, or master's degree rather than the microcredentials that are so often featured in the dialogue about higher education innovation. Insofar as the traditional degree remains the dominant currency in the job market, this is a strong enough result. Institutions have announced new experiments in credentialing on a monthly basis across 2015 and 2016, and most are just launching as of the writing of this book. By the time these pages are in your hands, there certainly will be a host of new developments, models, and terminologies to consider.

Given that it is the nascent stage in the development of a new, nondegree credential market, this is an opportunity for all parties in the ecosystem to shape the market's development. Universities have the capability to lead by experimenting. When considering noncredit offerings—not to mention the creative for-credit/degree precedents that are emerging at some highly selective and traditional institutions—the opportunities are nearly limitless. Yet, it is critical that the regulatory and quality assurance systems do not limit innovation in a system with entrenched standards and practices. We can find an example of the challenges that can emerge in the state-level cross-border regulation of distance education that is only now being somewhat resolved with interstate compacts, after new requirements emerged circa 2009–2010.[109] If higher education and governments can't agree on how to efficiently assess quality and protect consumers for a twenty-plus-year-old innovation—the online delivery of traditional degrees—how can we expect efficiency or consistency in new credentials and noninstitutional providers? With university credentialing moving toward a more micro level via fast-changing, market-oriented approaches, the ecosystem will certainly need new, more responsive modes of quality assurance.

Judith Eaton of CHEA believes that the new, emerging sector of postsecondary education offered by noninstitutional providers—for example, boot camps and MOOCs—represents "a revolution in what is meant by higher education in this country. We will grow to accept—like we've accepted online education—episodic online experiences as higher education . . . just like we got community colleges and for-profits. And employers are going to decide what they value or don't value. But how will that actually work? Perhaps they may become a little less degree minded going down the road."[110] Eaton continues, "Accommodations will be made; some accreditors will start doing nondegree activity; some won't. But there's no coherent vision. This emerging sector does do several things, from where I sit in this office of quality review: access, affordability, and disenchantment with higher education."[111] The growing convergence between traditional higher education and more episodic, industry-based professional learning indeed appears meaningful.

The question is whether employers will accept new credentials and models and how the interplay between universities, employers, students, regulators, and other parties in the ecosystem will play out. As Robert Kelchen of Seton Hall University notes, "One thing a lot of the regulators are missing is that the traditional system is not as homogeneous as people think. Even if you have a bachelor's degree in a certain field, that doesn't mean that it's the same across institutions. Employers are trying to get a handle on, What does a credential from this institution mean?—and by and large are looking at, How have people from that institution done in the workplace?"[112]

Having completed our journey through various thematic strands of the credentialing ecosystem, we will defer more our forward-looking analysis to the final chapter, as that is its focus: panning back and understanding what the key issues are; where traction is likely to occur; and how the ecosystem is likely to evolve, with some concrete conclusions and recommendations for interested parties.

# SEVEN

# Conclusions and Recommendations on the Future of University Credentials

This book began with the argument that developing a deeper, evidence-based understanding of the workings of the credentialing ecosystem was imperative for academic and government leaders, university administrators, boards, employers, investors, and others to understand and shape the future of university credentials. Various conclusions and analytical assessments have been woven throughout each chapter in our journey. The goal of this final chapter is to briefly synthesize and look forward—standing on the foundation of history, current trends, and market-based insights that we have built—to arrive at the implications, recommendations, and key questions and issues to consider for all parties with an interest in higher education's future and that of its credentials. This look at macro issues is presented in a thematic and modular format rather than a more traditional narrative.

*Little evidence exists that disruptive market forces will wash away universities and their credentials such as degrees anytime soon. While traditional credentials must evolve, they continue to have a special place in the job market.* The dominant narrative in the media and policy world over the past few years has suggested that degrees are endangered relics. While employers are often appropriately critical about how well universities and traditional educational approaches prepare students for the workforce, very few employers articulate a preference for new types of nondegree credentials in hiring, at least at this point in time. In the United States alone, tens of millions of job openings each year continue to prefer or require degrees, tens of millions of individuals continue to enroll in degree programs, and a strong college wage premium continues to exist. Certainly, the marketplace of credentials is diversifying and evolving in important ways, traditional higher education models are threatened by new alternatives, and higher education programs must deliver greater value relative to cost. However, there is little evidence to confirm the "death of the degree" meme that is the product of a Silicon Valley–centered worldview.

The highly competency-oriented approach to hiring that works well for *some* roles and segments within the IT industry does indeed offer a set of lessons for other sectors, but the realities of highly technical fields that can favor experience and capability over formal educational credentials are not translatable to all industries or academic disciplines. While some pundits seem to suggest that college students should drop out of school *en masse* to become coders by enrolling in a boot camp, it is interesting to note that nationwide, the employers who posted the largest number of job openings targeting bachelor's and graduate degree holders in 2015 included technology titans such as Oracle (#1), IBM (#9), Amazon (#12), and Hewlett-Packard (#14)—with tens of thousands of positions each, according to Burning Glass Technologies.[1]

*Despite the staying power of the degree, credentialing innovation is important and there is clear momentum for it, but realizing the potential of new higher-value university credentials will require fundamentally evolved strategies and practices.* Clear shifts *are*, however, taking place in how university credentials are constructed and delivered. The trends are from theoretical to practical, from traditional face-to-face instruction to online, from monolithic to short-form, from instructor-led to self-paced, from static to more adaptive, and from faculty-driven design alone to job-market-aligned. Creating new types of credentials and optimizing new approaches to credential delivery (such as competency-based education and new online models) will require universities to engage in new approaches to design, refresh programs more frequently, focus more intentionally on outcomes, and leverage the still-emerging interdisciplinary field of learning science. The landscape of new university credentials is still in an early phase of development, with most efforts in experimental and pilot form.

Today's experiments with new credential forms are fundamentally testing some of higher education's most enduring elements and attributes, and this is one of the many reasons that new credentialing approaches attract such interest. In MOOCs and the new programs they spawn, students often complete courses and programs without interacting with instructors. New competency-based direct assessment models entirely do away with the notion of the course and credit hours as units of learning. Also, as seen in the examples of Georgia Tech's online MS in computer science or the University of Illinois's iMBA, a segmentation is now beginning to occur as some institutions tier their product offerings based on variations in inputs and costs (such as faculty time), price, or services and value (such as extra cost for a for-credit track, access to advising, or a verified credential). One can envision a spectrum of options emerging that lead to the same or similar terminal credentials—ranging from a no-frills, low-cost version based on a MOOC, all the way to a premium, more traditional version that features the novel concept of access to live faculty. However, universities must be attentive to whether employers will view these nonpremium credential versions as of equal standing; early indications are that employers do not. While I personally believe that MOOC-based credential experiments (as just one example) are a step toward the technology-powered models of the future, as of early 2016, most university provosts remain fairly dubious, with only 12 percent believing that these models will "provide high-quality education to students."[2]

Any innovation agenda related to credentials must also recognize that employers themselves have deeply ensconced practices and cultural traditions when it comes to hiring, and that change management on that side of the equation is required just as much as new products from universities. The ability of students to mix and match a series of episodic learning experiences or microcredentials together via a portfolio and present this as a hiring qualification in lieu of a degree is many, many years away—if this vision ever arrives. Few employers foresee this future, and while entrepreneurs and some policy makers are calling for it, our existing higher education system, regulatory environment, and professional communities are not yet organized and structured to facilitate or support it.

*Given job market trends, higher education should prepare for a world of more advanced credential attainment and lifelong learning.* Today's dialogue related to educational attainment is often focused on the lower levels of postsecondary education, including prebaccalaureate credentials. There is certainly impact to be had in that segment of higher education and sound policy reasons to focus on it. However, we cannot deny the fact that job growth is forecast to be greatest at the advanced degree level, and that skills-biased technological change and employers' preference for degrees are driving the need for graduate-level credentials and more continuous lifelong learning.[3] Just as bachelor's degree attainment became more common in the first half of the twentieth century and enrollment in master's degree programs exploded late in its second half, formal postbaccalaureate education will continue to become much more common. This is important to note from a social and economic mobility perspective, as graduate degree programs have become preferred and direct pathways to many corporate leadership roles.[4] The "4+1" programs in which students earn a bachelor's degree coupled with an accelerated master's degree may have a role to play here although these programs must be carefully constructed to ensure that the graduate-level component has value versus a dilutive effect.[5]

The increasingly lifelong and episodic nature of postsecondary education suggests that there is indeed value to be created in student-professionals' ability to stack credentials with one smaller credential contributing to the earning of another; to transfer or have academic credits recognized across institutions; and to have non-institutional learning recognized for credit in some form, whether via a competency assessment or other means. However, this type of portability—a market in credentials and learning units, so to speak— requires a new emphasis on standards across the ecosystem; cooperation between parties; and technology systems to document, verify, exchange, and present evidence of learning. Perhaps more than anything, this vision will also require a cultural shift in higher education institutions' and faculty's willingness to accept outside credit. Creating credentials that are portable across institutions and contexts is a noble goal, but given how the credit transfer market has historically worked—with many institutions protective of their curriculum, brand, and revenue streams—portable credentials are a pipe dream without a new voluntary standards movement or systematic reform or legislative mandate. Even *within* a single institution, it can often be very difficult for students to transfer credit from one department or program to another, and many states have had to step in and regulate this process within their higher education systems.[6] In an age when competency-based direct assessment and MOOCs are in the spotlight, the notion of academic credit is increasingly fluid. In terms of how technology and government might play a role in standards that create more of a true market and level playing field, Matthew Pittinsky, the CEO of Parchment, offers the analog of how technology standards have shaped the evolution of banking and health care, noting that perhaps there is potential for an "electronic record exchange" of some sort.[7]

*Greater dialogue and cooperation are needed between universities, employers, and other parties in the ecosystem.* Countless employers interviewed for this book noted the opportunity for universities to engage in a more substantive dialogue or partnership with them. However, for most universities, the notion of aligning more tightly with employer needs has been relegated to vocational institutions. This thinking must change in a higher education market that recognizes the imperative of employability. Greater discussion and collaboration between all parties in this complex ecosystem—including vendors, government, investors, and so on—are necessary for the credential market to evolve effectively. Higher education in the United States has thrived on its diversity and institutional autonomy, yet this has created fragmented approaches to credentials across corporate, government, institutional, and other silos.

In 2015, the Lumina Foundation, for example, sponsored a national dialogue with more than eighty cosponsoring organizations tackling various issues in the credentialing ecosystem.[8] However, the most intense work and discussion related to the credentialing ecosystem is happening largely among a group of specialist, workforce-focused entities and scholars. This dialogue needs to be broader and much more central among higher education leaders, as well as in the employer community, which could use more intersection points with higher education. It is not only universities that need to leave their ivory towers: employers themselves could be more active in specifying what they need from institutions and seeking out partnerships. As Tom Hanna of Bosch Tool Company notes, "We businesses need to step up our game. We need to be driving some of those relationships, so it's incumbent on us also as the nature of talent acquisition changes over time. It becomes more of an outreach—more of a cooperative effort with the education system."[9]

*A more standardized taxonomy and a common language for naming, describing, and communicating new forms of credentials would be helpful in accelerating market adoption and ensuring value for both students and employers.* As exciting as the proliferation of new forms of credentials with interesting names like the *micromasters* is, it is also dangerous in that the wide range of terminologies potentially dilutes the value and utility of credentials as signals. Institutions and other organizations are certainly free to create their own terms and constructs to see what becomes accepted in the open market, but we have established that a common complaint among employers is that they are confused by the range and diversity of credentials that they are seeing on resumes. This also applies to various flavors of degree programs. The Lumina Foundation has made efforts to create a framework for what competencies a given *level of degree* might entail through its Degree Qualifications Profile (DQP), and it is interesting that this type of effort is needed even for classic degrees.[10]

The potential benefit of standardization is not to suggest that more regulation or accreditation is the answer, but that there is historical precedent for associations of higher education institutions coming together to define common standards in times of proliferating credentials, such as with the standardization movement related to bachelor's degrees in the early 1900s and efforts to standardize master's degrees later in the century.[11] Perhaps we might introduce new credential stations between the bachelor's and the master's or operate along two dimensions or more, in a scenario in which a certain terminology designates a credential's depth, complexity, or length. A new standardization movement also would align well with the current policy push for competency-based education. This standards dialogue could also extend to interoperability and formats for digital credentials.

*Meeting the need for more job-market-aligned higher education will require abandoning old constructs that pit traditional liberal arts approaches in opposition to professional and skills-focused learning.* Peter Stokes, managing director in the higher education practice of Huron Consulting Group and author of *Higher Education and Employability*, frames this challenge and opportunity in the following way, based on his experiences consulting across institutions and states.[12] "This issue about the tension between professional education and the liberal arts is a real tension in the market, but I do think many institutions recognize that it's not an either/or choice," Stokes notes.[13] "When we think about it from the state level and higher education administrative management, there's very much an interest in bringing these things together in thoughtful ways to address the labor market . . . state higher education officials I've spoken with do want to see these capabilities be brought into combination in more market-responsive ways. Having said that, despite the fact that some leaders get it, there's no question that many faculty feel threatened."[14] Joseph Aoun, president of Northeastern University, has argued for ending the false dichotomy between the liberal arts and practical education, advocating for an "experiential liberal arts" approach that appreciates the complexity and rigor of the study of human culture and behavior with practical application.[15]

Within a narrative that is so focused on technical skills, it should be fascinating that the skills employers both say and demonstrate (via their hiring activity) that they value most in higher education credentials include problem solving, communication, writing, analytical thinking, and so on—all outcomes and values that are core to a traditional liberal arts approach. Just as much as there is an opportunity for modular specialized and technical credentials, perhaps there is also an opportunity for credentials and professional development experiences that address these broader skills. Overall, it is important that universities consider the balance of skills and outcomes that make up a given credential, from general soft skills and breadth, to technical depth, and this is a mix that employers are highly attentive to. Historically, the general nature of undergraduate degrees has represented the base layer, with various postbaccalaureate specializations and certifications layered on top. Opportunities will exist to fundamentally reorganize this stack and its components.

*Rather than being based just on didactic models, the future of university credentials is increasingly experiential and project-based.* In hiring, employers clearly value work experience as much as education. As a result, they also greatly appreciate and are growing to expect applied experiences and projects as part of a higher education curriculum and credential. Whereas university credentials have historically represented the completion of an *educational* curriculum, there is a trend toward and opportunity for the incorporation and certification of real-world application and work experience. In a 2014 national survey by Northeastern University and FTI Consulting, 97 percent of business leaders believed that "integrating education programs with practical experience such as internships" was important.[16] Students are increasingly seeking experiences and practical application as part of their studies, as well. Northeastern's proprietary surveys of prospective working professional students have found that 70 percent are very interested in a program with an experiential employer project, internship, or career experience component.[17] As Gail Jacobs of RMS notes: "Universities are slow to respond to the needs of businesses, and in offering real hands-on work. If you're looking for a coder, you need someone with good, solid, hands-on experience."[18] Similarly, Felby Chen, technical recruiter at Facebook, comments: "A focus on group projects, consulting opportunities, and internships/co-ops would be useful in connecting learnings to practical scenarios. Ideally, these experiences encourage and teach students to be resourceful and self-sufficient."[19]

Indeed, one pattern in many of the new, leading-edge approaches to professional credentials (university-issued or otherwise) is to incorporate applied projects and capstone experiences as demonstrations that an individual has mastered a skill or body of knowledge. These experiences are also, of course, commonly woven into traditional professional master's degree programs. Evolving higher education in this direction will require much closer and more regular cooperation between universities and employers in aligning competencies, securing experiential work opportunities and real-world projects for students. It will also require shifting traditional academic mentalities to accept that work experience can be powerful when integrated with traditional instruction.

*New types of quality assurance entities and regulatory approaches operating at a program-specific level are needed. And to enable the development of a new credential market, regulatory constructs must adapt to encourage rather than inhibit innovation.* As acknowledged by groups ranging from the US Department of Education to accreditation agencies themselves, the accreditation system in the United States is built to assess institutions and their quality and longevity more than specific programs. Although there is strong momentum for new quality assurance entities, it is impossible to predict how this new layer or option of quality assurance, consumer protection, or regulation will develop. This means that we are in a critical and unique period when higher education institutions and other interests must play an active and vocal role in shaping this future.

It is promising that experimentation is often being encouraged, and it will be fascinating and important to monitor the emerging interplay between noninstitutional postsecondary education providers and universities. From a market perspective, it is important to keep in mind that it is universities' recognized accreditation, institutional longevity, and perception of quality that differentiates their credentials from various substitutes—arguably even when they may not be as high quality. If employers and consumers embrace more market-based recognition of quality, or if universities and noninstitutional providers compete on the same playing field in terms of the seals of approval that they carry, these dynamics will undoubtedly shift.

*Much more research is needed to better understand and shape how university credentials work in hiring and how the ecosystem can optimally evolve to deliver greater value.* As established at the outset of this book, relatively little contemporary research is being done on how employers make hiring decisions based on university credentials. Further, as we saw in our discussion of talent analytics, employers are still in the early stages of understanding employee performance and patterns in their development of human capital. Many scholars and thought leaders are making important contributions in analyzing job market outcomes, enrollment trends, and so on, but more can be done to specifically understand the role that higher education plays in hiring decisions as well as in organizational performance generally. Ideally, this would be interdisciplinary research that spans the fields of education, business, economics, sociology, statistics, and other domains. It is also important that the dialogue about the future of university credentialing—indeed, the future of higher education—be shaped by empirical evidence rather than speculation. This book has hopefully offered one small contribution.

*The United States higher education system can potentially learn lessons and import models from other nations.* The United States is, of course, not alone in its desire for innovation in credentialing and more workforce-aligned higher education. It is also very important to remember that the higher education market is still in the early stages of globalization, but this is progressing rapidly. One of the more interesting examples for our system, as educational researcher Cliff Adelman has documented, is the significant lessons that can be learned from the European Union's Bologna Process. This undertaking spanned many years, encompassed forty nations, and sought to harmonize disparate systems and degree standards by tuning credentials via qualification frameworks.[20] This approach is now being deployed in a number of states and contexts across the United States.[21] Meanwhile, in Canada, a robust market exists in which Canadian universities offer postgraduate diplomas and Canadian colleges offer postgraduate certificates, through which graduates can top off their undergraduate education with short, job-market-focused credentials. Countless other examples exist, and in an increasingly global market, US leaders should closely monitor developments in other nations. This is especially pertinent in terms of shaping the future of what has been growing international demand for US credentials and the aspirations of many US institutions to operate overseas.

*Universities' internal governance and new program development and approval processes must evolve to support faster-paced credential development and refreshing.* The employment landscape of today and tomorrow is demanding credentials that are nimble and shorter, and address skills and competencies that are quickly changing. However, the process of conceiving, approving, developing, and launching a new degree or certificate program within most universities typically takes twelve to eighteen months, and in many cases far longer. I am intimately familiar with these processes, having spent much of my career focused on new academic program development activities, including across scores of institutions both private and public. A curriculum must clear internal departmental review, political discussions across departments and colleges, provost's offices, faculty senates, boards of trustees, and state approval processes or accreditors. These quality control processes, checks and balances, and shared governance are critically valuable, but they are designed around annual review and the agrarian calendar rather than for a world of rapidly evolving job market needs and credentials. A faster pace—and the ability to quickly refresh and evolve credentials—is critical, especially as universities hope to compete with upstarts who are stepping in to fill gaps in areas driving the knowledge economy such as data science and analytics, software development, and so on. Scholars of university governance have noted that technology, competition, and consumerization pressures are challenging traditional models, and it will therefore be important for universities, their boards, states, and policy leaders to enhance institutions' ability to be more nimble in developing new credentials.[22] Speed-to-market and nimbleness are the primary advantages of noninstitutional providers. To cede the growing professional credential market to outside providers on this basis would be a loss to the role of the university in society. With appropriate adaptation and new structures, universities should be able to leverage their scale, prestige, capital, and centuries of expertise to compete more effectively.

*In a rapidly evolving and competitive market, universities will need to continuously reconsider their capabilities and core competencies, as well as the evolving nature of their relationships with privately capitalized outside providers.* Universities' credential-awarding authority is at the heart of their value and longevity in the marketplace. However, as we have explored, various activities that support the design and delivery of credentials are being outsourced and delivered in partnership with outside partners—often to useful effect.

Lawyer Michael Goldstein, cochair of the higher education practice at Cooley LLP, has written about and long put into practice—through innovative organizational designs and joint ventures—the notion that we can analyze and unpack the functions of a college or university in the way that we might crack open an egg. The yolk, or core of the egg, represents the essential functions of the university as an academic entity, including credentialing, developing and managing the curriculum, appointing and supervising faculty, ensuring appropriate admissions and student performance, and so on.[23] Outside of that defined yolk is the egg white—the activities that support the core but can be extricable from it and purchased in the service marketplace: activities such as marketing, facilities management, financial management, and online infrastructure, to name a few.[24] With the rise of enabling firms and various types of outside technology and service organizations, partnerships and joint ventures are increasingly common, and the future is likely more of a hybrid mix between traditional academia and private industry in this fashion.

As entering into partnerships and joint ventures becomes more common, universities must consider issues such as what activities they uniquely perform best in the value chain, how much value or equity will accrue to them versus a partner, and what level of oversight is necessary. In addition, institutions need to recognize their own capabilities and limitations. Accreditation leader Barbara Brittingham of CIHE of NEASC notes, "Part of what we ask is, 'What does the place have the capacity to do?' For example, talking to the heads of small residential colleges, maybe you don't have the capacity to start your own EdX; that's not going to come from your sector. Your sector is the coming-of-age educational experience. Understanding mission, understanding capacity, understanding risk—really paying attention to the numbers and what the realistic possibilities are: we've seen some places try things that they may not have the capacity to do."[25]

*With traditional higher education programs, professional credentialing, and lifelong learning increasingly converging, university credentials could be much more aligned with and integrate professional standards.* Over the past decade or so, a number of examples have emerged in which university credentials have been made more job-market-relevant via tight integration with professional certification standards. Perhaps the most prominent example is in project management, where the Project Management Professional (PMP) designation of the Project Management Institute (PMI) has been one of the most requested certifications by employers. In addition to maintaining the PMP certification standards, the Project Management Institute in 2001 developed its own higher-education-focused programmatic accreditation body that today accredits ninety-five degree programs around the world.[26] Other examples of alignment exist with the Certified Financial Planner (CFP) designation's "board-registered" university programs that satisfy this professional credential's educational requirements; and the APICS "blanket waiver" system in supply chain, logistics, and operations management certifications, among many others.[27] When degrees, certificates, and other university credentials are linked directly to professional standards through partnership, greater value is delivered for both the learner and employers.

*Talent analytics, prehire assessment, and other technology-driven approaches to hiring and outcomes assessment are likely to reshape the role of university credentials and therefore bear very close monitoring.* Degrees and other university credentials have operated as relatively useful but blunt proxies for ability. However, as we have analyzed at length, the use of data- and competency-based approaches to hiring—including at its extreme bypassing educational credentials entirely through prehire online assessment—could reshape the utility of university credentials work in the job market. Established organizations and start-ups are deploying hundreds of millions of dollars related to this effort.

Talent analytics and evolving employer approaches to on-campus recruiting will make strategic partnerships between universities and employers more important. In on-campus recruiting, many employers are moving to a core school model that is logically based on where they are having the most success finding talent. Employers are also eager to engage with universities and their students earlier in the educational process, which they characterize as an early talent strategy and see as a way to diversify their organizations, bringing in fresh skills and high potential employees. In addition, the list of institutions that they prefer to hire graduates from is increasingly being shaped by talent analytics. As employers become savvier about which institutions and programs are producing the best professionals in their organization, and as employers seek to partner more deeply with those institutions as a talent acquisition pipeline, this could create a system of haves and have-nots. Universities that are able to partner closely with employers, deliver relevant credentials, and have the data to prove it will be advantaged, whereas institutions without the appropriate career services interfaces or quality outcomes will suffer. Although this scenario may take many years to play out, in our increasingly transparent and data-driven world, this type of dynamic could bring about the consolidation of higher education institutions that many forecast. The vast middle, or at least the end of the bell curve—institutions with mediocre outcomes, credentials, and reputation—will be left behind. This is the reality of a performance-based market.

Just as the availability of data and web-based social reputation has shaped markets in other sectors, the availability of outcomes data and increased transparency will begin to shape the market for credentials. With today's social media platforms and networks, we live in a world awash in data and social reputations embedded in sites such as LinkedIn and Yelp. For years, college ranking systems have been influential, and many rankings have been moving toward a focus on student outcomes rather than inputs. Recently, many new rankings frameworks have been launched, and even more ranking and rating will be enabled by data and analytics, including publicly available data that can be sliced and diced in creative or proprietary ways—from salary surveys to LinkedIn data or social measures of reputation. As these large-scale systems grow in power, and as employers deploy their own talent analytics, new, outcomes-based assessments of reputation could emerge that might disrupt the status quo in terms of what are considered high-quality programs, institutions, and credentials. Likewise, this transparency will challenge the reputation or market value of institutions that lack quality, a distinct value proposition, or an ability to align with the job market.

*Better data is needed to create more relevant credentials and higher value connections between higher education and the workforce.* The use of analytics in higher education is still very immature compared to other sectors.[28] Before we arrive at predictive modeling and leveraging "big data," more *basic* data on educational outcomes and careers is needed. The market for talent operates in real time. The Integrated Postsecondary Education Data System (IPEDS) data that higher education relies on is at the institutional level and lags by a few years, and traditional labor market forecasts are relatively static. New real-time labor market information (LMI) systems such as those provided by Burning Glass Technologies and Career Builder/EMSI are useful tools and a step in the right direction—but only one part of the equation. For a decade there has been a debate about a federal student unit record system that would track individual students' credentials and workforce outcomes.[29] Any additional data that could connect higher education credentials and career outcomes would be highly useful in optimizing outcomes. In addition to this issue being a policy question, it is also a technology problem. Traditionally, higher education systems and human resources systems do not connect. And, if higher education and the government aren't able to create the systems that link higher education and its credentials and outcomes with careers, private companies such as LinkedIn—in which consumers are populating their own educational and career data—will do so, and they will own the value. As Allen Blue of LinkedIn describes, "Data is one thing we've barely scratched the surface on. We look at BLS, unemployment figures, and so on—all of those are for the most part still based on survey . . . LinkedIn can give us a better and more data-oriented portrait of what the talent marketplace actually looks like, and those are going to become more powerful over time. If we're able to build data interfaces to look at what the world actually looks like around me, you've got an opportunity to actually make decisions based on data . . . Companies—our customers—ask us questions like, 'Where should we put our next location because we want to put our next location where the talent is available?' So that will apply to not only hiring, but competitive decision making and strategic planning."[30] Similarly, as talent analytics expert Michael Housman notes, "HR is typically a late adopter; universities are often the latest adopter in terms of using new data science and technology. Universities should jump on this wave too—which is changing how people are hired."[31]

*The emergence of major employers as recognized credentialers in their own right could also be game changing.* All parties in the ecosystem should recognize the disruptive potential of employers to emerge as credentialers and certifiers of skill independent of academic constructs. Although there is limited momentum for this trend, it could be enabled by competency management systems such as LinkedIn or the concepts related to badging. Eric Korb, CEO of Accreditrust, explains a potential technology-enabled scenario: "You're going to have an employee record that's going to be portable. Today the employee record is locked up in the HR department, and when you leave, you can't take it with you. You will start to have a record of your skills and accomplishments, issued by the HR department, that you can use as social currency as you move throughout your career. Just like a transcript shows what you achieved in college through courses, you'll have an employee transcript, and control it as the employee, the credential owner."[32] At the same time, Michael Piwoni of Stanley Tool Company makes an interesting point on the core competencies of higher education institutions relative to corporations: "If the college system in this country someday disappeared because there's a better way to do it, maybe we could deal with it and move on, but I tend to think in the future if those training programs exist, the universities are probably best equipped to figure out how to produce them. Companies are good at what they do, but they get into trouble when they try to do things they're not built for—and education is not one of them."[33]

Additionally, with examples such as AT&T's sponsorship of Georgia Tech's online MS in computer science, we have emerging models (among a handful of other examples) for direct corporate sponsorship of higher education programs that meet talent needs and align with employer brands. Higher education has historically been skeptical of corporate sponsorship and influence, as Derek Bok discusses in *Universities in the Marketplace*.[34] At what rate will universities embrace this type of employer collaboration? To what extent will major employers step up with funding and intellectual contributions? Only time will tell.

*Universities should be cognizant of potential shifts in how brand, selectivity, and scale relate—and many institutions might benefit from a focus on programmatic excellence and differentiation.* Historically, universities have defined their brands based on selectivity and exclusivity. For example, at the undergraduate level, the top institutions in *U.S. News & World Report*'s popular college rankings enroll relatively small freshman classes and typically accept less than 10 percent of their applicants from among tens of thousands each year.[35] Admissions selectivity is, of course, also defining for elite graduate programs, and importantly, we recognize that employers value selectivity and pres-tige as a signal.[36] Yet, scale and access do not appear to harm repu-tation at the graduate level. For example, the highest volume issuers of master's degree credentials each year in the United States include Columbia University, Johns Hopkins, and Harvard—each with more than 4,000 graduates per year.[37] Part-time and executive MBA pro-grams at elite business schools often accept more than 70 percent of their applicants.[38] With traditional online degrees, many highly selective institutions have become comfortable enrolling thousands of students; and with MOOCs, while the credential is importantly typically delivered by a third party or set off as a sub-brand, there is also a movement toward scale rather than selectivity. It will be im-portant to watch whether or not employers or others continue to de-fine quality often based on selectivity or based on outcomes. We have seen that general reputational imprimatur doesn't always translate to novel forms of credentialing, and that employers are discerning and skeptical about what is the "real thing." In a marketplace that is trending toward a focus on discrete skills and programs, this offers an opportunity for higher education institutions to focus on being the best in certain differentiated areas—a distinction that employers notice and respect.[39]

*A golden age for noncredit courses and continuing education brings intense competition for universities with noninstitutional providers.* The explosion in online learning skills firms, MOOC providers, and boot camps—all of which are highly capitalized—heralds a new era in lifelong learning. Due to workforce and employer training trends, skill ac-quisition and learning and development are often now the responsi-bility of the learner, who will interact with many different providers in assembling a portfolio of courses, skills, and experiences. The key question is what types of credentials may account for that learning, and universities should have an important role to play here as ex-perts in and respected certifiers of learning. The fact that many of these online skill offerings are free also cannibalizes what was once a revenue-producing market for universities and other entities. As a result, universities will need to carefully consider how they compete—or partner with—these upstarts.

*Access to higher education as an enabler of economic opportunity and employee diversity are indeed critical social issues for a market that continues to be powered by prestige and tradition.* When considering alternative talent pipelines, many leading employers are clear that they are committed to the goal of having a more diverse workforce. Yet, Lauren Rivera's scholarship on the hiring process of employers in high-status industries—consistent with the findings of my own research—speaks to how employers value reputation and ranking, and prefer prestigious credentials due to their signaling ability, short of more competency-based hiring processes.[40] If the goal of government leaders, universities true to their particular missions, or foundations that seek to improve economic opportunity is to create a more fluid system of credentialing and access to jobs, the solution will not exclusively be found in mass-market microcredentials and competency-based education. Instead, it will require a broader rethinking of the way hiring, relationships within the ecosystem, and the role of brand and reputation work. Some employers are even beginning to experiment with blind hiring—a pure focus on competency—rather than hiring based on any resume-based work experience or educational information.[41] Perhaps rather than *inhibiting* equal opportunity, there are ways that prehire assessments can enable the identification of talent independent of the social constructs wrapped up in credentials. Broader, systematic innovations will be required. As economist Harry Patrinos of the World Bank comments on human capital theory, "When we interpret skills more broadly to include cognitive and behavioral skills, the college wage premium increases—which is great for people who are making these educational investments and taking advantage. But it's also worrying because it could further increase the gap, which in the long run is not as good for society . . . I worry about inequality and financing that isn't sustainable. It's either knee-jerk reactions—raise fees and let the rich benefit, or let's make college free—which will lower the average quality of degree—so we need more innovative financing mechanisms to take advantage of markets and expand the resource base."[42]

## CONCLUSION

The future of university credentials is exciting and dynamic, but it is also more complicated and nuanced than many believe. As of the writing of this book in 2016, the dominant narratives related to higher education in the United States reflect two highly polarized points of view. On one side of the spectrum are the increasingly vocal critics of higher education and a segment of the technology and entrepreneurial community who contend that a fundamental refashioning of the university credential market is already here, or is imminent. On the other side are traditionalists and incumbent institutions that believe that the status quo is likely to persist, and ignore the percolating signs of change and innovation. The likely future—rather than an either-or scenario—is somewhere in between these two views.

Significant evolution in the higher education credentialing function is indeed already here. Evolution is just occurring at a slower and steadier pace than some might predict or wish, given the nature of the ecosystem that we have analyzed, and especially the ensconced role of degrees in employers' talent acquisition process. It is certainly worth noting that rather than continuing down the path of slow, continuous evolution, the entire credentialing ecosystem could be quickly transformed by systematic, episodic change operating at the fundamental, structural level. This could include, for example, major shifts in national or state policy and funding, or perhaps the coordinated actions of a significant coalition of major employers or professions. The systematic embrace of new models—change by design—is, of course, what led to major structural innovations in US higher education. These innovations have included, for example, the creation of research universities in the German model and with them, graduate education; the birth of land-grant universities; and the genesis of the community college system.

This particular moment when technology is having a profound and accelerated impact in all areas of society makes it an especially exhilarating time for leaders, thinkers, and innovators who seek to tackle the challenges and opportunities posed by the evolution of credentialing—including those who wish to make the idea of the university relevant in the global economy for decades and centuries more to come. From a business strategy perspective, it is precisely this type of environment that creates opportunity: a large, fragmented market with many distinct segments experiencing shifting patterns in demand and drivers of value. Further, when we consider that the United States is the largest and most mature higher education market in the world, the rapidly growing global demand for higher education suggests additional layers of complexity and opportunity. Going forward, the future of US higher education and its credentialing function is more than ever very much intertwined with trends in *international* economies and employment dynamics, and it just so happens that US-based corporations remain the pace setters in the global market for talent—for now.

While our focus has been on higher education, a central theme and premise of this book is that higher education cannot neglect the role that employers and their hiring processes play in shaping the value of and demand for postsecondary education. Employers are not simply buyers of college-educated talent at the end of an educational pipeline; rather, they are active participants with great power and influence in shaping or even dictating in some sense how the higher education marketplace evolves in this age that recognizes university-level education as the dominant pathway to professional work. Thus, it is important to keep in mind that the world of work itself—also a global market, and also shaped by rapid technological innovation—is also evolving at a significant pace. Yet, it still appears to be the early innings of the university credential market's next chapter.

If the twentieth century was known as "the human capital century," the trends that are playing out fifteen years into the twenty-first century seem to ensure that it may be defined even more so by the role of human capital.[43] The role of university credentials in the workforce is pivotal in shaping the future of some of the major societal issues of our time, ranging from income inequality and globalization to the future role and value of human versus machine intelligence. As corporations continue to discover the importance of more refined talent strategies, and policy makers continue to recognize the primacy of credentials, this guarantees that the university credential will be a central character in the economic landscape of the decades ahead.

# NOTES

## PREFACE

1. John Dewey, *Democracy and Education* (New York, NY: Macmillan, 1916).
2. US Department of Education, "Total Fall Enrollment in Degree-granting Institutions, by Attendance Status, Sex, and Age: Selected Years, 1970 through 2021," https://nces.ed.gov/programs/digest/d12/tables/dt12_224.asp.
3. Harris Dellas and Plutarchos Sakellaris, "On the Cyclicality of Schooling: Theory and Evidence," *Oxford Economic Papers* (2003): 148–172.
4. US Department of Education, "Total Fall Enrollment in Degree-granting Postsecondary Institutions, by Attendance Status, Sex of Student, and Control of Institution: Selected Years, 1947 through 2023," https://nces.ed.gov/programs/digest/d13/tables/dt13_303.10.asp.
5. Jaison R. Abel, Richard Deitz, and Yaqin Su, "Are Recent College Graduates Finding Good Jobs?" *Current Issues in Economics and Finance*, 20, no. 1 (2014), https://www.newyorkfed.org/research/current_issues/ci20-1.html.
6. William James, "The Ph.D. Octopus," *Memories and Studies* (1903): 320–347.
7. Harold Wilensky, "The Professionalization of Everyone?" *American Journal of Sociology* 70, no. 2 (1964): 137–158.
8. Merrill Sheils, H. McGee, F. V. Boyd, and S. Monroe, "Who Needs College?," *Newsweek*, April (1976): 60–69.
9. M. G. Siegler, "Peter Thiel Has New Initiative to Pay Kids to 'Stop Out of School,'" *TechCrunch*, September 27, 2010, http://techcrunch.com/2010/09/27/peter-thiel-drop-out-of-school/.
10. Clayton M. Christensen and Henry J. Eyring, *The Innovative University: Changing the DNA of Higher Education from the Inside Out* (New York, NY: John Wiley & Sons, 2011).
11. Laura Pappano, "The Year of the MOOC," *New York Times*, November 2, 2012, http://www.nytimes.com/2012/11/04/education/edlife/massive-open-online-courses-are-multiplying-at-a-rapid-pace.html.
12. Andrew Rice, "Anatomy of a Campus Coup," *New York Times*, September 11, 2012, http://www.nytimes.com/2012/09/16/magazine/teresa-sullivan-uva-ouster.html.
13. Kevin Carey, *The End of College: Creating the Future of Learning and the University of Everywhere* (New York: Riverhead Books, 2015); Jeffrey Selingo, *College (Un)bound: The Future of Higher Education and What It Means for Students* (Boston,

MA: Houghton Mifflin Harcourt, 2013); Ryan Craig, *College Disrupted: The Great Unbundling of Higher Education* (New York, NY: St. Martin's Press, 2015).

14. S. A. Ginder, J. E. Kelly-Reid, and F. B. Mann, *Postsecondary Institutions and Cost of Attendance in 2014–15; Degrees and Other Awards Conferred, 2013–14; and 12-Month Enrollment, 2013–14: First Look* (Washington, DC: US Department of Education, 2015), http://nces.ed.gov/pubs2015/2015097.pdf.

15. George Keller, *Academic Strategy: The Management Revolution in American Higher Education* (Baltimore, MD: Johns Hopkins University Press, 1983); Robert Zemsky, Gregory Wegner, and William Massy, *Remaking the American University: Market-Smart and Mission-Centered* (New Brunswick, NJ: Rutgers University Press, 2005); Lloyd Armstrong, "Changing Higher Education," http://www.changinghighereducation.com.

16. Sheila Slaughter and Gary Rhoades, *Academic Capitalism and the New Economy: Markets, State, and Higher Education* (Baltimore, MD: Johns Hopkins University Press, 2004).

17. Adrianna Kezar and Peter Eckel, "Meeting Today's Governance Challenges," *Journal of Higher Education* 75, no. 4 (2004): 371–399; Jun Ma and Zelimir Todorvic, "Making Universities Relevant: Market Orientation as a Dynamic Capability Within Institutions of Higher Learning," *Academy of Marketing Studies Journal* 15, no. 2 (2011): 1–15.

18. Sean Gallagher, "Yes, Master's: A Graduate Degree's Moment in the Age of Higher Education Innovation," *New England Journal of Higher Education*, August 5, 2014, http://www.nebhe.org/thejournal/yes-masters-a-graduate -degrees-moment-in-the-age-of-higher-education-innovation/; American Community Survey, US Census Bureau, 2015, https://www.census.gov /programs-surveys/acs/.

19. Josh Bersin, "Workday Recruiting: Will It Disrupt the Talent Acquisition Software Market?," *Forbes*, May 6, 2014, http://www.forbes.com/sites /joshbersin/2014/05/06/workday-recruiting-will-it-disrupt-the-talent -acquisition-software-market/; Anthony Carnevale, Jeff Strohl, and Artem Gulish, *College Is Just the Beginning: Employers' Role in the $1.1 Trillion Postsecondary Education and Training System* (Washington, DC: Georgetown University, 2015), https://cew.georgetown.edu/wp-content/uploads/2015/02 /Trillion-Dollar-Training-System-.pdf.

## INTRODUCTION

1. Yahoo Finance, "CREE Key Statistics," http://finance.yahoo.com/q/ks?s =CREE+Key+Statistics; Cree, Inc., "Cree Employment," https://careers -cree.icims.com/jobs/search?pr=1.

2. Scott A. Ginder, Janice E. Kelly-Reid, and Farrah B. Mann, *Postsecondary Institutions and Cost of Attendance in 2014–15; Degrees and Other Awards Conferred, 2013–14; and 12-Month Enrollment, 2013–14: First Look* (Washington, DC: US Department of Education, 2015), http://nces.ed.gov/pubs2015/2015097.pdf.

3. Tom Mathews (Senior Vice President, Human Resources, Cree, Inc.), in discussion with the author, October 2015.

4. Jerry W. Miller and L. E. Boswell, "Assessment, and the Credentialing of Educational Accomplishment," *Journal of Higher Education* 50, no. 2 (1979): 219–225.

5. David Bills, "Credentials, Signals and Screens: Explaining the Relationship Between Schooling and Job Assignment," *Review of Educational Research* 73, no. 4 (2003): 441–469.

6. David Baker, "Forward and Backward, Horizontal and Vertical: Transformation of Occupational Credentialing in the Schooled Society," *Research in Social Stratification and Mobility* 29 (2011): 5–29.

7. Ibid.

8. David Autor, "Skills, Education, and the Rise of Earnings Inequality Among the 'Other 99 Percent,'" *Science* 344, no. 6186 (2014): 843–851.

9. US Department of Education, "Enrollment, Staff, and Degrees/Certificates Conferred in Degree-Granting and Non-Degree-Granting Postsecondary Institutions, by Control and Level of Institution, Sex of Student, Type of Staff, and Level of Degree: Fall 2010, Fall 2011, and 2011–12," https://nces.ed.gov/programs/digest/d13/tables/dt13_301.10.asp.

10. Stephanie Ewert and Robert Kominski, *Measuring Alternative Educational Credentials: 2012* (Washington, DC: US Census Bureau), https://www.census.gov/prod/2014pubs/p70-138.pdf.

11. US Department of Education, "Total Fall Enrollment in Degree-Granting Postsecondary Institutions, by Attendance Status, Sex of Student, and Control of Institution: Selected Years, 1947 through 2023," https://nces.ed.gov/programs/digest/d13/tables/dt13_303.10.asp.

12. Institute for International Education, "Open Doors 2014: International Students in the United States and Study Abroad by American Students Are at All-Time High," http://www.iie.org/Who-We-Are/News-and-Events/Press-Center/Press-Releases/2014/2014-11-17-Open-Doors-Data.

13. Michael R. Sandler, *Social Entrepreneurship in Education: Private Ventures for the Public Good* (Lanham, MD: Rowman & Littlefield Education, 2010).

14. Jones International University, "Accreditation," http://www.jiu.edu/about-jiu/accreditation.

15. Lisa Bransten, "Something Ventured," *Wall Street Journal*, March 12, 2001, http://www.wsj.com/articles/SB984067888892312186.

16. University Business, "What Went Wrong with AllLearn?," June 2006, http://www.universitybusiness.com/article/what-went-wrong-alllearn.

17. House of Commons Education and Skills Committee, *UK e-University: Third Report of Session 2004–05* (London, UK: Parliament of the United Kingdom), http://www.publications.parliament.uk/pa/cm200405/cmselect/cmeduski /205/205.pdf.

18. Lisa Gubernick, "I Got My Degree Through E-Mail," *Forbes Magazine*, June 16, 1997, http://www.forbes.com/forbes/1997/0616/5912084a.html; Anna Muoio, "Cisco's Quick Study," *Fast Company*, September 30, 2000, http:// www.fastcompany.com/41492/ciscos-quick-study.

19. Cliff Adelman, *A Parallel Postsecondary Universe: The Certification System in Information Technology* (Washington, DC: US Department of Education, 2000), http://www2.ed.gov/pubs/ParallelUniverse/universe.pdf.

20. Ibid.

21. Emily Hollis, "Trends in Online Higher Education," *Chief Learning Officer*, April 13, 2004, http://www.clomedia.com/articles/trends_in_online _higher_education.

22. Scott Duke Harris, "Penny-Pinching Entrepreneurs Changing World of Venture Capital," *San Jose Mercury News*, August 10, 2007, http://www .mercurynews.com/ci_6593343.

23. Harris Dellas and Plutarchos Sakellaris, "On the Cyclicality of Schooling: Theory and Evidence," *Oxford Economic Papers* (2003): 148–172.

24. US Department of Education, "Total Fall Enrollment."

25. Brian T. Prescott and Peace Bransberger, *Knocking at the College Door: Projections of High School Graduates*, 8th ed. (Boulder, CO: Western Interstate Commission for Higher Education, 2012), http://www.wiche.edu/info /publications/knocking-8th/ch2.pdf.

26. Matthew T. Lambert, *Privatization and the Public Good: Public Universities in the Balance* (Cambridge, MA: Harvard Education Press, 2014).

27. Ibid.

28. Anthony P. Carnevale, "College for All?," *Change* 40, no. 1 (2008): 22–31.

29. Jonathan James, "The College Wage Premium," *Economic Commentary* 2012-10 (2012), https://www.clevelandfed.org/en/Newsroom%20and %20Events/Publications/Economic%20Commentary/2012/ec%20201210 %20the%20college%20wage%20premium.aspx.

30. Ibid.

31. Anthony P. Carnevale, Tamara Jayasundera, and Ban Cheah, *The College Advantage: Weathering the Economic Storm* (Washington, DC: Georgetown

University, 2014), https://cew.georgetown.edu/wp-content/uploads /2014/11/CollegeAdvantage.ExecutiveSummary.081412.pdf.

32. Adam Stoll, *The Higher Education Act: Reauthorization Status and Issues* (Washington, DC: Congressional Research Service, 2005), http://www .oswego.edu/~ruddy/Educational%20Policy/CRS%20Reports/Higher %20Education%20Act-Reauthorization%20Issues.pdf.

33. US Department of Education, "Secretary Spellings Announces New Commission on the Future of Higher Education," http://immagic.com /eLibrary/ARCHIVES/GENERAL/US_ED/E050919G.pdf; Margaret Spellings, *A Test of Leadership: Charting the Future of U.S. Higher Education* (Washington, DC: US Department of Education, 2006), http://www2.ed.gov /about/bdscomm/list/hiedfuture/reports/final-report.pdf.

34. Spellings, *A Test of Leadership*, 7.

35. *Postsecondary Education Success Plan Brochure* (Seattle, WA: Bill & Melinda Gates Foundation, 2005), https://docs.gatesfoundation.org/Documents /postsecondary-education-success-plan-brochure.pdf.

36. Lumina Foundation, "Goal 2025," http://www.luminafoundation.org /goal_2025.

37. "Remarks of President Barack Obama—Address to Joint Session of Congress," The White House, February 24, 2009, https://www.whitehouse.gov /the-press-office/remarks-president-barack-obama-address-joint-session -congress.

38. Linda Hoffman and Travis Reindl, *Complete to Compete: Improving Postsecondary Attainment Among Adults* (Washington, DC: National Governors Association, 2011), http://www.nga.org/files/live/sites/NGA/files/pdf /1102POSTSECONDARYATTAINMENT.pdf.

39. Alene Russell, *A Guide to Major U.S. College Completion Initiatives* (Washington, DC: American Association of State Colleges and Universities, 2011), http:// www.isac.org/dotAsset/dbf0788e-4c9b-4ccd-8649-65361d6ff059.pdf.

40. Josh Zumbrun, "Class of 2015 Is Summa Cum Lucky in the Job Market," *Wall Street Journal*, May 28, 2015, http://www.wsj.com/articles/class-of -2015-is-summa-cum-lucky-in-the-job-market-1432866602; US Bureau of Labor Statistics, "The Job Market for Recent College Graduates in the United States," April 5, 2013, http://www.bls.gov/opub/ted/2013/ted _20130405.htm.

41. Steve Kowolich, "Career Centers See More Students and Fewer Recruiters in a Tight Job Market," *Chronicle of Higher Education*, February 13, 2009, http://chronicle.com/article/Career-Centers-See-More/36485/.

42. John Pryor, Kevin Eagan, Laura Palucki Blake, Sylvia Hurtado, Jennifer Berdan, and Matthew Case, *The American Freshman: National Norms Fall*

*2012* (Los Angeles, CA: Higher Education Research Institute, UCLA, 2012), http://heri.ucla.edu/monographs/TheAmericanFreshman2012.pdf.

43. Northeastern University, "Innovation Imperative: Enhancing the Talent Pipeline," http://www.northeastern.edu/innovationsurvey/pdfs/Pipeline _keyfindings.pdf.

44. Mona Mourshed, Diana Farrell, and Dominic Barton, *Education to Employment: Designing a System That Works* (New York, NY: McKinsey & Company), http://mckinseyonsociety.com/downloads/reports/Education/Education -to-Employment_FINAL.pdf.

45. Peter Stokes, *Higher Education and Employability: New Models for Integrating Study and Work* (Cambridge, MA: Harvard Education Press, 2015).

46. Cathy Sandeen, *Signals and Shifts in the Postsecondary Landscape: Presidential Innovation Lab White Paper* (Washington, DC: American Council on Education, 2014), http://www.acenet.edu/news-room/Documents/Signals -and-Shifts-in-the-Postsecondary-Landscape.pdf; Brian D. Voss, *Massive Open Online Courses (MOOCs): A Primer for University and College Board Members* (Washington, DC: Association of Governing Boards of Universities and Colleges, 2013), http://agb.org/sites/default/files/legacy/report_2013 _MOOCs.pdf.

47. Harvard Business School, "HBX CORe: The Language of Business," http://hbx.hbs.edu/hbx-core.

48. Coursera, "Data Science Certificate," https://www.coursera.org/ specializations/jhudatascience.

49. Paul Fain, "Establishment Goes Alternative," *Inside Higher Ed*, August 14, 2015, https://www.insidehighered.com/news/2015/08/14/group-seven -major-universities-seeks-offer-online-microcredentials.

50. "NEXT: The Credentials Craze," *Chronicle of Higher Education*, September 14, 2015, http://chronicle.com/section/NEXT-The-Credentials-Craze/885/.

51. John Cassidy, "College Calculus," *New Yorker*, September 7, 2015, http:// www.newyorker.com/magazine/2015/09/07/college-calculus.

52. "Higher Education Forum," *Economist*, October 22, 2015, http://www .economist.com/events-conferences/americas/education-2015; "Teaching Tomorrow," *Economist*, September 5, 2015, http://www.economist .com/news/technology-quarterly/21662654-sebastian-thrun-pioneer -googles-autonomous-cars-wants-teach-people-how.

53. Kelly Field, "New Players Could Be in Line to Receive Federal Aid," *Chronicle of Higher Education*, July 2, 2015, http://chronicle.com/article /New-Players-Could-Be-in-Line/231333/.

54. US Department of Education, "About Us: Federal Student Aid," https:// studentaid.ed.gov/sa/about.

55. "Remarks by the President at the National League of Cities Conference," The White House, March 9, 2015, https://www.whitehouse.gov/the -press-office/2015/03/09/remarks-president-national-league-cities -conference.

56. Michael Winters and Tyler McNally, "2014 US Edtech Funding Hits $1.36B," *EdSurge*, https://www.edsurge.com/news/2014-12-23-2014-us -edtech-funding-hits-1-36b.

57. CB Insights, "2014 Ed Tech Review—The Largest Financings and Most Active VCs in Ed Tech," https://www.cbinsights.com/blog/ed-tech-venture -capital-financings-2014/.

58. CrunchBase, "Parchment," https://www.crunchbase.com/organization /parchment; CrunchBase, "Degreed," https://www.crunchbase.com /organization/degreed.

59. Jeff Weiner, "2014 LinkedIn Company Presentation" (presented at Morgan Stanley Technology, Media, and Telecom Conference, March 3, 2014), http://www.slideshare.net/linkedin/2014-linkedin-company -presentation.

60. LinkedIn, "LinkedIn to Acquire Lynda.com," https://press.linkedin.com /site-resources/news-releases/2015/linkedin-to-acquire-lyndacom.

61. Peter Cappelli, *Will College Pay Off?* (New York, NY: PublicAffairs, 2015).

62. Peter Cappelli, *Why Good People Can't Get Jobs: The Skills Gap and What Companies Can Do About It* (Philadelphia, PA: Wharton Digital Press, 2012); Josh Bersin, "Spending on Corporate Training Soars: Employee Capabilities Now a Priority," *Forbes*, February 4, 2015, http://www.forbes.com/sites /joshbersin/2014/02/04/the-recovery-arrives-corporate-training-spend -skyrockets/.

63. EY, "EY Transforms Its Recruitment Selection Process for Graduates, Undergraduates and School Leavers," http://www.ey.com/UK/en/Newsroom /News-releases/15-08-03---EY-transforms-its-recruitment-selection -process-for-graduates-undergraduates-and-school-leavers.

64. Marc Orlitzky, "Recruitment Strategy," in *The Oxford Handbook of Human Resource Management*, ed. P. Boxall et al. (Oxford, UK: Oxford University Press), 273–299.

65. Lauren A. Rivera, *Pedigree: How Elite Students Get Elite Jobs* (Princeton, NJ: Princeton University Press, 2015); David Brown and David Bills, "An Overture for the Sociology of Credentialing: Empirical, Theoretical, and Moral Considerations," *Research in Social Stratification and Mobility* 29 (2011): 133–138.

66. Michael Staton, "The Degree Is Doomed," *Harvard Business Review,* January 8, 2014, https://hbr.org/2014/01/the-degree-is-doomed.

## CHAPTER 1

1. Gordon Lee, "The Morrill Act and Education," *British Journal of Educational Studies* 12, no. 1 (1963): 19–40.

2. Julie Reuben, *The Making of the Modern University* (Chicago, IL: University of Chicago Press, 1996).

3. Ibid.

4. Ibid.

5. National Center for Education Statistics, *120 Years of American Education: A Statistical Portrait* (Washington DC: US Department of Education, 1993), http://nces.ed.gov/pubs93/93442.pdf.

6. David Brown, *Degrees of Control: A Sociology of Educational Expansion and Occupational Credentialism* (New York: Teachers College Press, 1995).

7. Judith Glazer-Raymo, *Professionalizing Graduate Education: The Master's Degree in the Marketplace* (Hoboken, NJ: Association for the Study of Higher Education, 2005).

8. Steven Brint, *Schools and Societies* (Palo Alto, CA: Stanford University Press, 2006).

9. Claudia Goldin, "America's Graduation from High School: The Evolution and Spread of Secondary Schooling in the Twentieth Century," *Journal of Economic History* 58, no. 2 (1998): 345–374.

10. Brown, *Degrees of Control*.

11. Timothy Noah, *The Great Divergence: America's Growing Inequality Crisis and What We Can Do About It* (New York, NY: Bloomsbury Press, 2013).

12. Catherine Rampbell, "College Enrollment Rate at Record High," *New York Times*, April 28, 2010, http://economix.blogs.nytimes.com/2010/04/28/college-enrollment-rate-at-record-high/?_r=0.

13. US Census Bureau, "College Enrollment Declines for Second Year in a Row, Census Bureau Reports," http://www.census.gov/newsroom/press-releases/2014/cb14-177.html.

14. Ibid.

15. Randall Collins, *The Credential Society: A Historical Sociology of Education and Stratification* (New York, NY: Academic Press, 1979).

16. James Forest and Kevin Kinser, *Higher Education in the United States: An Encyclopedia* (Santa Barbara, CA: ABC-CLIO, 2002).

17. Ibid.

18. Steven Brint and Jerome Karabel, *The Diverted Dream: Community Colleges and the Promise of Educational Opportunity in America, 1900–1985* (Oxford, UK: Oxford University Press, 1989).

19. Arthur Cohen, Florence Brawer, and Carrie Kisker, *The American Community College* (San Francisco, CA: Jossey-Bass, 2013).

20. Glazer-Raymo, *Professionalizing Graduate Education*.
21. Ibid.
22. Judith Glazer, *The Master's Degree: Tradition, Diversity, Innovation* (Washington, DC: Association for the Study of Higher Education, 1986).
23. National Center for Education Statistics, "Total Fall Enrollment in Degree Granting Institutions," http://nces.ed.gov/programs/digest/d12/tables/dt12_198.asp.
24. National Center for Education Statistics, "Degrees Conferred by Degree-Granting Institutions, by Level of Degree and Sex of Student: Selected Years, 1869–70 through 2021–22," https://nces.ed.gov/programs/digest/d12/tables/dt12_310.asp.
25. Ibid.
26. National Center for Education Statistics, "Integrated Postsecondary Education Data System: Glossary," http://nces.ed.gov/ipeds/glossary/index.asp?searchtype=term&keyword=certificate&Search=Search.
27. Ann Leigh Spiker, "The Association of American Universities: A Century of Service to Higher Education," The Association of American Universities, https://www.aau.edu/WorkArea/DownloadAsset.aspx?id=1090.
28. Roger Geiger, *History of Higher Education Annual: 1986* (Piscataway, NJ: Transaction Publishers, 1986).
29. Judith Eaton, "U.S. Accreditation: Meeting the Challenges of Accountability and Student Achievement," *Evaluation in Higher Education* 5, no. 1 (2011): 1–20.
30. Ibid.
31. Catherine Morris, "Senate Committee Taking a Closer Look at Education Accreditation Process," *Diverse Issues in Higher Education*, June 17, 2015, http://diverseeducation.com/article/73897/.
32. Claudia Goldin and Lawrence Katz, *The Race Between Education and Technology* (Cambridge, MA: Harvard University Press, 2008).
33. Ibid.
34. Ian Wyatt and Daniel Hecker, "Occupational Changes During the 20th Century," *Monthly Labor Review*, March (2006): 35–57.
35. Anthony Carnevale and Stephen Rose, *The Economy Goes to College* (Washington, DC: Georgetown University, 2015), https://cew.georgetown.edu/wp-content/uploads/EconomyGoesToCollege.pdf.
36. David Baker, "The Educational Transformation of Work: Towards a New Synthesis," *Journal of Education and Work*, 22, no. 3 (2009): 163–191.
37. Carnevale and Rose, *The Economy Goes to College*.
38. David Autor, *The Polarization of Job Opportunities in the U.S. Labor Market* (Washington, DC: The Center for American Progress and The Hamilton Project, 2010).

39. Harold Wilensky, "The Professionalization of Everyone?," *American Journal of Sociology*, 70, no. 2 (1964): 137–158.
40. Stephanie Ewert and Robert Kominski, *Measuring Alternative Educational Credentials: 2012* (Washington, DC: US Census Bureau), https://www.census.gov/prod/2014pubs/p70-138.pdf.
41. David Baker, "Forward and Backward, Horizontal and Vertical: Transformation of Occupational Credentialing in the Schooled Society," *Research in Social Stratification and Mobility*, 29 (2011): 5–29.
42. Ibid.
43. US Bureau of Labor Statistics, "Employment 2012 and Projected 2022, by Typical Entry-Level Education and Training Assignment," http://www.bls.gov/emp/ep_table_education_summary.htm.
44. Ibid.
45. Nick Timraos, "Why Job Growth Could Get Even Worse for Men Without College Degrees," *Wall Street Journal*, December 31, 2015, http://blogs.wsj.com/economics/2015/12/31/why-job-growth-could-get-even-worse-for-men-without-college-degrees/.
46. Ibid.
47. US Bureau of Labor Statistics, "Fastest Growing Occupations, 2014–24," http://www.bls.gov/news.release/ecopro.t05.htm.
48. Ibid.
49. National Association of Colleges and Employers, "Job Outlook: Hiring Outlook Positive for Class of 2016," http://www.naceweb.org/s07222015/job-outlook-spring-update-positive-for-class-of-2016.aspx.
50. National Association of Colleges and Employers, "M.B.A. Job Market Continues to Grow," http://www.naceweb.org/s09022015/mba-job-market-grows.aspx.
51. Collegiate Employment Research Institute, *Recruiting Trends 2015–16, 45th Edition: Hiring Outlook for the Class of 2015–16, Including Hiring Plans by Organizational Size* (East Lansing, MI: Michigan State University, 2015), http://msutoday.msu.edu/_/pdf/assets/2015/brief-1-hiring-outlook.pdf.
52. US Bureau of Labor Statistics, "Educational Attainment for Workers 25 and Older by Detailed Occupation," http://www.bls.gov/emp/ep_table_111.htm.
53. Ibid.
54. Burning Glass Technologies, "LaborInsight Database," http://laborinsight.burning-glass.com/jobs/us#/.
55. US Census Bureau, "Educational Attainment in the United States: 2014—Detailed Tables," http://www.census.gov/hhes/socdemo/education/data/cps/2014/tables.html.

56. Burning Glass Technologies, *Moving the Goalposts: How Demand for a Bachelor's Degree Is Reshaping the Workforce* (Boston, MA: Burning Glass Technologies, 2014), http://burning-glass.com/wp-content/uploads/Moving_the _Goalposts.pdf.

57. Ibid.

58. Ibid.

59. Liz Dwyer, "The Reason Why Peggy Olson Would Never Get Hired Today," *Takepart*, April 6, 2015, http://www.takepart.com/article/2015/04/06 /reason-why-peggy-olson-would-never-get-hired-today.

60. HighBeam Research, "Business and Secretarial Schools: SIC 8244," http:// business.highbeam.com/industry-reports/business/business-secretarial -schools.

61. International Association of Administrative Professionals, "History of the Secretarial Profession," http://backlundn.faculty.mjc.edu/313/history %20of%20sec.pdf.

62. Indeed.com, "Executive Assistant Jobs in New York, NY," http://www .indeed.com/jobs?q=%22executive+assistant%22&l=new+york%2C+ny.

63. OECD, *Education at a Glance 2011: OECD Education Indicators* (Paris, France: Organization for Economic Cooperation and Development, 2011), http://www.oecd.org/education/skills-beyond-school/48630696.pdf.

64. Harry Patrinos (Practice Manager, Education, the World Bank), in discussion with the author, December 2015.

65. US Bureau of Labor Statistics, "Earnings and Unemployment Rates by Educational Attainment," http://www.bls.gov/emp/ep_table _001.htm.

66. Ibid.

67. Anthony Carnevale, Tamara Jayasundera, and Ban Cheah, *The College Advantage: Weathering the Economic Storm* (Washington, DC: Georgetown University, 2012), http://files.eric.ed.gov/fulltext/ED534455.pdf.

68. Anthony P. Carnevale, "College for All?," *Change* 40, no. 1 (2008): 22–31.

69. Ibid.

70. David Autor, "Skills, Education, and the Rise of Earnings Inequality Among the 'Other 99 Percent'," *Science* 344, no. 6186 (2014): 843–851.

71. US Bureau of Labor Statistics, "Earnings and Unemployment Rates by Educational Attainment."

72. Jaison Abel and Richard Deitz, "Do the Benefits of College Still Outweigh the Costs?," *Federal Reserve Bank of New York Current Issues in Economics and Finance* 20, no. 3 (2014): 1–11, http://www.ny.frb.org/research/current _issues/ci20-3.pdf.

73. Mina Dadgar and Madeline Joy Trimble, "Labor Market Returns to Sub-Baccalaureate Credentials: How Much Does a Community College Degree or Certificate Pay?," *Educational Evaluation and Policy Analysis* 43, no. 4 (2015): 380–406.

74. Autor, "Skills, Education, and the Rise of Earnings Inequality," 843–851.

75. National Center for Education Statistics, "Fast Facts: Educational Institutions," https://nces.ed.gov/fastfacts/display.asp?id=84; National Center for Education Statistics, "Classification of Instructional Programs (CIP)," http://nces.ed.gov/ipeds/cipcode/searchresults.aspx?y=55&sw=1,2,3&ct =3&ca=1,2,5,3,4.

76. Abel and Deitz, "Do the Benefits of College Still Outweigh the Costs?," 1–11.

77. Anthony Carnevale, Ban Cheah, and Andrew Hanson, *The Economic Value of College Majors* (Washington, DC: Georgetown University), https://cew .georgetown.edu/wp-content/uploads/The-Economic-Value-of-College -Majors-Full-Report-Web.compressed.pdf.

78. Ibid.

79. National Association of Colleges and Employers, "Master's Degrees Mean Higher Salary Payoff," http://www.naceweb.org/s09262012/ masters-salary/.

80. Katie Zaback, Andy Carlson, and Matt Crellin, *The Economic Benefit of Post-secondary Degrees* (Boulder, CO: State Higher Education Executive Officers, 2012), http://www.sheeo.org/resources/publications/economic-benefit -postsecondary-degrees.

81. Joni Hersch, "Catching Up Is Hard to Do: Undergraduate Prestige, Elite Graduate Programs, and the Earnings Premium," *Vanderbilt Law and Economics Research Paper No 14-23* (2014), http://papers.ssrn.com/sol3/papers .cfm?abstract_id=2473238.

82. David Deming, Noam Yuchtman, Amira Abulafi, Claudia Goldin, and Lawrence Katz, "The Value of Postsecondary Credentials in the Labor Market: An Experimental Study" (National Bureau of Economic Research Working Paper no. 20528, 2014), http://www.nber.org/papers/w20528.pdf.

83. Dale Belman and John Haywood, "Sheepskin Effects by Cohort: Implications of Job Matching in a Signaling Model," *Oxford Economic Papers* 49, no. 4 (1997): 623–637.

## CHAPTER 2

Portions of the text and research in this chapter—including various anonymous quotes from corporate hiring leaders—draw from the author's doctoral research study completed and published in 2014 and cited throughout. The interviews conducted with HR/hiring leaders for this study over the course of 2013–2014 were done so anonymously: as a result, the names of the interviewees and their organizations are withheld by mutual agreement. Generally, these were Fortune 500 corporations, with interview participants in the study representing organizations that total $1 trillion in revenue and collectively employ three million individuals. By contrast, the majority of the fifty+ interviews conducted specifically for this book in 2015–2016 are all attributed throughout the book, with just a handful that were off-the-record or not ultimately cited.

1. Lee Bolman and Terrance Deal, *Reframing Organizations: Artistry, Choice, and Leadership* (San Francisco, CA: Jossey-Bass, 1997).
2. PricewaterhouseCoopers, *2015 US CEO Survey: Leading in Extraordinary Times* (New York: PricewaterhouseCoopers, 2015), http://www.pwc.com/us/en/ceo-survey/img/human-capital-finding.pdf.
3. US Department of Labor, "Job Openings and Labor Turnover—August 2015," http://www.bls.gov/news.release/jolts.nr0.htm.
4. Allen Blue (VP Product Management and Cofounder, LinkedIn), in discussion with the author, November 2015.
5. Bersin by Deloitte, "Bersin and Associates' New U.S. Research Finds Dramatic Shift in Recruitment Spending Towards Professional and Social Networks and Away from Agencies and Job Boards," http://www.bersin.com/News/Content.aspx?id=14998.
6. Josh Bersin (Principal and Founder, Bersin by Deloitte), in discussion with the author, December 2015.
7. Gerald Calvasina, Richard Calvasina, and Eugene Calvasina, "Making More Informed Hiring Decisions: Policy and Practice Issues for Employers," *Journal of Legal, Ethical, & Regulatory Issues* 11, no. 1 (2008): 95–107.
8. Heather Boushey and Sarah Jane Glynn, *There Are Significant Business Costs to Replacing Employees* (Washington, DC: Center for American Progress, 2012), https://www.americanprogress.org/wp-content/uploads/2012/11/CostofTurnover.pdf.
9. Chuck Edward (Head of Global Talent Acquisition, Microsoft), in discussion with the author, October 2015.
10. Tom Hanna (Staffing Manager, Robert Bosch Tool Company), in discussion with the author, December 2015.
11. Marc Orlitzky, "Recruitment Strategy," in *The Oxford Handbook of Human Resources Management*, ed. P. Boxall et al. (Oxford, UK: Oxford University Press, 2007), 273–299.
12. James Breaugh, "Employee Recruitment: Current Knowledge and Important Areas for Future Research," *Human Resource Management Review* 18 (2008): 103–118.

13. Peter Cappelli, *Why Good People Can't Get Jobs: The Skills Gap and What Companies Can Do About It* (Philadelphia, PA: Wharton Digital Press, 2012).
14. Ibid.
15. Sara Rynes, Marc Orlitzky, and David Bretz, "Experienced Hiring Versus College Recruiting: Practices and Emerging Trends," *Personnel Psychology* 50, no. 2 (2007): 309–339.
16. Ibid.; Sara Rynes and John Boudreau, "College Recruiting in Large Organizations: Practice, Evaluation, and Research Implications," *Personnel Psychology* 39, no. 4 (1986): 729–757.
17. Tim Howe (Process Excellence Leader, GE Distributed Power), in discussion with the author, November 2015.
18. Adrienne Alberts (Director of Talent Acquisition Programs and Operations, American Red Cross), in discussion with the author, January 2016.
19. Sean Gallagher, "Major Employers' Hiring Practices and the Evolving Function of the Professional Master's Degree" (EdD dissertation, Northeastern University, 2014).
20. Felby Chen (Technical Recruiter, Facebook), in e-mail correspondence with the author, November 2015.
21. Gallagher, "Major Employers' Hiring Practices."
22. Ibid.
23. David Bills, "Credentials and Capacities: Employers' Perceptions of the Acquisition of Skills," *Sociological Quarterly*, 29, no. 3 (1988): 439–449; David Bills, "Credentials, Signals, and Screens: Explaining the Relationship Between Schooling and Job Assignment," *Review of Educational Research* 73, no. 4 (2003): 441–469.
24. Dale Belman and John Haywood, "Sheepskin Effects by Cohort: Implications of Job Matching in a Signaling Model," *Oxford Economic Papers* 49, no. 4 (1997): 623–637.
25. Tom Mathews (SVP Human Resources, Cree, Inc.), in discussion with the author, October 2015.
26. Tom McCleary (VP for Strategic Partner Alliances at Salesforce.com), in discussion with the author, November 2015.
27. Burning Glass Technologies, "LaborInsight Database," http://laborinsight .burning-glass.com/jobs/us#/reports/display.
28. Gallagher, "Major Employers' Hiring Practices."
29. Patrick Walsh (Director of Operations HR and Talent Acquisition, Pizza Hut), in discussion with the author, November 2015.
30. Gallagher, "Major Employers' Hiring Practices."
31. Tom Mathews, in discussion with the author.
32. Gallagher, "Major Employers' Hiring Practices"; Rynes and Boudreau, "College Recruiting," 729–757; John Storey and Keith Sisson, *Managing*

*Human Resources and Industrial Relations* (Buckingham, UK: Open University Press, 1993); Dave Ulrich, "A New Mandate for Human Resources," *Harvard Business Review* 76, no. 1 (1998): 124–134.

33. Gallagher, "Major Employers' Hiring Practices."
34. Ibid.
35. Ibid.
36. Ibid.
37. US Equal Employment Opportunity Commission, "Prohibited Employment Policies/Practices," http://www.eeoc.gov/laws/practices/.
38. Miller & Martin PLLC, "Another EEOC Landmine," http://www.jdsupra.com/legalnews/another-eeoc-landmine-40266/.
39. David Bills, "Employers' Use of Job History Data for Making Hiring Decisions: A Fuller Specification of Job Assignment and Status Assignment," *Sociology Quarterly* 31, no. 1 (1990): 23–35.
40. Bills, "Credentials, Signals, and Screens," 441–469.
41. Bryan O'Keefe and Richard Vedder, *Griggs vs. Duke Power: Implications for College Credentialing* (Raleigh, NC: Pope Center for Higher Education Policy, 2008), http://www.popecenter.org/acrobat/Griggs_vs_Duke_Power.pdf; Jeremy Arkes, "What Do Educational Credentials Signal and Why Do Employers Value Credentials?," *Economics of Education Review*, 18 (1999): 131–141; Peter Cappelli, "Colleges, Students, and the Workplace: Assessing Performance to Improve the Fit," *Change* 24 no. 6 (1992): 54.
42. O'Keefe and Vedder, *Griggs vs. Duke Power.*
43. Ibid.
44. Lawrence Ashe, Jr. (Senior Counsel, Parker Hudson Rainier & Dobbs Law Firm), in conversation with the author, December 2015.
45. Bills, "Employers' Use of Job History," 23–35.
46. Harry Patrinos (Practice Manager, Education, the World Bank), in discussion with the author, December 2015.
47. Jacob Mincer, "Investment in Human Capital and Personal Income Distribution," *Journal of Political Economy* 66 (1958): 282–302; Theodore Schultz, "Investment in Human Capital," *American Economic Review* 51, no. 1 (1961): 1–17; Gary Becker, *Human Capital: A Theoretical and Empirical Analysis, with Special Reference to Education* (New York, NY: National Bureau of Economic Research).
48. John Smart, *Higher Education: Handbook of Theory and Research,* (New York, NY: Springer, 2004).
49. Bills, "Credentials, Signals, and Screens," 441–469.
50. Ibid.; David Baker, "Forward and Backward, Horizontal and Vertical: Transformation of Occupational Credentialing in the Schooled Society," *Research in Social Stratification and Mobility*, 29 (2011): 5–29.

51. Kenneth Arrow, "Higher Education as Filter," *Journal of Public Economics* 2 (1973): 193–216; Joseph Stiglitz, "The Theory of 'Screening' Education, and the Distribution of Income," *American Economic Review* 65 (1975): 283–300.

52. Michael Spence, *Market Signaling: Informational Transfer in Hiring and Related Processes* (Cambridge, MA: Harvard University Press, 1974).

53. Gallagher, "Major Employers' Hiring Practices."

54. Harry Patrinos, in discussion with the author.

55. Bills, "Credentials and Capacities," 439–449; Lauren Rivera, "Hiring as Cultural Matching: The Case of Elite Professional Services Firms," *American Sociological Review* 77 (2012): 999–1022; Lauren Rivera, "Ivies, Extracurriculars, and Exclusion: Elite Employers' Use of Educational Credentials," *Research in Social Stratification and Mobility* 29 (2012): 71–90.

56. Lauren A. Rivera, *Pedigree: How Elite Students Get Elite Jobs* (Princeton, NJ: Princeton University Press, 2015).

57. Paul Edelman (Managing Director, Edelman & Associates), in discussion with the author, October 2015.

58. Arkes, "What Do Educational Credentials Signal?," 131–141.

59. Ivar Berg, *Education and Jobs: The Great Training Robbery* (New York, NY: Praeger, 1970); Randall Collins, *The Credential Society: A Historical Sociology of Education and Stratification* (New York, NY: Academic Press, 1979).

60. Cappelli, *Why Good People Can't Get Jobs.*

61. Bills, "Credentials, Signals, and Screens," 441–469.

62. Ibid.; Bills, "Credentials and Capacities," 439–449.

63. Baker, "Forward and Backward," 5–29.

64. Bills, "Credentials, Signals, and Screens," 441–469.

65. David Bills, "The Mutability of Educational Credentials as Hiring Criteria: How Employers Evaluate Atypically Highly Credentialed Candidates," *Work and Occupations* 19, no. 1 (1992): 79–95.

66. Ibid.

67. Ibid.

68. Ibid.

69. National Association of Colleges and Employers, "The Skills/Qualities Employers Want in New College Graduate Hires," http://www.naceweb.org /about-us/press/class-2015-skills-qualities-employers-want.aspx.

70. Burning Glass Technologies, "LaborInsight Database."

71. Sharon Paranto and Mayuresh Kelkar, "Employer Satisfaction with Job Skills of Business College Graduates and Its Impact on Hiring Behavior," *Journal of Marketing for Higher Education* 9, no. 3 (1999): 73–89; Gallagher, "Major Employers' Hiring Practices."

72. Gallagher, "Major Employers' Hiring Practices."

73. Stanley Litow (VP of Corporate Citizenship, Corporate Affairs, and President, IBM International Foundation), in discussion with the author, November 2015.

74. Ibid.

75. Tom McCleary, in discussion with author.

76. National Association of Colleges and Employers, "The Skills/Qualities Employers Want."

77. Gallagher, "Major Employers' Hiring Practices."

78. Cappelli, "Colleges, Students, and the Workplace"; Rivera, "Ivies, Extracurriculars, and Exclusion," 71–90; Rivera, "Hiring as Cultural Matching," 999–1022.

79. Adam Bryant, "In Head-Hunting, Big Data May Not Be Such a Big Deal," *New York Times*, June 19, 2013, http://www.nytimes.com/2013/06/20/business/in-head-hunting-big-data-may-not-be-such-a-big-deal.html.

80. Chuck Edward, in discussion with the author.

81. Stephanie Pallante (AVP Global College Recruiting, Aramark), in discussion with the author, December 2015.

82. Shelly Holt (Senior Director, Global Leadership Development & Learning, Concur Technologies), in discussion with the author, October 2015.

83. Melissa Korn, "Giant Resumes Fail to Impress Employers," *Wall Street Journal*, February 5, 2014, http://on.wsj.com/N592tQ.

84. Bianca Delgado-Marquez and Nuria Hurtado-Torres, "Being Highly Internationalized Strengthens Your Reputation: An Empirical Investigation of Top Higher Education Institutions," *Higher Education* 66 (2013): 619–633.

85. Robert Zemsky, Gregory Wegner, and William Massy, *Remaking the American University: Market Smart and Mission-Centered* (New Brunswick, NJ: Rutgers University Press, 2005).

86. Alexander Leischnig and Margit Enke, "Brand Stability as a Signaling Phenomenon—An Empirical Investigation in Industrial Markets," *Industrial Marketing Management*, 40, no. 7 (2011): 1116–1122.

87. Rivera, *Pedigree*.

88. Gallagher, "Major Employers' Hiring Practices."

89. Ibid.

90. Ibid.

91. Ibid.

92. Michael Housman (Workforce Scientist in Residence, hiQ Labs), in discussion with the author, October 2015.

93. Gallagher, "Major Employers' Hiring Practices."

## CHAPTER 3

1. M. Corey Goldman, "Labor Market Seen as Tight," *CNN Money*, January 6, 2000, http://money.cnn.com/2000/01/06/economy/jobs_preview/.

2. US Department of Labor, "Databases, Tables, Calculators by Subject: Unemployment," http://www.bls.gov/data/#unemployment.

3. Sharita Forrest, "NCSA Web Browser 'Mosaic' Was Catalyst for Internet Growth," *Inside Illinois* (University of Illinois at Urbana–Champaign News Bureau), April 17, 2003, http://news.illinois.edu/II/03/0417/mosaic.html; Thomas York, "The Future of IT: 1999 IT Career Outlook," *Infoworld*, November 30, 1999, 90.

4. National Research Council, *Building a Workforce for the Information Economy: Executive Summary* (Washington, DC: The National Academies Press, 2001).

5. Julie Hatch and Angela Clinton, "Job Growth in the 1990s, a Retrospect," *Monthly Labor Review*, December 2000, http://www.bls.gov/opub/mlr /2000/12/art1full.pdf.

6. Clifford Adelman, *A Parallel Postsecondary Universe: The Certification System in Information Technology* (Washington, DC: US Department of Education, 2000), https://www.edpubs.gov/document/ed001454p.pdf?ck=1.

7. David Raths, "Directory of Certification Programs," *Infoworld*, September 20, 1999, 82–83.

8. Ibid.

9. Adelman, *Parallel Postsecondary Universe*.

10. Ibid.

11. Kevin Currie (Special Assistant to the Dean, Northeastern CPS), in conversation with the author, December 2015.

12. Brad Reese, "Terry Slattery—The Very First Cisco CCIE in History," *Network World*, January 25, 2008, http://www.networkworld.com/article /2350537/cisco-subnet/terry-slattery---the-very-first-cisco-ccie-in-history .html.

13. Cisco, "Cisco Issues 2 Millionth Certification; Celebrates 20th Anniversary of Industry-Leading CCIE," press release, August 20, 2013, http://news-room.cisco.com/press-release-content?articleId=1240408.

14. David Lucey (Vice President, Talent Acquisition, Epsilon), in discussion with the author, November 2015.

15. "Careers—Qualifications—Do They Measure Up?" *Computing*, March 23, 2000, 57.

16. Alice Lipwicz, "When Hiring Techies, Check the Certificate: MCP? CCNA? It's Hard to Gauge an Employee's Skills Without a Guidebook," *Crain's New York Business*, August 7, 2000, 31.

17. Mark Johnson (Director of Talent, Fresenius Medical Care), in discussion with the author, November 2015.

18. Adam Newman, Abigail Callahan, and Sean Gallagher, *Strategies for Supporting Off-Campus Growth* (Washington, DC: EDUCAUSE Center for Applied Research, 2002), https://net.educause.edu/ir/library/pdf/ers0203/rs /ers0203w.pdf; Anthony Lease and Thomas Brown, "Distance Learning Past, Present, and Future," *International Journal of Instructional Media* 36, no. 4 (2009), 415–426.

19. Lease and Brown, "Distance Learning, " 415–426; Matt Novak, "Predictions for Educational TV in the 1930s," *Smithsonian.com*, May 29, 2012, http://www.smithsonianmag.com/history/predictions-for-educational -tv-in-the-1930s-107574983/?no-ist.

20. Michael G. Moore, *Handbook of Distance Education* (London, UK: Routledge, 2012).

21. "Correspondence School via Computer Is Planned," *New York Times*, September 13, 1983, http://www.nytimes.com/1983/09/13/us/correspondence -school-via-computer-is-planned.html.

22. John Ebersole (President, Excelsior College), in discussion with the author, December 2015.

23. University of Phoenix, "University of Phoenix Online Education," http:// www.phoenix.edu/about_us/media-center/just-the-facts/online -education.html.

24. Badrul H. Khan and Mohamed Ally, *International Handbook of E-Learning Volume 1* (London, UK: Routledge, 2015), 54.

25. Alfred P. Sloan Foundation, "Recently Completed Programs: Anytime, Anyplace Learning," http://www.sloan.org/major-program-areas /recently-completed-programs/anytime-anyplace-learning/.

26. Frank Mayadas, "Asynchronous Learning Networks: A Sloan Foundation Perspective," *Journal of Asynchronous Learning Networks*, 1, no. 1 (1997): 1–16.

27. University of Illinois, "Special Area of Emphasis: LEEP," http://accreditation .lis.illinois.edu/leep.htm.

28. Micah Schneider, "Turning B-School into E-School," *Bloomberg Business-Week*, October 18, 1999, http://www.businessweek.com/1999/99_42 /b3651033.htm.

29. Nina Schuyler, "Class Dismissed?," *Stanford Alumni Magazine*, May/June 2001, https://alumni.stanford.edu/get/page/magazine/article/?article _id=39153.

30. Michael R. Sandler, *Social Entrepreneurship in Education: Private Ventures for the Public Good* (Lanham, MD: Rowman & Littlefield Education, 2010).

31. "WebCT Announces $70 Million Equity Investment; Munder NetNet Fund Closes Round Led by Thomson Learning and SCT," *BusinessWire*, November 20, 2000, http://www.thefreelibrary.com/WebCT+Announces+$70 +Million+Equity+Investment%3B+Munder+NetNet+Fund...-a067129407.

32. Roger Hughlett, "Blackboard's Success May Erase Bad Feelings about Dot-Coms," *Washington Business Journal*, August 11, 2003, http://www .bizjournals.com/washington/stories/2003/08/11/story6.html.

33. Andy Wang, "Stock Watch: eCollege IPO Has Decent Showing," *E-Commerce Times*, December 16, 1999, http://www.ecommercetimes.com /story/2020.html; "Pearson Agrees to Buy eCollege for $477 mln," *Reuters*, October 16, 2012, http://www.reuters.com/article/us-pearson-ecollege-idUSL145989420070514; Robert Budden, "Pearson Acquires Embanet Compass for $650m," *Financial Times*, October 16, 2012, http://www.ft.com /cms/s/0/a39a9e92-17b3-11e2-9530-00144feabdc0.html#axzz3tDgFgIzm.

34. Pensare, "Pensare Announces Partnership with Duke University's Fuqua School of Business to Develop Internet-Enabled 'Top-Ten' Accredited MBA Program," press release, October 11, 1999, http://www.cs.trinity. edu/rjensen/000aaa/Pensare2.htm.

35. Ibid.; Goldie Blumenstyk, "Company That Sells Duke's Online MBA Courses Files for Bankruptcy," *Chronicle of Higher Education*, June 1, 2001, http://chronicle.com/article/Company-That-Sells-Dukes/109000.

36. Ibid.

37. Martha Woodall, "Wharton Embarks on Distance-Learning Program If Students Can't Come to the Business School, It Will Go to Them. Classes Will Be Broadcast Live, Via Digital Satellites, to 30 Sites," *Philadelphia Inquirer*, April 24, 1998, http://articles.philly.com/1998-04-24/business/25767594 _1_wharton-s-executive-education-wharton-faculty-wharton-school.

38. Neil Irwin, "Caliber Learning Says Cash Is Low," *Washington Post*, May 23, 2001, https://www.washingtonpost.com/archive/business/2001/05/23 /caliber-learning-says-cash-is-low/d2e5f005-575c-42e1-b286-10c377bb9e6a/.

39. While this section is based entirely on publicly available sources referenced throughout, I had unique first-hand experience with and special interest in UNext, having worked with the firm as one of my clients at Eduventures, and also earning my MBA through its partnership with the New York Institute of Technology. It was a fantastic program, and I can say well ahead of its time based on my experiences with online courses across a host of providers.

40. Barbara Rose, "UNext Wants to Alter Deals with Universities," *Chicago Tribune*, August 9, 2001, http://articles.chicagotribune.com/2001-08-09 /business/0108090247_1_cardean-university-investors-support-restructure;

James Robinson, "Stanford Announces Participation in UNext.com," June 30, 1999, http://news.stanford.edu/news/1999/june30/unext-630.html; "E-Learning Firm Lays Off Half Its Workers," *Times Higher Education*, September 21, 2001, https://www.timeshighereducation.com/news/e-learning -firm-lays-off-half-its-workers/164938.article.

41. Arlyn Tobias Gajilan, "An Education Revolution? Investors Like Michael Milken and Larry Ellison Are Betting That Chicago's UNext Can Change the Face of College Online," *Fortune Small Business*, December 1, 2000, http://money.cnn.com/magazines/fsb/fsb_archive/2000/12/01/294025/.

42. Ibid.

43. Unext.com, "UNext.com Names Former Stanford University Vice Provost Geoffrey M. Cox Provost of Cardean University," press release, July 24, 2000, http://www.prnewswire.com/news-releases/unextcom-names-former -stanford-university-vice-provost-geoffrey-m-cox-provost-of-cardean -university-72491182.html.

44. William S. Baer, "Competition and Collaboration in Online Distance Learning," in *Digital Academe: The New Media and Institutions of Higher Education and Learning*, eds. William H. Dutton and Brian D. Loader (New York: Routledge, 2002), 169–184.

45. Ibid.

46. Tobias Gajilan, "An Education Revolution?"

47. UNext.com, "UNext Unveils New Series of Executive Education Courses with 'Get The Net,'" press release, September 25, 2000, http://www .prnewswire.com/news-releases/unext-unveils-new-series-of-executive -education-courses-with-get-the-net-73400747.html.

48. Tobias Gajilan, "An Education Revolution?"

49. UNext.com, "Cardean University Approved to Grant Degrees and to Operate in Illinois," press release, June 6, 2000, http://www.prnewswire.com /news-releases/cardean-university-approved-to-grant-degrees-and-to -operate-in-illinois-73463752.html.

50. Stephen Pizzo, "Barbarians at the University Gate," *Forbes*, September 10, 2001, http://www.forbes.com/asap/2001/0910/064s01.html.

51. Barbara Rose, "UNext to Launch Online MBAs," *Chicago Tribune*, August 6, 2002, http://articles.chicagotribune.com/2002-08-06/business/0208060217 _1_cardean-university-unext-chairman-internet-courses.

52. Jennifer Rewick, "Off Campus," *Wall Street Journal*, March 12, 2001 , http:// www.wsj.com/articles/SB984068778432368823.

53. General Motors "General Motors and UNext Form Innovative E-Learning Alliance," press release, April 4, 2001, https://archives.media.gm.com/news /releases/010403gm_Unet.html.

54. Billy Neo, "'Inhospitable' Climates Forces Layoffs at UNext," *Columbia Spectator*, October 3, 2001, http://columbiaspectator.com/2001/10/03/inhospitable-climates-forces-layoffs-unext.
55. Sarah Carr, "Rich in Cash and Prestige, UNext Struggles in Its Search for Sales," *Chronicle of Higher Education*, May 4, 2001, http://chronicle.com/article/Rich-in-CashPrestige/15860.
56. Columbia University, "Columbia and Five Other Institutions Create Premier Knowledge Web Site, Fathom.com," *Columbia University Record*, April 7, 2000, http://www.columbia.edu/cu/record/archives/vol25/19/2519_Fathom.html; Jeffrey R. Young, "Universitas 21 Moves Forward with Plans for Online University," *Chronicle of Higher Education*, September 21, 2001, http://chronicle.com/article/Universitas-21-Moves-Forward/1721; Scott Carlson, "Distance-Education Alliance Backed by Oxford, Stanford, and Yale Will Offer Courses to the Public," *Chronicle of Higher Education*, August 22, 2002, http://chronicle.com/article/Distance-Education-Alliance/116393.
57. Karen Arensen, "Columbia's Internet Concern Will Soon Go Out of Business," *New York Times*, http://www.nytimes.com/2003/01/07/nyregion/columbia-s-internet-concern-will-soon-go-out-of-business.html.
58. "Alliance to Fill Gap in Online Market," *Times Higher Education*, July 4, 2003, https://www.timeshighereducation.com/news/alliance-to-fill-gap-in-online-market/177823.article.
59. "What Went Wrong with AllLearn?," *University Business*, June 2006, http://www.universitybusiness.com/article/what-went-wrong-alllearn.
60. "Corporate Training," *Forbes*, September 18, 2000, http://www.forbes.com/global/2000/0918/0318122a.html.
61. Nunzio Quacquarelli, "Financing an MBA: Does It Make Sense?," *Guardian*, http://www.theguardian.com/education/2003/apr/07/mbas.highereducation; Krysten Crawford, "A Degree of Respect for Online MBAs," *Business 2.0*, December 1, 2005, http://money.cnn.com/magazines/business2/business2_archive/2005/12/01/8364611/.
62. UNext.com, "NYIT and UNext Launch Online College for Working Adults," press release, September 16, 2003, http://www.prnewswire.com/news-releases/nyit-and-unext-launch-online-college-for-working-adults-71086577.html.
63. Jack Stripling, "Breaking Up Is Hard to Do," *InsideHigherEd*, December 9, 2008, https://www.insidehighered.com/news/2008/12/09/ellis; Steve Kolowich, "Glimpse into the Future," *InsideHigherEd*, May 25, 2001, https://www.insidehighered.com/news/2011/05/25/ellis_university_losing_regional_accreditation_highlights_modern_challenges_for_colleges_and_accreditors.

64. New York Institute of Technology, "New York Institute of Technology: Consolidated Financial Statements August 31, 2004 and 2003,"

65. Stripling, "Breaking Up Is Hard to Do."

66. Patrice M. Jones and Ron Grossman, "U. Of C. Sets Controversial Course to Provide On-line Business Classes," *Chicago Tribune*, May 13, 1999, http://articles.chicagotribune.com/1999-05-13/news/9905130163_1_on-line -michael-milken-unext.

67. Derek Bok, *Universities in the Marketplace: The Commercialization of Higher Education* (Princeton, NJ: Princeton University Press, 2009), 80.

68. "Caliber Learning IPO Raises $79.8 million," *Baltimore Sun*, May 6, 1998, http://articles.baltimoresun.com/1998-05-06/business/1998126002_1 _caliber-training-programs-mci.

## CHAPTER 4

1. Goldie Blumenstyk, "Temple U. Shuts Down For-Profit Distance-Education Company," *Chronicle of Higher Education*, July 20, 2001, http://chronicle.com/article/Temple-U-Shuts-Down/23877.

2. Ibid.

3. Robert Zemsky and William F. Massy, *Thwarted Innovation: What Happened to e-Learning and Why* (Philadelphia, PA: The Learning Alliance for Higher Education at the University of Pennsylvania), http://immagic.com/eLibrary /ARCHIVES/GENERAL/UPENN_US/P040600Z.pdf.

4. Richard S. Ruch, *Higher Ed, Inc.: The Rise of the For-Profit University* (Baltimore, MD: Johns Hopkins University Press, 2002); William G. Tierney and Guilbert C. Hentschke, *New Players, Different Game: Understanding the Rise of For-Profit Colleges and Universities* (Baltimore, MD: Johns Hopkins University Press, 2007).

5. Apollo Group, "Apollo Education Group SEC Filing PRER14A," July 21, 2000, http://investors.apollo.edu/phoenix.zhtml?c=79624&p=irol -SECText&TEXT=aHR0cDovL2FwaS50ZW5rd2l6YXJkLmNvbS9maWxpbg mcueG1sP2lwYWdlPTExNTcyNzQmRFNFUT0xJlNFUT0zJlNRREVTVQz 1TRUNUSU9OX1BBR0UmZXhwPSZzdWJzaWQ9NTc%3D.

6. Jennifer Rewick, "Off Campus," *Wall Street Journal*, March 12, 2001 , http://www.wsj.com/articles/SB984068778432368823; Apollo Group, "Apollo Group Inc. Reports Fiscal 2003 Third Quarter Results," press release, June 23, 2003, http://investors.apollo.edu/phoenix.zhtml?c=79624&p=irol -newsArticle_print&ID=424593.

7. William Symonds, "Online Extra: University of Phoenix Online: Swift Rise," *Bloomberg BusinessWeek*, June 22, 2003, http://www.bloomberg.com/bw /stories/2003-06-22/online-extra-university-of-phoenix-online-swift-rise.

8. Sean Gallagher and Basar Poroy, *Online Distance Education Market Update 2005: Growth in the Age of Competition* (Boston, MA: Eduventures, Inc., 2005).

9. Sean Gallagher, "Online Education: Marketing Benchmarks and Trends—Channels, Costs, and Competitive Differentiation in an Evolving Market" (presentation for a Sloan-C Online Seminar, July 2005).

10. Sean Gallagher, "Maximum Profit and ROI in Distance Ed: Planning to Refine or Launch Your Online Learning Programs? Learn from the Winners," *University Business*, May 2003, 47–48.

11. Sean Gallagher and Adam Newman, *Distance Learning at the Tipping Point: Critical Success Factors to Growing Fully Online Distance Learning Programs* (Boston, MA: Eduventures, Inc., 2002); Gallagher, "Maximum Profit and ROI," 47–48.

12. Gallagher and Poroy, *Online Distance Education Market Update 2005*.

13. Sheri Qualters, "Traditional Colleges Court Online Learners for New Revenue," *Boston Business Journal*, December 1, 2003, http://www.bizjournals .com/boston/stories/2003/12/01/story1.html.

14. Ibid.

15. Gallagher and Poroy, *Online Distance Education Market Update 2005*.

16. I. Elaine Allen and Jeff Seaman, *Making the Grade: Online Education in the United States, 2006* (Needham, MA: The Sloan Consortium, 2006), http:// www.onlinelearningsurvey.com/reports/making-the-grade.pdf.

17. Gallagher and Poroy, *Online Distance Education Market Update 2005*.

18. Eduventures, Inc., "Eduventures Finds More Than 75% of Students Are Interested in Online Education," press release, June 14, 2005, http://www .businesswire.com/news/home/20050614005801/en/Eduventures-Finds -75-Students-Interested-Online-Education.

19. Ibid.

20. Sean Gallagher and Peter Stokes, *Developing Effective Channels to Corporate and Government Markets* (Boston, MA: Eduventures, Inc., 2005).

21. Ibid.

22. Ibid.

23. Jonathan Adams and Margaret H. DeFleur, "The Acceptability of Online Degrees Earned as a Credential for Obtaining Employment," *Communication Education* 55, no. 1 (2006): 32–45.

24. "University of Westfield Online," *Saturday Night Live,* from a performance televised by NBC in Season 35, 2009, http://www.nbc.com/saturday-night -live/video/university-of-westfield-online/n12560.

25. I. Elaine Allen and Jeff Seaman, *Online Nation: Five Years of Growth in Online Learning* (Needham, MA: The Sloan Consortium, 2007), http://www .onlinelearningsurvey.com/reports/online-nation.pdf.

26. Jeff Seaman (Director, Babson Survey Research Group), in discussion with the author, December 2015.
27. US Department of Education, "Distance Education Demonstration Program," http://www2.ed.gov/programs/disted/index.html.
28. Ibid.
29. US House Education & the Workforce Committee News Update, "Boehner, McKeon Call Attention to New Report Showing Distance Education Can Expand Access to Higher Education," April 12, 2005, http://archives.republicans.edlabor.house.gov/archive/press/press109/first/04apr/disted041205.htm.
30. Sam Dillon, "Online Colleges Receive a Boost from Congress," *New York Times*, March 1, 2006, http://www.nytimes.com/2006/03/01/national/01educ.html?pagewanted=all&_r=0.
31. Andrea L. Foster, "Texas Weights Bill to Allow Graduates of Online Law Schools to Take Bar Exam," *Chronicle of Higher Education*, March 11, 2005, http://chronicle.com/article/Texas-Weighs-Bill-to-Allow/3160.
32. Mike Offerman (Former President, Capella University), in discussion with the author, December 2015.
33. Author's own analysis, unpublished, 2010.
34. Ibid.
35. Doug Lederman, "Online Learning, Upscale (and Scaled Up)," *InsideHigherEd*, September 12, 2008, https://www.insidehighered.com/news/2008/09/12/2tor.
36. US Securities & Exchange Commission, "2U, Inc. Form S-1," http://www.sec.gov/Archives/edgar/data/1459417/000104746914001172/a2218267zs-1.htm.
37. Merrill Balassone, "USC Embraces Online Graduate Education," *USC News*, September 17, 2012, https://news.usc.edu/41400/usc-embraces-online-graduate-education/.
38. Joel Shapiro (former Northwestern University School of Continuing Studies Associate Dean of Academics), in correspondence with author, December 2015.
39. Gabriel Kahn, "The Amazon of Higher Education," *Slate*, January 2, 2014, http://www.slate.com/articles/life/education/2014/01/southern_new_hampshire_university_how_paul_leblanc_s_tiny_school_has_become.html; "Liberty University Hits 100,000 Enrolled, Ranks Among Nation's Top 5 Online Educators," *Liberty University News Service*, June 4, 2013, http://www.liberty.edu/news/?PID=18495&MID=94203.
40. Society for Human Resource Management (SHRM), "SHRM Poll: Hiring Practices and Attitudes: Traditional vs. Online Degree Credentials,"

August 18, 2010, http://secure-us.imrworldwide.com/cgi-bin/b?ci=us
-shrm&cg=powerpoint&tu=http://www.shrm.org/Research/Survey
Findings/Articles/Documents/SHRMPoll_OnlineDegrees_Final.PPTX.

41. Jeff Seaman, in discussion with the author.

42. Author's own analysis, unpublished, 2011.

43. Ibid.

44. Ibid.

45. Terri Taylor Straut and Russ Poulin, "Highlights of Distance Education
Enrollment Trends from IPEDS Fall 2014," WICHE Cooperative for Educational Technologies, December 21, 2015, https://wcetblog.wordpress
.com/2015/12/21/ipeds-fall-2014-de-highlights/.

46. Mike Offerman, in discussion with the author.

47. Max Chafkin, "Udacity's Sebastian Thrun, Godfather of Free Online
Education, Changes Course," *Fast Company*, January 2014, http://www
.fastcompany.com/3021473/udacity-sebastian-thrun-uphill-climb; John
Markoff, "Virtual and Artificial, but 58,000 Want Course," *New York
Times*, August 15, 2011, http://www.nytimes.com/2011/08/16/science
/16stanford.html.

48. Liz Gannes, "Stanford Professors Launch Coursera with $16M from
Kleiner Perkins and NEA," *All Things D*, April 18, 2012, http://allthingsd
.com/20120418/stanford-professors-launch-coursera-with-16m-from
-kleiner-perkins-and-nea/.

49. Massachusetts Institute of Technology, "MIT Launches Online Learning
Initiative," December 19, 2011, http://news.mit.edu/2011/mitx-education
-initiative-1219; Meg P. Bernhard and Ignacio Sabate, "The Founders: The
Evolution of edX at Harvard and MIT," *Harvard Crimson*, May 28, 2015,
http://www.thecrimson.com/article/2015/5/28/the-founders/.

50. Rosanna Tamburri, "An Interview with Canadian MOOC Pioneer George
Siemens," *University Affairs*, February 12, 2014, http://www.universityaf-
fairs.ca/features/feature-article/an-interview-with-canadian-mooc
-pioneer-george-siemens/.

51. Coursera, "12 New Universities Join Coursera!," July 17, 2012, http://blog
.coursera.org/post/27394575240/12-new-universities-join-coursera; EdX,
"The University of Texas System Joins Harvard, MIT and UC Berkeley in
Not-for-Profit Online Learning Collaborative," October 15, 2012, https://
www.edx.org/press/university-texas-system-joins-edx.

52. Laura Pappano, "The Year of the MOOC," *New York Times*, November 2,
2012, http://www.nytimes.com/2012/11/04/education/edlife/massive
-open-online-courses-are-multiplying-at-a-rapid-pace.html; Jordan Weiss-
mann, "The Single Most Important Experiment in Higher Education,"

*Atlantic*, July 18, 2012, http://www.theatlantic.com/business/archive/2012
/07/the-single-most-important-experiment-in-higher-education/259953/.

53. Jeffrey R. Young, "Providers of Free MOOC's Now Charge Employers for
Access to Student Data," *Chronicle of Higher Education*, December 4, 2012,
http://chronicle.com/article/Providers-of-Free-MOOCs-Now/136117/.

54. Ibid.

55. Steve Kolowich, "EdX Drops Plans to Connect MOOC Students with Employers," *Chronicle of Higher Education*, December 16, 2013, http://chronicle.
com/blogs/wiredcampus/edx-drops-plans-to-connect-mooc-students-with
-employers/48987.

56. Ibid.

57. Dhawal Shah, "MOOCs in 2015: Breaking Down the Numbers," *EdSurge*,
December 28, 2015, https://www.edsurge.com/news/2015-12-28-moocs
-in-2015-breaking-down-the-numbers.

58. Northeastern University, "Preparing Graduates for Global Success
Toplines Report," http://www.northeastern.edu/test/innovationsurvey
/pdfs/toplines_report.pdf.

59. Ibid.

60. Peter Stokes and Sean Gallagher, "Year of the Backlash," *InsideHigherEd*,
December 13, 2013, https://www.insidehighered.com/views/2013/12/13
/have-moocs-hurt-public-perception-online-education-essay.

61. Tom Hanna (Staffing Manager, Robert Bosch Tool Company), in discussion with the author, December 2015.

62. Tom Mathews (Senior Vice President, Human Resources, Cree, Inc.), in
discussion with the author, October 2015.

63. *Training Magazine*, "2014 Training Industry Report," https://trainingmag
.com/sites/default/files/magazines/2014_11/2014-Industry-Report.pdf.

64. Adrienne Alberts (Director of Talent Acquisition Programs and Operations, American Red Cross), in discussion with the author, January 2016.

65. American Council on Education, "ACE Launches Presidential Innovation
Lab," July 2, 2013, http://www.acenet.edu/news-room/Pages/ACE-
Launches-Presidential-Innovation-Lab-.aspx.

66. Cathy Sandeen, *Signals and Shifts in the Postsecondary Landscape* (Washington,
DC: American Council on Education, 2014), http://www.acenet.edu/news
-room/Documents/Signals-and-Shifts-in-the-Postsecondary-Landscape
.pdf; Cathy Sandeen, *Beyond the Inflection Point: Reimagining Business Models
for Higher Education* (Washington, DC: American Council on Education,
2014), http://www.acenet.edu/news-room/Documents/Beyond-the-
Inflection-Point-Reimagining-Business-Models-for-Higher-Education
.pdf; Cathy Sandeen, *Unbundling Versus Designing Faculty Roles* (Washington

DC: American Council on Education, 2014), http://www.acenet.edu/news
-room/Documents/Unbundling-Versus-Designing-Faculty-Roles.pdf.
67. Tom Mathews, in discussion with the author.
68. Adrienne Alberts, in discussion with the author.
69. Gail Jacobs (Senior Director Talent Acquisition and HR Operations, RMS), in discussion with the author, November 2015.
70. Sean Gallagher, "Major Employers' Hiring Practices and the Evolving Function of the Professional Master's Degree" (EdD dissertation, Northeastern University, 2014).
71. Ibid.
72. Ibid.
73. Ibid.
74. Shelly Holt (Senior Director, Global Leadership Development & Learning, Concur Technologies), in discussion with the author, October 2015.
75. Paul Edelman (Managing Director, Edelman & Associates), in discussion with the author, October 2015.
76. Chuck Edward (Head of Global Talent Acquisition, Microsoft), in discussion with the author, October 2015.

CHAPTER 5

1. Marc Andreessen, "Why Software Is Eating the World," *Wall Street Journal*, August 20, 2011, http://www.wsj.com/articles/SB10001424053111903480904576512250915629460.
2. Steve Dee, "Why You Shouldn't Lose Sleep over the Tech Boom," *Forbes*, August 13, 2015, http://www.forbes.com/sites/greatspeculations/2015/08/13/why-you-shouldnt-lose-sleep-over-the-tech-boom/.
3. National Venture Capital Association, "Annual Venture Capital Investment Tops $48 Billion in 2014, Reaching Highest Level in Over a Decade, According to the MoneyTree Report," January 16, 2015, http://nvca.org/pressreleases/annual-venture-capital-investment-tops-48-billion-2014-reaching-highest-level-decade-according-moneytree-report/.
4. "Goldrush 2012: Why Venture Capital $$$ Is Flooding into the EdTech Startup Market," *Wired Academic*, September 12, 2012, http://www.wiredacademic.com/2012/09/goldrush-2012-why-venture-capital-is-flooding-into-the-edtech-startup-market/?share=email; Michael Winters and Tyler McNally, "US Edtech Funding Hits $1.36B," *EdSurge*, December 23, 2014, https://www.edsurge.com/news/2014-12-23-2014-us-edtech-funding-hits-1-36b; Michael Winters, "Christmas Bonus! US Edtech Sets Record with $1.85 Billion Raised in 2015," *EdSurge*, December 21, 2015, https://www.edsurge.com/news/2015-12-21-christmas-bonus-us-edtech-sets-record-with-1-85-billion-raised-in-2015.

5. Bersin by Deloitte, "HR Technology for 2016: Ten Disruptions on the Horizon," October 22, 2015, http://www.bersin.com/Blog/post/HR -Technology-For-2016-Ten-Disruptions-On-The-Horizon.aspx.
6. Peter Cappelli, "Why We Love to Hate HR . . . and What HR Can Do About It," *Harvard Business Review*, July–August 2015, https://hbr.org/2015/07 /why-we-love-to-hate-hr-and-what-hr-can-do-about-it.
7. Matt Greenfield (Managing Director, Rethink Education), in discussion with the author, November 2015.
8. Ibid.
9. Paul Basken, "Electronic Portfolios May Answer Calls for More Account- ability," *Chronicle of Higher Education*, April 18, 2008, http://chronicle.com /article/Electronic-Portfolios-May/20892.
10. Digication, "Digication," https://www.digication.com/about.html; Cen- gage Learning, "Cengage Learning Acquires Pathbrite's Best-In-Class ePortfolio Solution," October 27, 2015, http://news.cengage.com/corporate /cengage-learning-acquires-pathbrites-best-in-class-eportfolio-solution/.
11. Chris Ward and Chris Moser, "E-Portfolios as a Hiring Tool: Do Employ- ers Really Care?," *EDUCAUSE Quarterly*, November 17, 2008, http://er .educause.edu/articles/2008/11/eportfolios-as-a-hiring-tool-do-employers -really-care.
12. Melissa Korn, "Giant Résumés Fail to Impress Employers," *Wall Street Journal*, February 5, 2014, http://on.wsj.com/N592tQ.
13. Gail Jacobs (Senior Director Talent Acquisition and HR Operations, RMS), in discussion with the author, November 2015.
14. Adrienne Alberts (Director of Talent Acquisition Programs and Opera- tions, American Red Cross), in discussion with the author, January 2016.
15. Ryan Craig, *College Disrupted: The Great Unbundling of Higher Education* (New York: St. Martin's Press, 2015), 106.
16. Leila Meyer, "California State University System Makes E-Portfolios Avail- able to All Students and Alumni," *Campus Technology*, October 19, 2015, https://campustechnology.com/articles/2015/10/19/california-state -university-system-makes-e-portfolios-available-to-all-students-and -alumni.aspx.
17. Portfolium, "Portfolium for Educators," https://portfolium.com /educators.
18. Portfolium, "Portfolium for Employers—The Search Engine for College Recruiting," http://employers.portfolium.com.
19. Jim Milton (VP of Customer Development, Portfolium), in discussion with the author, January 2016.
20. The Lumina Foundation, "Grants Database," https://www.lumina foundation.org/grants-database/strategy/create-new-credentialing-systems.

21. American National Standards Institute, "Major Grant Made to Increase the Transparency and Value of Industry Credentials and Degrees," July 8, 2015, https://www.ansi.org/news_publications/news_story.aspx?menuid =7&articleid=5fbc67a7-cde0-4c3a-9517-478d74ba6fb5.
22. Parchment, "Mission," http://www.parchment.com/company/.
23. Crunchbase, "Parchment—Crunchbase," https://www.crunchbase.com /organization/parchment#/entity.
24. Parchment, "Matthew Pittinsky, Ph.D.," http://www.parchment.com /matthew-pittinsky/.
25. Matthew Pittinsky (Chief Executive Officer, Parchment), in discussion with the author, January 2016.
26. Ibid.
27. Accreditrust, "TrueCred—Secure Credentials," https://www.accreditrust .com/truecred-framework.
28. Eric Korb (Chief Executive Officer, Accreditrust), in discussion with the author, December 2015.
29. Ibid.
30. David Baker, "Forward and Backward, Horizontal and Vertical: Transformation of Occupational Credentialing in the Schooled Society," *Research in Social Stratification and Mobility*, 29 (2011): 5–29.
31. Gail Jacobs, in discussion with the author.
32. Steve Knox (Global Talent Acquisition Leader, General Electric), in discussion with the author, November 2015.
33. Degreed, "Mission," https://degreed.com/about.
34. Degreed, "Degreed for Me," https://degreed.com/for-me.
35. vcaonline.com, "Degreed Raises $21M Series B to Make All Professional and Lifelong Learning Matter," January 5, 2016, http://www.vcaonline .com/news/news.asp?ID=2016010503#.Vo0Eguw8KnN.
36. Josh Bersin, John Houston, and Boy Kester, "Talent Analytics in Practice," *Deloitte University Press*, March 7, 2014, http://dupress.com/articles/hc -trends-2014-talent-analytics/?id=gx:el:dc:dup684:cons:awa:hct14.
37. Ibid.
38. Shelly Holt (Senior Director, Global Leadership Development & Learning, Concur Technologies), in discussion with the author, October 2015.
39. Josh Bersin (Principal and Founder, Bersin by Deloitte), in discussion with the author, December 2015.
40. Shelly Holt, in discussion with the author.
41. Michael Piwoni (Human Resources Director, Stanley Tool Company), in discussion with the author, December 2015.
42. Tom Mathews (SVP Human Resources, Cree, Inc.), in discussion with the author, October 2015.

43. Roy Mauer, "The Holy Grail of Recruiting: How to Measure Quality of Hire," *Society for Human Resource Management,* November 18, 2015, http:// www.shrm.org/hrdisciplines/staffingmanagement/articles/pages/how-to -measure-quality-of-hire.aspx#sthash.u4pB50op.dpuf.

44. Chuck Edward (Head of Global Talent Acquisition, Microsoft), in discussion with the author, October 2015.

45. Stephanie Pallante (AVP Global College Recruiting, Aramark), in discussion with the author, December 2015.

46. Ibid.

47. Luke Weaver (Human Resources Director, PepsiCo), in discussion with the author, December 2015.

48. Ibid.

49. Ibid.

50. Mark Johnson (Director of Talent, Fresenius Medical Care), in discussion with the author, November 2015.

51. Yahoo Finance, "Form 10-Q for LinkedIn Corp: October 2015," October 29, 2015, http://biz.yahoo.com/e/151029/lnkd10-q.html.

52. Yahoo Finance, "LinkedIn Corporation (LNKD)," http://finance.yahoo .com/q?s=lnkd&ql=1.

53. Yahoo Finance, "Form 10-K for LinkedIn Corp: February 2015," February 12, 2015, http://biz.yahoo.com/e/150212/lnkd10-k.html.

54. Jeff Weiner, "2014 LinkedIn Company Presentation" (presented at Morgan Stanley Technology, Media, and Telecom Conference, March 3, 2014), http://www.slideshare.net/linkedin/2014-linkedin-company-presentation.

55. ICEF Monitor, "LinkedIn Rolls Out New School Selection Services for Prospective Students," January 16, 2015, http://monitor.icef.com/2015/01 /linkedin-rolls-new-school-selection-services-prospective-students/.

56. LinkedIn, "Skill Endorsements—Overview," https://help.linkedin.com/app /answers/detail/a_id/31888/~/skill-endorsements---overview.

57. Michael Piwoni, in discussion with the author.

58. Ibid.

59. Allen Blue (VP Product Management and Cofounder, LinkedIn), in discussion with the author, November 2015.

60. Ibid.

61. Ibid.

62. Dan Shapero, "Showcase Your Professional Certifications on LinkedIn in One Click," LinkedIn (blog), November 20, 2014, http://blog.linkedin.com/2014 /11/20/showcase-your-professional-certifications-on-linkedin-in-one-click/.

63. LinkedIn, "Top 100 Certification Providers," https://addtoprofile.linkedin .com/cert/ranking?trk=li_corpblog_corp_danshapero_showcase professionalcertification.

64. Shapero, "Showcase Your Professional Certifications."
65. Ryan Craig, "LinkedIn Eats the University," *VentureBeat*, April 16, 2015, http://venturebeat.com/2015/04/16/linkedin-eats-the-university-2/.
66. Curt Woodward, "Smarterer Sold to Utah-Based Pluralsight for $75M," *Xconomy*, November 19, 2014, http://www.xconomy.com/boston/2014/11/19/smarterer-sold-to-utah-based-pluralsight-for-75m/.
67. Dave Balter (Head of Transactions, Pluralsight), in discussion with the author, December 2015.
68. Matt Greenfield, in discussion with the author.
69. Allen Smith, "Target Will Pay $2.8M over Employment Tests," *Society for Human Resource Management*, August 25, 2015, http://www.shrm.org/legalissues/federalresources/pages/target-employment-tests.aspx.
70. Bersin by Deloitte, "Pre-Hire Assessments: The Game Has Changed," March 25, 2010, http://www.bersin.com/blog/post/Pre-Hire-Assessments-The-Game-Has-Changed.aspx.
71. Charles A. Handler, *Talent Assessment 2014/2015: Market Analysis, Vendor Classification, and Market Opportunity* (New Orleans, LA: Rocket-Hire LLC, 2014), http://www.slideshare.net/rockethire/rockethire-talent-assessment-market-overview-20142015; Josh Bersin, "Pre-Hire Assessment Science Revealed: Value for Employers, Value for Candidates," Bersin by Deloitte (blog), April 2, 2013, http://www.bersin.com/Blog/post/Pre-Hire-Assessment-Science--Value-for-Employers2c-Value-for-Job-Candidates.aspx; Sarah Halzack, "Online Tests Are the Latest Gateway to Landing a New Job," *Washington Post*, May 8, 2014, https://www.washingtonpost.com/business/capitalbusiness/online-tests-are-the-latest-gateway-to-landing-a-new-job/2014/05/08/c5eebc6a-cb2d-11e3-95f7-7ecdde72d2ea_story.html.
72. Zach Lahey, *An Asset for HR in the Age of the Candidate* (Boston, MA: Aberdeen Group, 2015), http://www.aberdeen.com/research/10326/10326-RR-advanced-prehire-assessments.aspx/content.aspx.
73. Mark Johnson, in discussion with the author.
74. Kevin Oakes (Chief Executive Officer, Institute for Corporate Productivity), in discussion with the author, December 2015.
75. Lawrence Ashe, Jr. (Senior Counsel, Parker Hudson Rainer & Dobbs), in discussion with the author, December 2015.
76. Gail Jacobs, in discussion with the author.
77. Paul Barsness (Associate, Parker Hudson Rainer & Dobbs), in discussion with the author, December 2015.
78. David Lucey (VP Talent Acquisition, Epsilon), in discussion with the author, November 2015.

79. Hacker Rank, "Hacker Rank for Work," https://www.hackerrank.com /work; Codility, "Codility: Hiring Programmers Made Easy," https:// codility.com.
80. Michael Piwoni, in discussion with the author.
81. Mark Johnson, in discussion with the author.
82. Adrienne Alberts, in discussion with the author.
83. Claudio Fernandez-Araoz, "21ˢᵗ Century Talent Spotting," *Harvard Business Review*, June 2014, https://hbr.org/2014/06/21st-century-talent-spotting.
84. Stephanie Pallante, in discussion with the author.
85. Steve Knox, in discussion with the author.
86. Josh Bersin, "People Analytics Takes Off: Ten Things We've Learned," LinkedIn (blog), October 19, 2015, https://www.linkedin.com/pulse /people-analytics-takes-off-ten-things-weve-learned-josh-bersin.

CHAPTER 6

1. New England Association of Schools and Colleges, Commission on Institutions of Higher Education, "FAQs About Accreditation," https://cihe .neasc.org/information-public/faqs-about-accreditation.
2. Eric Kelderman, "U.S. to Put New Requirements on Accreditors," *Chronicle of Higher Education,* November 6, 2015, http://chronicle.com/article/US-to -Put-New-Requirements/234082.
3. Barbara Brittingham (President of the Commission on Institutions of Higher Education, NEASC), in discussion with the author, December 2015.
4. Ibid.
5. Council for Higher Education Accreditation, "Council for Higher Education Accreditation," http://www.chea.org.
6. Judith Eaton (President of the Council for Higher Education Accreditation), in discussion with the author, January 2016.
7. Ibid.
8. Council for Higher Education Accreditation, "The Quality Platform: External Review of Alternative Providers of Higher Education," http://www .chea.org/pdf/Quality%20Platform%20-%20Summary%20Doc.pdf.
9. "Upstart Auditor for Boot Camp Experiment," *Inside Higher Ed,* November 12, 2015, https://www.insidehighered.com/quicktakes/2015/11/12/upstart -auditor-boot-camp-experiment.
10. Ted Mitchell, "Innovation and Quality in Higher Education," US Department of Education, http://blog.ed.gov/2015/07/innovation-and-quality -in-higher-education/.
11. Federal Register, "Notice Inviting Postsecondary Educational Institutions to Participate in Experiments Under the Experimental Sites Initiative;

Federal Student Financial Assistance Programs Under Title IV of the Higher Education Act of 1965, as Amended," https://www.federalregister .gov/articles/2015/10/15/2015-26239/notice-inviting-postsecondary -educational-institutions-to-participate-in-experiments-under-the.

12. Ibid.

13. Ibid.

14. David Soo (Senior Policy Advisor, US Department of Education), in discussion with the author, January 2016.

15. Ibid.

16. Kevin Carey, "Here's What Will Truly Change Higher Education: Online Degrees That Are Seen as Official," *New York Times*, March 5, 2015, http:// www.nytimes.com/2015/03/08/upshot/true-reform-in-higher-education -when-online-degrees-are-seen-as-official.html?_r=0.

17. Arne Duncan, "Digital Badges for Learning: Remarks by Secretary Duncan at 4th Annual Launch of the MacArthur Foundation Digital Media and Lifelong Learning Competition," US Department of Education, September 15, 2011, http://www.ed.gov/news/speeches/digital-badges-learning.

18. Jeffrey R. Young, "'Badges' Earned Online Pose Challenge to Traditional College Diplomas," *Chronicle of Higher Education*, January 8, 2012, http:// chronicle.com/article/Badges-Earned-Online-Pose/130241/.

19. Peer 2 Peer University, The Mozilla Foundation, and The MacArthur Foundation, "An Open Badge System Framework," https://docs.google .com/document/d/1xGuyK4h7DLVeOrFPeegB4ORMutblJf9xVRZCizgx _j8/edit?hl=en&authkey=CNarn4U.

20. The Mozilla Foundation, "About: Open Badges," http://openbadges.org /about/.

21. IMS Global Learning Consortium, "IMS Global Announces Initiative to Establish Digital Badges as Common Currency for K-20 and Corporate Education," https://www.imsglobal.org/pressreleases/pr150421.html.

22. Pearson Education, "Open Badges for Higher Education," https://www .pearsoned.com/wp-content/uploads/Open-Badges-for-Higher-Education.pdf.

23. Edward Abeyta, "We Don't Need No Stinking Badges . . . Or Do We?," *The Evolllution*, December 8, 2015, http://evolllution.com/programming/ credentials/we-dont-need-no-stinking-badges-or-do-we/.

24. Paul Fain, "Badging from Within," *Inside Higher Ed*, January 3, 2014, https:// www.insidehighered.com/news/2014/01/03/uc-daviss-groundbreaking -digital-badge-system-new-sustainable-agriculture-program.

25. The Mozilla Foundation, "Participating Issuers," http://openbadges.org /participating-issuers/; University of Illinois, "Who's Issuing Badges?," http://news.badges.illinois.edu/campus-efforts/.

26. Ibid.

27. Harper College, "Digital Badges," http://goforward.harpercollege. edu/ce/certificate/digital-badges.php; Santa Barbara City College, "Career Institute Digital Badges," http://sccrcolleges.org/sbcc-catalog.

28. The Mozilla Foundation, "Participating Issuers."

29. Pearson Education, "Fast-Track Your Institution's Badging Program with Acclaim," http://home.pearsonhighered.com/content/dam/ped/penak12 /US/pearsonhighered/documents/Acclaim_Community_College_Flyer.pdf.

30. Peter Janzow (Senior Director Business and Market Development, Acclaim), in discussion with the author, December 2015.

31. IBM, "IBM Open Badges," http://www.slideshare.net/JimDaniels2/ibm -open-badge-program-leading-the-industry.

32. Peter Janzow, in discussion with the author.

33. Nicola Soares (Vice President and Managing Director, Product Strategy, Kelly Services), in discussion with the author, December 2015.

34. Matthew Pittinsky (CEO, Parchment), in discussion with the author, January 2016.

35. IBM, "IBM Open Badges."

36. David Leaser (Senior Program Manager, Innovation and Growth Initiatives, IBM), January 2016.

37. Liz Eggleston and Tre Jones, "2014 Programming Bootcamp Survey," *Course Report*, April 30, 2014, https://www.coursereport.com/2014 -programming-bootcamp-survey.pdf.

38. Ibid.

39. Liz Eggleston, "Course Report Bootcamp Graduate Demographics & Outcomes Study," *Course Report*, https://www.coursereport.com/resources /course-report-bootcamp-graduate-demographics-outcomes-study.

40. "Remarks by the President at the National League of Cities Conference," The White House, March 9, 2015, https://www.whitehouse.gov/the -press-office/2015/03/09/remarks-president-national-league-cities -conference.

41. David Lucey (Vice President Talent Acquisition, Epsilon), in discussion with the author, November 2015.

42. Chuck Edward (Head of Global Talent Acquisition, Microsoft), in discussion with the author, October 2015.

43. Gail Jacobs (Senior Director Talent Acquisition and HR Operations, RMS), in discussion with the author, November 2015.

44. Ibid.

45. Galvanize, "About," http://www.galvanize.com/about/#.VpvMhHhqk1I.

46. University of New Haven, "Galvanize Launches Accredited Master's Degree Program in the Field of Data Science," October 23, 2014, http://www .newhaven.edu/news-events/news-releases/2014-2015/827025/.

47. Galvanize, "University of New Haven Partnership," http://www.galvanizeu .com/unh-partnership.
48. Paul Fain, "College Credit for a Boot Camp," October 9, 2015, https:// www.insidehighered.com/news/2015/10/09/lynn-university-and-general -assembly-team-credit-bearing-study-abroad.
49. Ibid.
50. Pamme Boutsells, "SNHU Partners with Flatiron School to Increase Access to Coding Bootcamps," Southern New Hampshire University, October 28, 2015, http://www.snhu.edu/about-us/news-and-events/2015 /10/snhu-partners-with-flatiron-school-to-increase-access-to-coding -bootcamps.
51. "Rutgers' First Coding Boot Camp Launches in Fall," *Rutgers Today*, August 28, 2015, http://news.rutgers.edu/news-release/rutgers'-first-coding -boot-camp-launches-fall/20150828#.VpvSQXhqk1I.
52. Rutgers University, "Rutgers Coding Bootcamp," http://www.rutgers codingbootcamp.com/#faq; Ibid.
53. Northeastern University, "Level Analytics Bootcamp," http://www .leveledu.com.
54. Ibid.
55. Nick Ducoff (Vice President for New Ventures, Northeastern University), in discussion with the author, January 2016.
56. Ryan Craig, "Coursera, Udacity and the Future of Credentials," *Forbes*, September 30, 2015, http://www.forbes.com/sites/ryancraig/2015/09/30 /coursera-udacity-and-the-future-of-credentials/#2715e4857a0b500c 56079215.
57. Udacity, "Nanodegree Programs for Jobs in Technology," https://www .udacity.com/nanodegree.
58. Leena Rao, "Udacity's New Degree Comes with a Money Back Guarantee," *Fortune*, January 13, 2016, http://fortune.com/2016/01/13/udacity -nanodegree-jobs/?utm_content=bufferc27e4&utm_medium=social&utm _source=twitter.com&utm_campaign=buffer.
59. John A. Byrne, "Coursera CEO: Reports of Mass Disruption to Higher Ed Greatly Exaggerated," *Poets & Quants*, May 6, 2015, http://poetsandquants. com/2015/05/06/coursera-ceo-employers-recognizing-the-value-of -online-learning/.
60. University of Pennsylvania, "Wharton 'Business Foundations' Now Available as a Specialization on Coursera," February 11, 2015, https:// news.wharton.upenn.edu/press-releases/2015/02/wharton-business -foundations-now-available-as-a-specialization-on-coursera/.
61. Byrne, "Coursera CEO."

62. University of Pennsylvania, "Wharton 'Business Foundations.'"

63. Coursera "Data Science," https://www.coursera.org/specializations/jhu
    -data-science/1?utm_medium=listingPage.

64. Ira Gooding, "Johns Hopkins Data Science Specialization Top Perform-
    ers," *SimplyStats*, http://simplystatistics.org/2015/02/05/johns-hopkins
    -data-science-specialization-top-performers/.

65. Johns Hopkins University, "Johns Hopkins Bloomberg School of Public
    Health's Data Science Specialization MOOC Series Launches Industry
    Collaboration with SwiftKey," August 19, 2014, http://dev13.jhsph.nts
    .jhu.edu/news/news-releases/2014/johns-hopkins-bloomberg-school-of
    -public-healths-data-science-specialization-mooc-series-launches-industry
    -collaboration-with-swiftkey.html.

66. Harvard Business School, "Harvard Business School Launches First On-
    line Offering," March 21, 2014, http://www.hbs.edu/news/releases/Pages
    /hbs-launches-first-online-offering-hbx.aspx.

67. Harvard Business School, "CORe FAQs," http://hbx.hbs.edu/hbx-core
    /core-faqs.html.

68. Harvard Business School, "CORe Credential," http://hbx.hbs.edu/hbx
    -core/core-credential.html.

69. John A. Byrne, "Harvard Pitching MBA Admits at Rival Schools," *Poets
    & Quants*, February 26, 2015, http://poetsandquants.com/2015/02/26
    /harvard-pitching-mba-admits-at-rival-schools/2/.

70. Harvard Business School, "HBX and Harvard Extension School Announce
    College-Level Credit for HBX CORe," September 10, 2015, http://www
    .prnewswire.com/news-releases/hbx-and-harvard-extension-school
    -announce-college-level-credit-for-hbx-core-300140924.html; Harvard
    Business School, "CORe FAQs."

71. Dennis Di Lorenzo (Dean, NYU School of Professional Studies), in discus-
    sion with the author, November 2015.

72. Ibid.

73. Ibid.

74. New York University, "NYU SPS Diplomas Programs—Professional Diplo-
    mas," http://sps.nyu.edu/diplomaprograms/professionaldiplomas.html

75. Ibid.

76. New York University, "NYU SPS Diploma Programs—Advanced Diplo-
    mas," http://sps.nyu.edu/diplomaprograms/advanceddiplomas.html.

77. Ibid.

78. Ibid.

79. Ibid.

80. Ibid.

81. Peter Stokes, *Higher Education and Employability: New Models for Integrating Study and Work* (Cambridge, MA: Harvard Education Press, 2015).
82. Melissa Korn, "Online Degree Hits Learning Curve," December 13, 2015, *Wall Street Journal*, http://www.wsj.com/articles/online-degree-hits-learning -curve-1450055726.
83. Stokes, *Higher Education and Employability*.
84. Korn, "Online Degree Hits Learning Curve."
85. Dhawal Shah, "Coursera Partners with University of Illinois to Launch iMBA," *Class Central*, https://www.class-central.com/report/coursera-imba/.
86. University of Illinois, "Frequently Asked Questions," https://onlinemba .illinois.edu/faq/; University of Illinois, "Application Requirements," https://onlinemba.illinois.edu/admissions/.
87. University of Illinois, "FAQ: Courses for University of Illinois Credit," https://onlinemba.illinois.edu/faq/courses-for-illinois-credit/.
88. Julie Wurth, "Coursera CEO: iMBA a Glimpse at the Future," *News-Gazette*, December 3, 2015, http://www.news-gazette.com/news/local/2015-12-03 /coursera-chief-imba-glimpse-future.html.
89. Massachusetts Institute of Technology, "Online Courses + Time on Campus = A New Path to an MIT Master's Degree," October 7, 2015, https:// news.mit.edu/2015/online-supply-chain-management-masters-mitx -micromasters-1007.
90. Massachusetts Institute of Technology, "FAQs on MIT's New Path to a Master's Degree," October 7, 2015, http://news.mit.edu/2015/faqs-mit-new -path-masters-degree-micromasters-1007.
91. Massachusetts Institute of Technology, "Online Courses + Time on Campus."
92. Ibid.
93. Massachusetts Institute of Technology, *Institute-Wide Task Force on the Future of MIT Education* (Cambridge, MA: Massachusetts Institute of Technology, 2014), http://web.mit.edu/future-report/TaskForceFinal_July28.pdf.
94. Pamela Tate and Rebecca Klein-Collins, *PLA and CBE on the Competency Continuum* (Chicago, IL: Council for Adult & Experiential Learning, 2015), http://www.cael.org/pdfs/cael-views-on-cbe-and-pla-oct-2015.
95. Ibid.
96. Paul Fain, "Beyond the Credit Hour," *Inside Higher Ed*, March 19, 2013, https://www.insidehighered.com/news/2013/03/19/ feds-give-nudge-competency-based-education.
97. Chip Franklin and Robert Lytle, *Employer Perspectives on Competency-Based Education* (Washington, DC: American Enterprise Institute, 2015), http:// www.aei.org/wp-content/uploads/2015/04/Employer-Perspectives-on- Competency-Based-Education.pdf, 11.

98. Sean Gallagher, "Major Employers' Hiring Practices and the Evolving Function of the Professional Master's Degree" (EdD dissertation, Northeastern University, 2014); Lauren A. Rivera, *Pedigree: How Elite Students Get Elite Jobs* (Princeton, NJ: Princeton University Press, 2015).

99. Ibid.

100. Scott Jaschik, "The 2016 Inside Higher Ed Survey of Chief Academic Officers," *Inside Higher Ed,* January 22, 2016, https://www.insidehighered.com /news/survey/2016-inside-higher-ed-survey-chief-academic-officers.

101. Robert Kelchen, *The Landscape of Competency-Based Education* (Washington, DC: American Enterprise Institute, 2015), https://www.aei.org/publication /landscape-competency-based-education-enrollments-demographics -affordability/.

102. Kelchen, *The Landscape of Competency-Based Education.*

103. Southern New Hampshire University, "A Milestone for Competency-Based Higher Ed," April 18, 2013, http://collegeforamerica.org/a-milestone-for -competency-based-higher-ed/.

104. Southern New Hampshire University, "College for America FAQs," http:// collegeforamerica.org/about-college-for-america/everything-you-need-to -know-about-college-for-america/.

105. Ibid.

106. Julian Alssid, "Proof Points: Competency-Based Education Stacks Up," *LinkedIn,* December 17, 2015, https://www.linkedin.com/pulse/proof -points-competency-based-education-stacks-up-julian-alssid?published=t; Southern New Hampshire University, "Co-Op Empowers Small Businesses to Offer Affordable College Degrees to Employees," January 14, 2016, http://www.prweb.com/releases/2016/01/prweb13164662.htm.

107. Keith Button, "7 Competency-Based Higher Ed Programs to Keep an Eye On," *Education Dive,* November 4, 2014, http://www.educationdive .com/news/7-competency-based-higher-ed-programs-to-keep-an-eye-on /328382/.

108. University of Maryland University College, "University of Maryland University College—Institutional Participants—Competency-Based Education Network," http://www.cbenetwork.org/about/institutional-participants /university-of-maryland-university-college/.

109. Excelsior College, "Excelsior College Receives $300,000 Grant from Lumina Foundation," http://news.excelsior.edu/excelsior-college-receives -300000-grant-from-lumina-foundation/; US Department of Education, "Program Integrity Questions and Answers—State Authorization," http://www2.ed.gov/policy/highered/reg/hearulemaking/2009/sa.html.

110. Judith Eaton, in discussion with the author.

111. Ibid.
112. Robert Kelchen (Assistant Professor, Higher Education, Seton Hall University), in discussion with the author, January 2016.

CHAPTER 7

1. Burning Glass Technologies, "LaborInsight Database," http://laborinsight .burning-glass.com/jobs/us#/.
2. Scott Jaschik, "The 2016 Inside Higher Ed Survey of Chief Academic Officers," *Inside Higher Ed*, January 22, 2016, https://www.insidehighered.com /news/survey/2016-inside-higher-ed-survey-chief-academic-officers.
3. Nick Timraos, "Why Job Growth Could Get Even Worse for Men Without College Degrees," *Wall Street Journal*, December 31, 2015, http://blogs.wsj. com/economics/2015/12/31/why-job-growth-could-get-even-worse-for -men-without-college-degrees/.
4. Sean Gallagher, "Major Employers' Hiring Practices and the Evolving Function of the Professional Master's Degree" (EdD dissertation, Northeastern University, 2014).
5. Ibid.
6. "Tracking States on Transfer," *Inside Higher Ed*, January 19, 2016, https:// www.insidehighered.com/quicktakes/2016/01/19/tracking-states-transfer.
7. Matthew Pittinsky (Chief Executive Officer, Parchment), in discussion with the author, January 2016.
8. Lumina Foundation, "Reimagining Credentials Through a National Conversation," http://connectingcredentials.org/national-dialogue/.
9. Tom Hanna (Staffing Manager, Robert Bosch Tool Company), in discussion with the author, December 2015.
10. Lumina Foundation, "The Degree Qualifications Profile," https://www .luminafoundation.org/files/resources/dqp.pdf.
11. Judith Glazer, *The Master's Degree: Tradition, Diversity, Innovation* (Washington, DC: Association for the Study of Higher Education, 1986); Roger Geiger, *History of Higher Education Annual: 1986* (Piscataway, NJ: Transaction Publishers, 1986).
12. Peter Stokes, *Higher Education and Employability: New Models for Integrating Study and Work* (Cambridge, MA: Harvard Education Press, 2015).
13. Peter Stokes (Managing Director, Huron Consulting Group), in discussion with the author, December 2015.
14. Ibid.
15. Joseph Aoun, "A Complete Education," *Inside Higher Ed*, April 20, 2015, https://www.insidehighered.com/views/2015/04/20/essay-calls-ending -divide-between-liberal-arts-and-practical-education.

16. Northeastern University and FTI Consulting, "Business Elite National Poll, 3rd Installment of the Innovation Imperative Polling Series," http://www.northeastern.edu/innovationsurvey/pdfs/Pipeline_toplines.pdf.
17. Northeastern University analysis, unpublished, 2013.
18. Gail Jacobs (Senior Director Talent Acquisition and HR Operations, RMS), in discussion with the author, November 2015.
19. Felby Chen (Technical Recruiter, Facebook), in e-mail correspondence with the author, November 2015.
20. Clifford Adelman, *The Bologna Process for U.S. Eyes: Re-Learning Higher Education in the Age of Convergence* (Washington, DC: Institute for Higher Education Policy, 2009), http://degreeprofile.org/press_four/wp-content/uploads/2014/09/Eyes-Final.pdf.
21. Lumina Foundation, "Degree Qualifications Profile."
22. Peter Eckel, "The Role of Shared Governance in Institutional Hard Decisions: Enabler or Antagonist?," *The Review of Higher Education* 24, no. 1 (2000): 15–39.
23. Michael Goldstein, "Cracking the Egg: Preserving the College While Protecting the Core," *Trusteeship Magazine*, January/February 2010, http://agb.org/trusteeship/2010/januaryfebruary/cracking-the-egg-preserving-the-college-while-protecting-the-core.
24. Ibid.
25. Barbara Brittingham (President of the Commission on Institutions of Higher Education, NEASC), in discussion with the author, December 2015.
26. Project Management Institute, "About the GAC," http://www.pmi.org/gac/about-gac.aspx.
27. CFP Board, "College Degree and Certificate Programs," http://www.cfp.net/for-education-partners/college-degree-certificate-programs; APICS, "Professional Designation in Logistics and Supply Chain Management (PLS) Academic Waiver Programs," http://www.apics.org/careers-education-professional-development/certification/logistics/pls/pls-academic-waiver-programs.
28. EDUCAUSE, "Analytics in 2015," http://www.educause.edu/library/resources/analytics-higher-education-2015.
29. Michael Stratford, "One Dupont & Unit Records," *Inside Higher Ed*, March 11, 2014, https://www.insidehighered.com/news/2014/03/11/new-america-report-takes-aim-private-college-lobby-student-unit-record-system.
30. Allen Blue (Vice President, Product Management and Cofounder, LinkedIn), in discussion with the author, November 2015.
31. Michael Housman (Workforce Scientist in Residence, hiQ Labs), in discussion with the author, October 2015.

32. Eric Korb (Chief Executive Officer, Accreditrust), in discussion with the author, December 2015.
33. Michael Piwoni (Human Resources Director, Stanley Tool Company), in discussion with the author, December 2015.
34. Derek Bok, *Universities in the Marketplace: The Commercialization of Higher Education* (Princeton, NJ: Princeton University Press, 2009).
35. "National Universities Rankings," *U.S. News and World Report*, http://colleges.usnews.rankingsandreviews.com/best-colleges/rankings/national-universities/data.
36. Lauren A. Rivera, *Pedigree: How Elite Students Get Elite Jobs* (Princeton, NJ: Princeton University Press, 2015); Gallagher, "Major Employers' Hiring Practices."
37. "Master's Degrees Awarded," *Washington Post*, https://www.washingtonpost.com/apps/g/page/local/masters-degrees-awarded/159/.
38. Jonathan Rodkin and Francesca Levy, "Best Business Schools 2015," *Bloomberg Businessweek*, http://www.bloomberg.com/bschools/rankings.
39. Gallagher, "Major Employers' Hiring Practices."
40. Rivera, *Pedigree*.
41. Rachel Feintzeig, "The Boss Doesn't Want Your Resume," *Wall Street Journal*, January 5, 2016, http://www.wsj.com/articles/the-boss-doesnt-want-your-resume-1452025908.
42. Harry Patrinos (Practice Manager, Education, the World Bank), in discussion with the author, December 2015.
43. Claudia Goldin and Lawrence Katz, *The Race Between Education and Technology* (Cambridge, MA: Harvard University Press, 2008).

# ACKNOWLEDGMENTS

This book would not have been possible without the experience of my own professional and educational journey and the tremendous support of so many colleagues, mentors, friends, and family along the way. In particular, I am indebted to my editor at Harvard Education Press, Doug Clayton, who saw the potential in this project and guided me throughout the way; and leaders at Northeastern University such as Philomena Mantella and Joseph Aoun, for their support and encouragement in my pursuit of this work.

Perhaps most significantly, I must also thank the many employer leaders and others who so graciously shared their time and insights through the interviews that are at the core of this book.

I owe substantial gratitude to my doctoral committee of John LaBrie (chair), Peter Stokes, and Joe Cronin, as they strongly encouraged and inspired me to pursue scholarship on top of my day-to-day administrative responsibilities—and Peter in particular for his example of writing a high-impact book part-time, and as a mentor and friend whom I have enjoyed working with and discussing these issues over many years.

The formative chapter of my career at Eduventures must also be acknowledged, including in particular, founder Michael Sandler, another author, mentor, and great friend of many years; as well as Tom Dretler, Adam Newman, Tom Evans, Brian Bright, Abigail Callahan, Emily Trask, Kristen Holmstrand, Eric Bassett, and countless others who partnered with and enabled me to develop as an analyst and writer. In a similar way, I have appreciated the tutelage of professors such as Joe McNabb, Leslie Hitch, Daniel Rogers, and Andrew Grobman.

My colleagues from Northeastern, including Bill Boozang, Kevin Bell, Brian Murphy Clinton, Seamus Harreys, Kerry Salerno, Chris Mallett, Nick Ducoff, Seema Mishra, Marina Brauch, and Yvonne Rogers, among many others, have been partners in the experiences and empirical study that led to many of the perspectives in this book, as well as creative sounding boards.

Lastly, I want to acknowledge the inspiration from the community of scholars and commentators focused on higher education and its future that I have been privileged to share in this critical dialogue and journey with.

# ABOUT THE AUTHOR

DR. SEAN GALLAGHER is the Chief Strategy Officer for Northeastern University's Global Network. Sean is a nationally recognized expert on strategy and innovation in higher education, with more than fifteen years of experience as a consultant, manager, and administrator. Since joining Northeastern in 2009, Sean has built a central strategy function unique among major US universities, working across colleges and academic domains to catalyze and launch new programs and initiatives and enter new geographic markets. Prior to Northeastern, Sean worked for nearly ten years at research/consulting firm Eduventures, where he played an instrumental role in growing the company by launching and leading many of its research practices while advising top industry executives and investors. Sean is frequently invited to speak at conferences and events, and his analysis and commentary have been featured in leading media outlets such as the *Wall Street Journal*, CBS Television, and the *New York Times*. Sean's research has been cited in numerous academic papers and books. Sean also serves as a member of the Board of Trustees of Bay State College, and holds a lecturer appointment in Northeastern's College of Professional Studies. He holds a Doctor of Education (EdD) degree from Northeastern University, an MBA from the New York Institute of Technology, and a BS in Marketing from Northeastern.

# INDEX

hard skills, 58–60
Harper, William Rainey, 25
Harper College (Illinois) digital
  badges, 144
*Harvard Business Review,* 112
Harvard Business School
  HBX CORe (credential of readi-
  ness), 15, 154
  partnership with Harvard Extension
  School, 154
Harvard Extension School, 15
  partnership with Harvard Business
  School, 154
Harvard University
  EdX, 101
  master's degrees, 183
  as research university, 23
Haywood, John, 50
HBX CORe (credential of readiness),
  16, 154
Hennessy, John, 75
Hersch, Joni, 42–43
Hewlett-Packard, 166
Heywood, John, 43
higher education
  advanced credentials and lifelong
    learning, 168–169
  analytics, 180–181
  applied experiences and projects,
    173
  attainment, 12–13
  bachelor's degree, 25
  business and academic mindsets, xv
  business model, xiii, xv, 3
  certificates, 27–28
  classic academic values, xv
  countercyclical enrollment, 9
  credentialing, xiv, 20
  cultural shift in, 169
  degrees as qualifications, xiv
  digital badges, 144
  distance learning, 73
  doctoral and professional degrees,
    26
  dot-com era, xiv
  ebay-like marketplaces, xiv

economic opportunity, 184–185
educating the masses, 23
enrollment, xii
filter, 55
4+1 programs, 168
funding, 10
globalization, 175
growth, 24–25
high school graduates, 24
hiring, vii, xi–xvii, 13–14, 175
human capital, 31
information age, 67–85
innovation, xiii, 99
international models, 175
Internet shaping, 75–77
job market, xi–xii, 7–14, 30, 171–172
land grant colleges and universities, 23
massified, 24
master's degree, 26
online learning, xiii
peer effects, 99
postsecondary information technology (IT) certifications, 8–9
private capital, 100
quality assurance and governmental
  bodies, 28–29
refashioning credentials, 185
reputation and prestige, 61–64
reshaping, xiii–xiv, 11–12
role, vii
scaling up, 12
skills, viii, 14
socialization, 55
status quo, 185
students as customers, xv
sustainability, xiii
technology-driven transformations
  and innovations, 7–8
television, 73
traditional programs, 178
tuition, 10
United States system, 23
value, xii–xiii
vocal critics, 185
workforce, 11–12, 180–181

Spellings, Margaret, 11
Spellings Commission, 11–12
Stanford University, 8
  global start-up ecosystem, 101
  Learning Technology and Extended
    Education, 77
  online course delivery, 80
  online master's degree in engineer-
    ing, 75
  partnering with UNext.com, 77
Stanley Infrastructure, 121, 124, 132
Stanley Tool Company, 182
Starbucks, 152
state universities, 23
Stiglitz, Joseph, 55
Stokes, Peter, 14, 171–172
strategic dynamism, xiii
Strategic Partner Alliances, 50
Strayer, 88
Struthers, Sally, 74
sub-baccalaureate credentials, 40–41
success profiles, 132–134
Sullivan, Theresa, xiii
SwiftKey collaboration with John's
  Hopkins University, 154
Sylvan Learning Systems, 76–77

**T**
talent analytics, 120–123, 179
Target, 128–129
TechHire, 16
technical occupations, 30
technical skills, 59–60
technological innovation, 4, 111
technology, 68
  boot camps, 147–152
  changes and jobs, 46, 67
  credentials, 112–113
  digital badges, 143
  economy, 111, 186
  investments in, 111
  transformations, 30
technology-driven approaches reshaping role of university credentials,
  178–180
Telelearning Systems, 73

television and higher education, 73
Temple University's Virtual Temple, 87
testing candidates for hire, 129–131
Thiel, Peter, xiii
Thiel Fellowship program, xiii
Thomson Corporation, 79
Thrun, Sebastian, 101
*Thwarted Innovation: What Happened to e-
  Learning and Why"* report (Zemsky
  and Massy), 88
*Time Magazine*, 33
Time Warner Cable, 2
traditional universities and online edu-
  cation, 92–93
training, 31, 54, 70
Training Finder, viii
Trimble, Madeline Joy, 40–41
2Tor, 95
2U, 95–96
two-year colleges enrollment, 25

**U**
UCLA's Higher Education Research
  Institute, 14
Udacity, 15, 16, 101, 102, 153
  nanodegrees, 108
  partnership with Georgia Institute
    of Technology, 157–158
UK eUniversities, 8
UMass Online, 90
UMUConline.com, 87
UNext.com, 78–79
  accredited university spin-off, 82
  affiliating with New York Institute
    of Technology (NYIT), 82
  bridge between two epochs, 80–81
  Cardean University, 8, 77, 78
  contracts, 83
  enrollment, 79
  failures, 79
  fees, 97
  funding, 77
  learning community, 78
  MBA, 81–82
  online marketing, 81
  partners, 77, 79